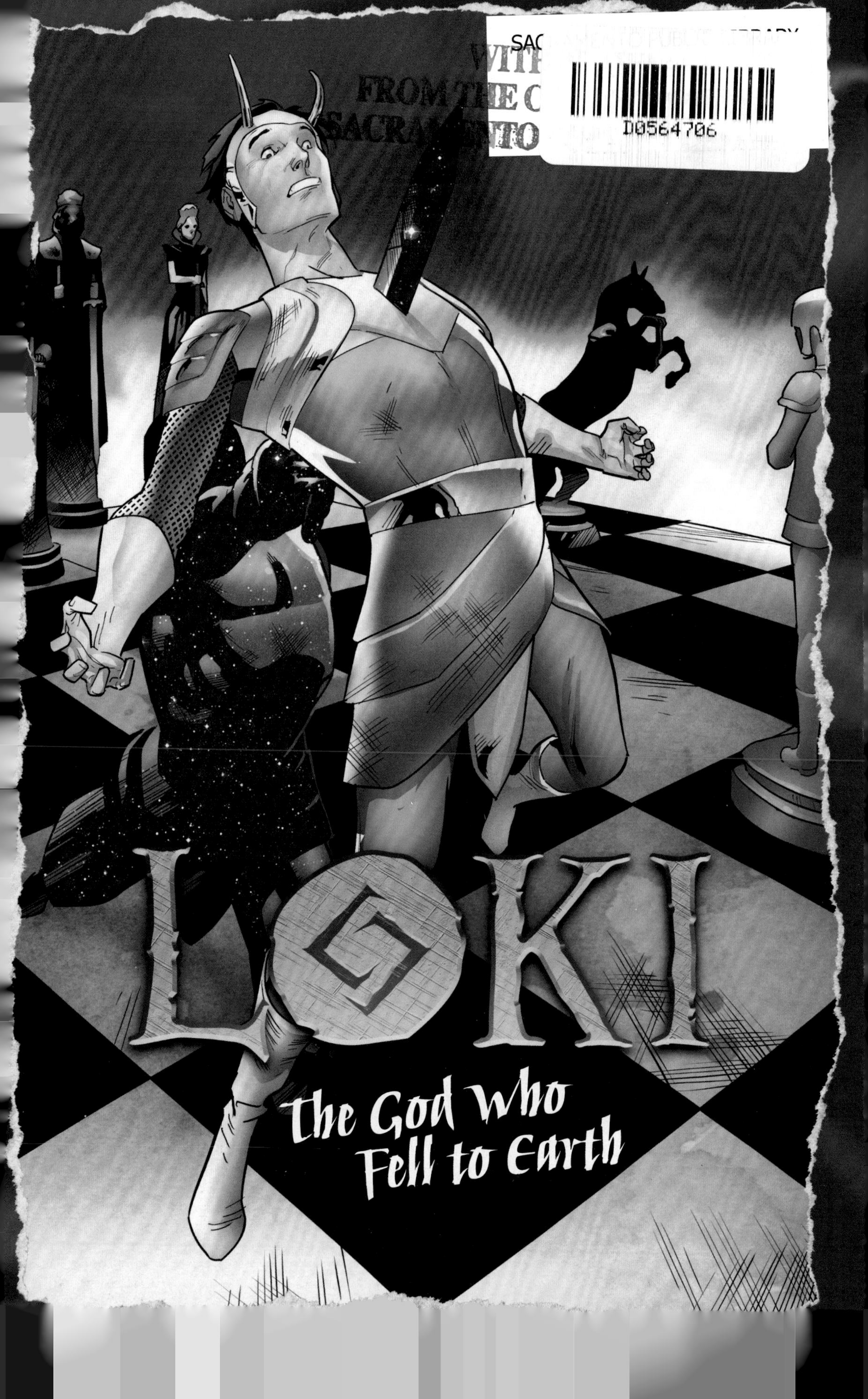
LOKI
The God Who
Fell to Earth

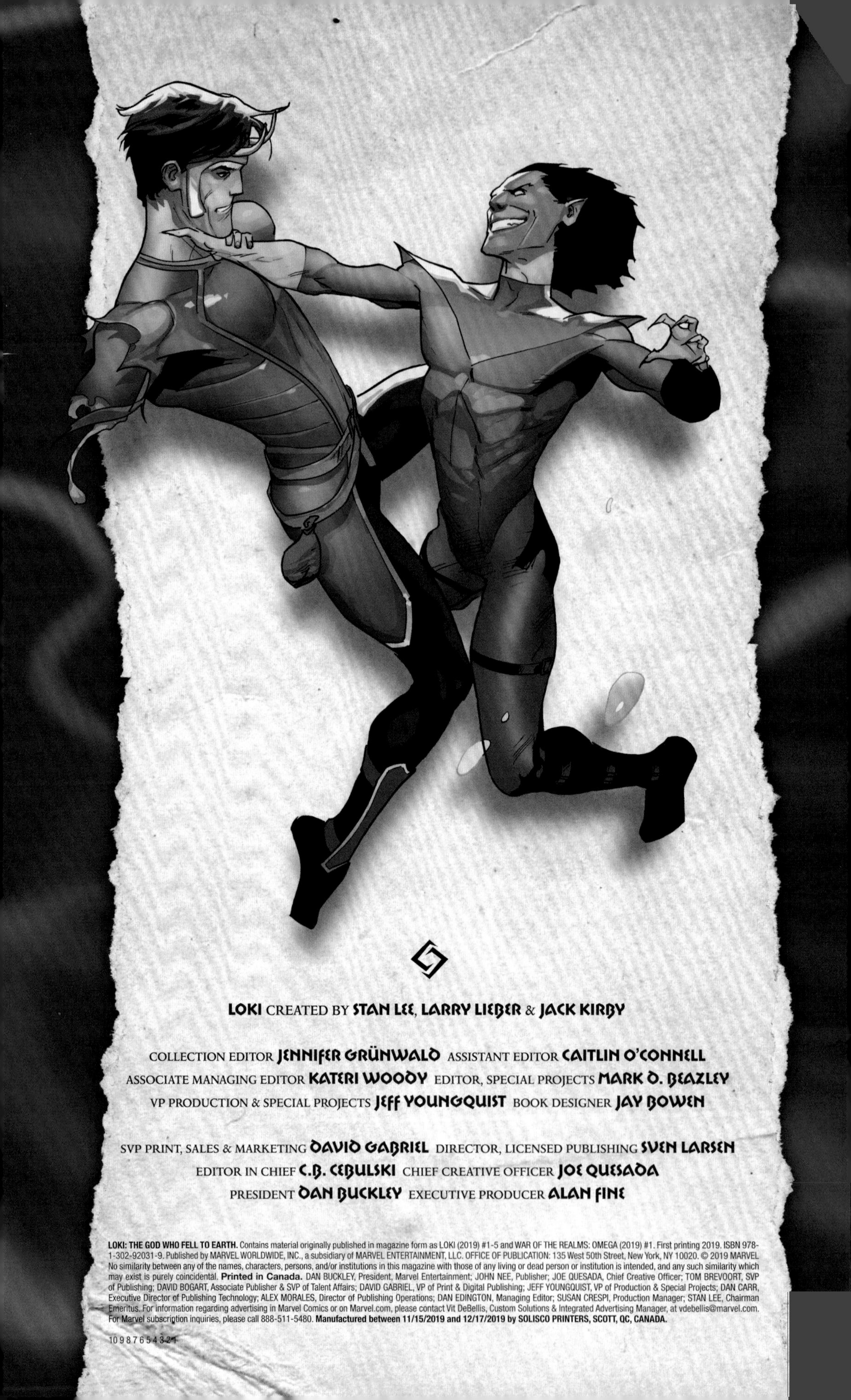

LOKI CREATED BY **STAN LEE**, **LARRY LIEBER** & **JACK KIRBY**

COLLECTION EDITOR **JENNIFER GRÜNWALD** ASSISTANT EDITOR **CAITLIN O'CONNELL**
ASSOCIATE MANAGING EDITOR **KATERI WOODY** EDITOR, SPECIAL PROJECTS **MARK D. BEAZLEY**
VP PRODUCTION & SPECIAL PROJECTS **JEFF YOUNGQUIST** BOOK DESIGNER **JAY BOWEN**

SVP PRINT, SALES & MARKETING **DAVID GABRIEL** DIRECTOR, LICENSED PUBLISHING **SVEN LARSEN**
EDITOR IN CHIEF **C.B. CEBULSKI** CHIEF CREATIVE OFFICER **JOE QUESADA**
PRESIDENT **DAN BUCKLEY** EXECUTIVE PRODUCER **ALAN FINE**

LOKI: THE GOD WHO FELL TO EARTH. Contains material originally published in magazine form as LOKI (2019) #1-5 and WAR OF THE REALMS: OMEGA (2019) #1. First printing 2019. ISBN 978-1-302-92031-9. Published by MARVEL WORLDWIDE, INC., a subsidiary of MARVEL ENTERTAINMENT, LLC. OFFICE OF PUBLICATION: 135 West 50th Street, New York, NY 10020. **Printed in Canada.** DAN BUCKLEY, President, Marvel Entertainment; JOHN NEE, Publisher; JOE QUESADA, Chief Creative Officer; TOM BREVOORT, SVP of Publishing; DAVID BOGART, Associate Publisher & SVP of Talent Affairs; DAVID GABRIEL, VP of Print & Digital Publishing; JEFF YOUNGQUIST, VP of Production & Special Projects; DAN CARR, Executive Director of Publishing Technology; ALEX MORALES, Director of Publishing Operations; DAN EDINGTON, Managing Editor; SUSAN CRESPI, Production Manager; STAN LEE, Chairman Emeritus. For information regarding advertising in Marvel Comics or on Marvel.com, please contact Vit DeBellis, Custom Solutions & Integrated Advertising Manager, at vdebellis@marvel.com. For Marvel subscription inquiries, please call 888-511-5480. **Manufactured between 11/15/2019 and 12/17/2019 by SOLISCO PRINTERS, SCOTT, QC, CANADA.**

10 9 8 7 6 5 4 3 2 1

Recently, the God of Lies—born a Frost Giant, raised an Asgardian, the enemy of his adoptive brother Thor and of the Ten Realms themselves — finally got what he deserved.

He was eaten, and he died.

Then he came back to life. Bursting through the stomach of his father, King Laufey, Loki ended the Frost Giant invasion of New York, saved the lives of countless civilians and heroes and helped bring about the end of the War of the Realms.

Now the savior of Midgard sits on the cold throne of Jotunheim as the new king of the Frost Giants —parallel to his brother Thor, the new All-Father of Asgard. Two kings. Two heroes.

And one hell of a story to be told.

LOKI

The God Who Fell to Earth

DANIEL KIBBLESMITH
WRITER

OSCAR BAZALDUA (#1-4) & ANDY MacDONALD (#5)
PENCILERS

OSCAR BAZALDUA (#1-4) & ANDY MacDONALD (#5)
WITH VICTOR OLAZABA (#4)
INKERS

DAVID CURIEL
WITH CARLOS LOPEZ (#4)
COLOR ARTISTS

VC's CLAYTON COWLES
LETTERER

OZGUR YILDIRIM (#1-5) & PHIL NOTO (WAR OF THE REALMS: OMEGA)
COVER ART

SARAH BRUNSTAD
ASSOCIATE EDITOR

WIL MOSS
EDITOR

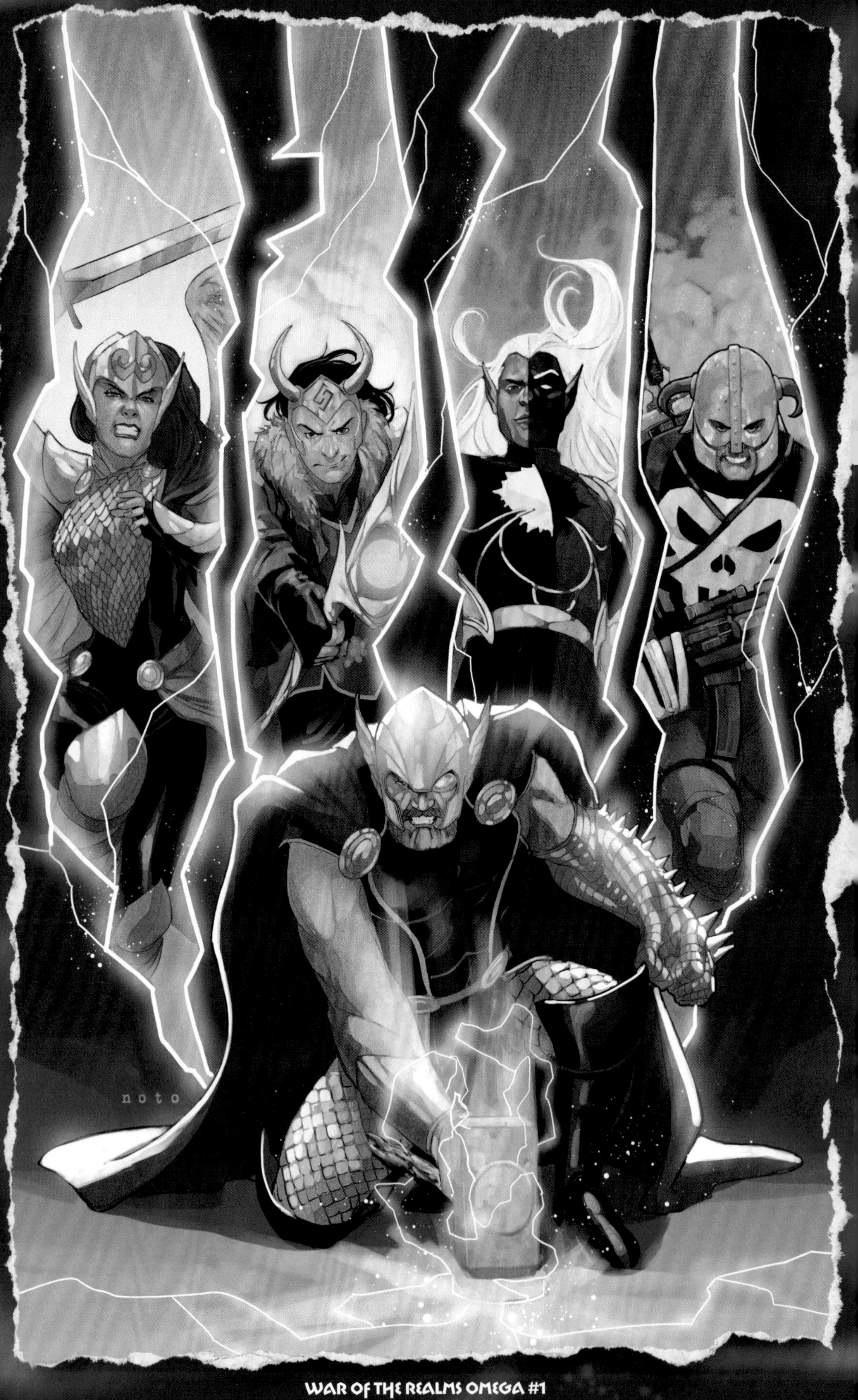
noto

WAR OF THE REALMS OMEGA #1

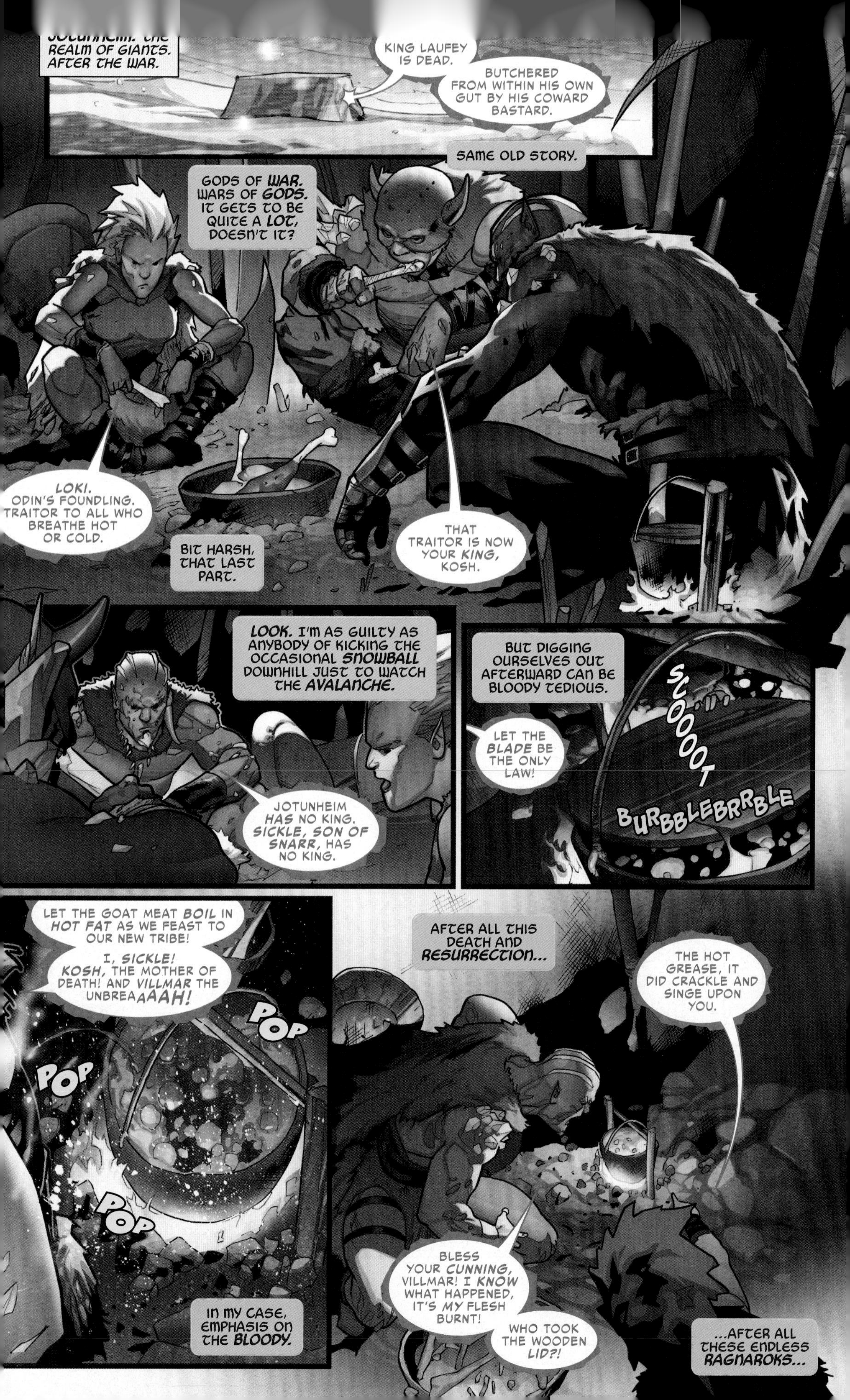
REALM OF GIANTS. AFTER THE WAR.
KING LAUFEY IS DEAD.
BUTCHERED FROM WITHIN HIS OWN GUT BY HIS COWARD BASTARD.
SAME OLD STORY.
GODS OF WAR. WARS OF GODS. IT GETS TO BE QUITE A LOT, DOESN'T IT?
LOKI. ODIN'S FOUNDLING. TRAITOR TO ALL WHO BREATHE HOT OR COLD.
BIT HARSH, THAT LAST PART.
THAT TRAITOR IS NOW YOUR KING, KOSH.
LOOK. I'M AS GUILTY AS ANYBODY OF KICKING THE OCCASIONAL SNOWBALL DOWNHILL JUST TO WATCH THE AVALANCHE.
JOTUNHEIM HAS NO KING. SICKLE, SON OF SNARR, HAS NO KING.
BUT DIGGING OURSELVES OUT AFTERWARD CAN BE BLOODY TEDIOUS.
LET THE BLADE BE THE ONLY LAW!
STOOOOT
BURBBLEBRRBLE
LET THE GOAT MEAT BOIL IN HOT FAT AS WE FEAST TO OUR NEW TRIBE!
I, SICKLE! KOSH, THE MOTHER OF DEATH! AND VILLMAR THE UNBREAAAAH!
POP
POP
POP
IN MY CASE, EMPHASIS ON THE BLOODY.
AFTER ALL THIS DEATH AND RESURRECTION...
THE HOT GREASE, IT DID CRACKLE AND SINGE UPON YOU.
BLESS YOUR CUNNING, VILLMAR! I KNOW WHAT HAPPENED, IT'S MY FLESH BURNT!
WHO TOOK THE WOODEN LID?!
...AFTER ALL THESE ENDLESS RAGNAROKS...

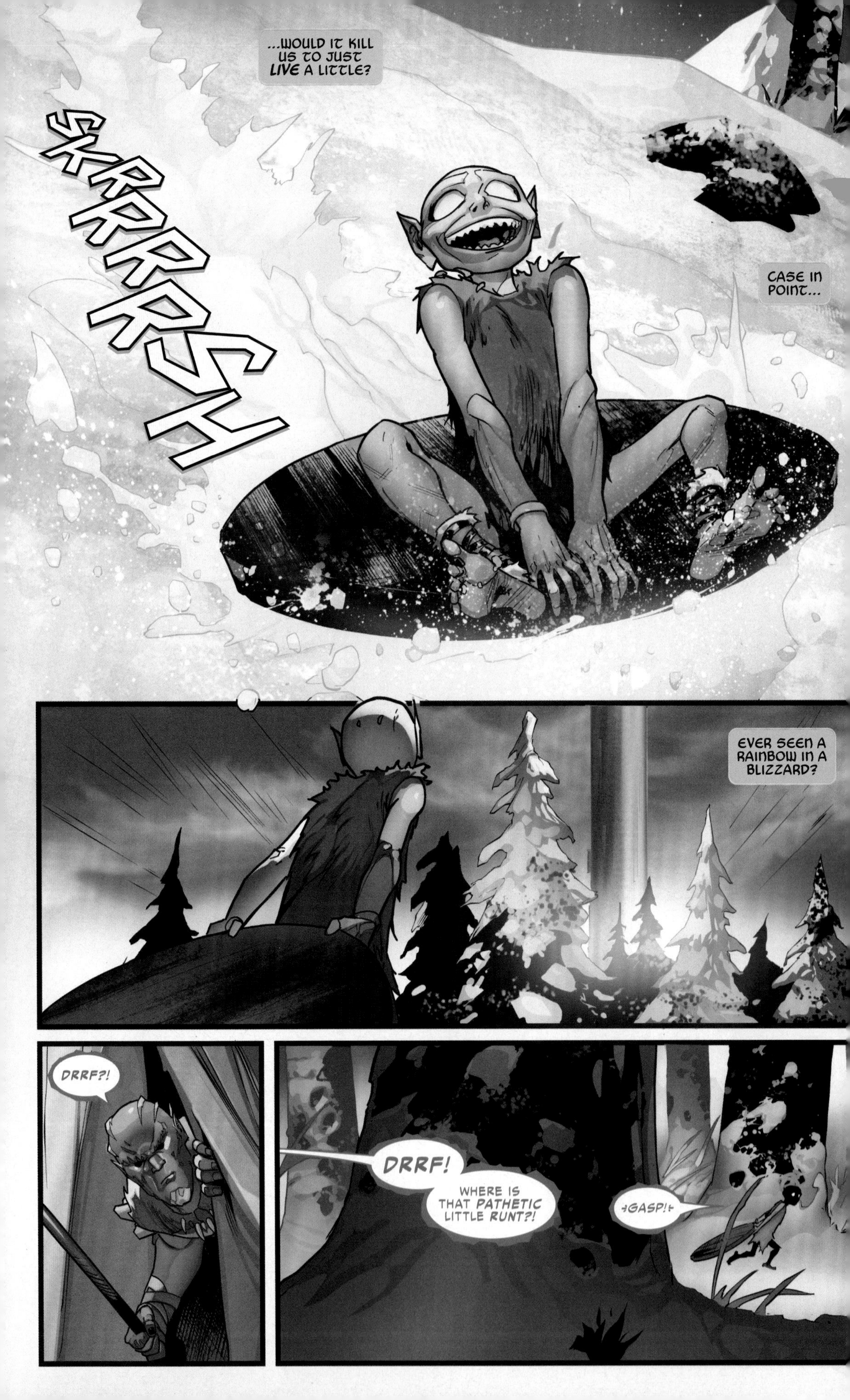
...WOULD IT KILL US TO JUST LIVE A LITTLE?
SKRRRSH
CASE IN POINT...
EVER SEEN A RAINBOW IN A BLIZZARD?
DRRF?!
DRRF!
WHERE IS THAT PATHETIC LITTLE RUNT?!
GASP!

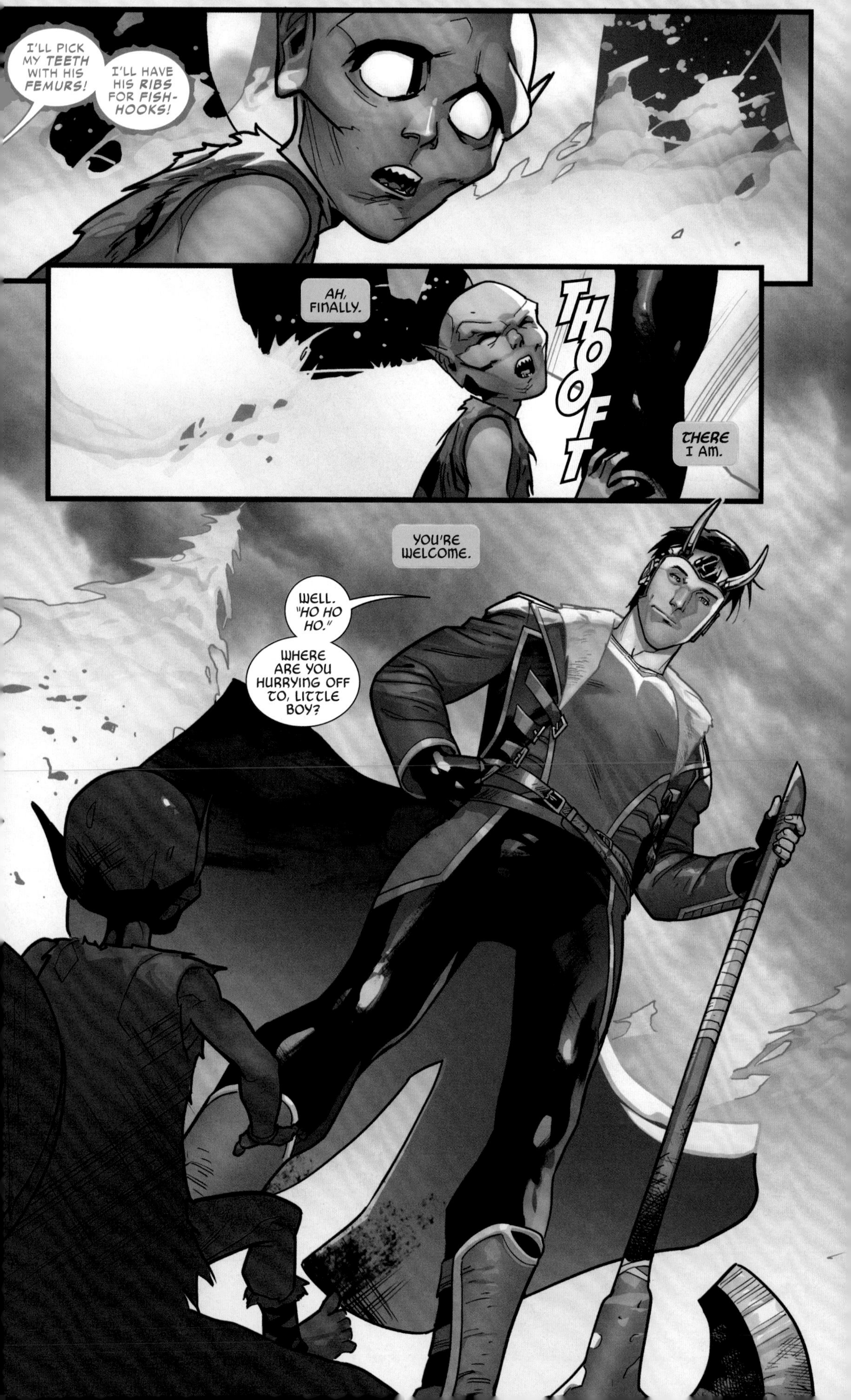

I'LL PICK MY TEETH WITH HIS FEMURS!
I'LL HAVE HIS RIBS FOR FISH-HOOKS!
AH, FINALLY.
THOOFT
THERE I AM.
YOU'RE WELCOME.
WELL. "HO HO HO."
WHERE ARE YOU HURRYING OFF TO, LITTLE BOY?

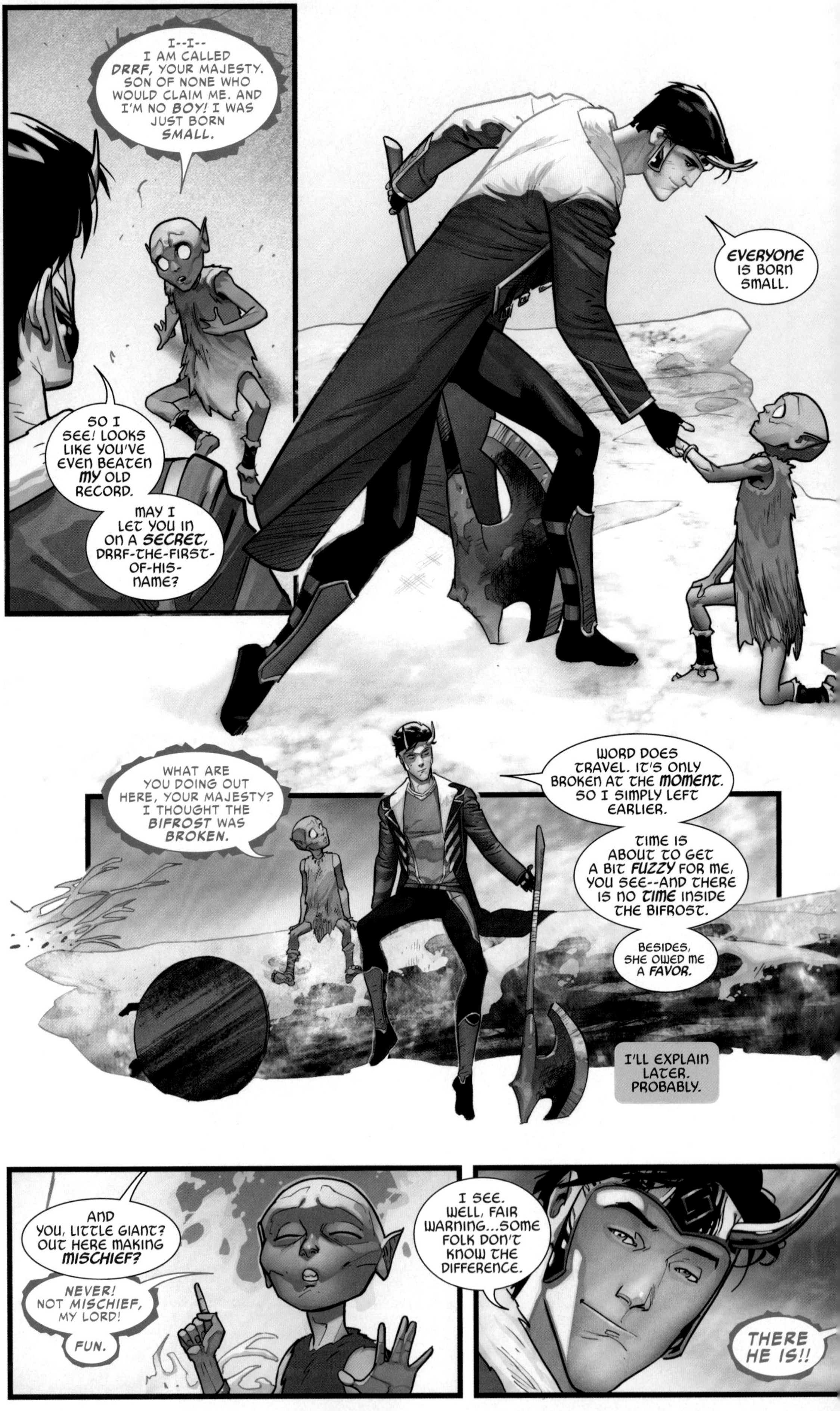
I--I-- I AM CALLED DRRF, YOUR MAJESTY. SON OF NONE WHO WOULD CLAIM ME. AND I'M NO BOY! I WAS JUST BORN SMALL.
SO I SEE! LOOKS LIKE YOU'VE EVEN BEATEN MY OLD RECORD.
MAY I LET YOU IN ON A SECRET, DRRF-THE-FIRST-OF-HIS-NAME?
EVERYONE IS BORN SMALL.
WHAT ARE YOU DOING OUT HERE, YOUR MAJESTY? I THOUGHT THE BIFROST WAS BROKEN.
WORD DOES TRAVEL. IT'S ONLY BROKEN AT THE MOMENT. SO I SIMPLY LEFT EARLIER.
TIME IS ABOUT TO GET A BIT FUZZY FOR ME, YOU SEE--AND THERE IS NO TIME INSIDE THE BIFROST.
BESIDES, SHE OWED ME A FAVOR.
I'LL EXPLAIN LATER. PROBABLY.
AND YOU, LITTLE GIANT? OUT HERE MAKING MISCHIEF?
NEVER! NOT MISCHIEF, MY LORD!
FUN.
I SEE. WELL, FAIR WARNING...SOME FOLK DON'T KNOW THE DIFFERENCE.
THERE HE IS!!

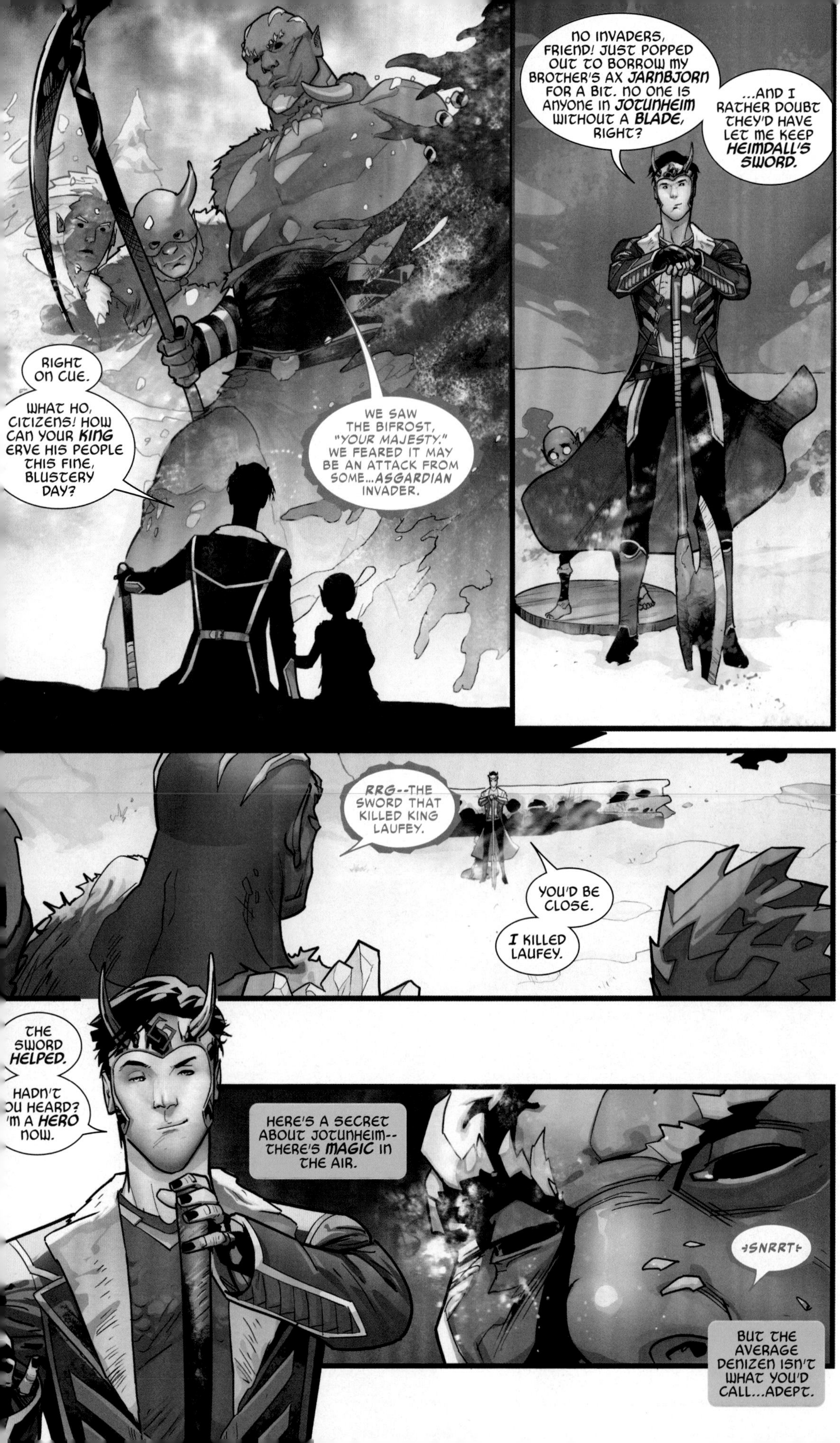
RIGHT ON CUE.
WHAT HO, CITIZENS! HOW CAN YOUR KING ERVE HIS PEOPLE THIS FINE, BLUSTERY DAY?
WE SAW THE BIFROST, "YOUR MAJESTY." WE FEARED IT MAY BE AN ATTACK FROM SOME...ASGARDIAN INVADER.
NO INVADERS, FRIEND! JUST POPPED OUT TO BORROW MY BROTHER'S AX JARNBJORN FOR A BIT. NO ONE IS ANYONE IN JOTUNHEIM WITHOUT A BLADE, RIGHT?
...AND I RATHER DOUBT THEY'D HAVE LET ME KEEP HEIMDALL'S SWORD.
RRG--THE SWORD THAT KILLED KING LAUFEY.
YOU'D BE CLOSE.
I KILLED LAUFEY.
THE SWORD HELPED.
HADN'T OU HEARD? 'M A HERO NOW.
HERE'S A SECRET ABOUT JOTUNHEIM--THERE'S MAGIC IN THE AIR.
SNRRT
BUT THE AVERAGE DENIZEN ISN'T WHAT YOU'D CALL...ADEPT.

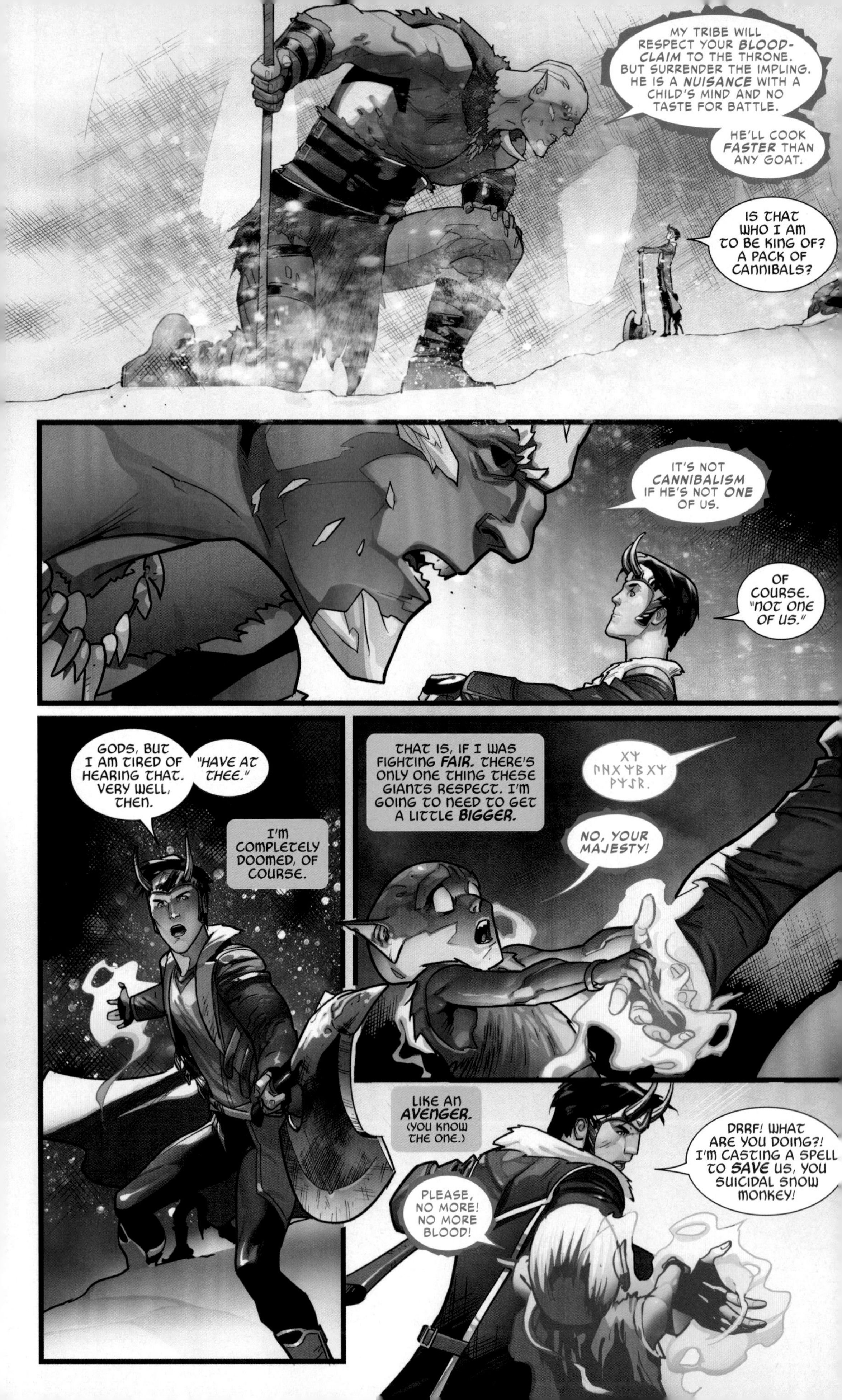

MY TRIBE WILL RESPECT YOUR BLOOD-CLAIM TO THE THRONE. BUT SURRENDER THE IMPLING. HE IS A NUISANCE WITH A CHILD'S MIND AND NO TASTE FOR BATTLE.
HE'LL COOK FASTER THAN ANY GOAT.
IS THAT WHO I AM TO BE KING OF? A PACK OF CANNIBALS?
IT'S NOT CANNIBALISM IF HE'S NOT ONE OF US.
OF COURSE. "NOT ONE OF US."
GODS, BUT I AM TIRED OF HEARING THAT. VERY WELL, THEN.
"HAVE AT THEE."
I'M COMPLETELY DOOMED, OF COURSE.
THAT IS, IF I WAS FIGHTING FAIR. THERE'S ONLY ONE THING THESE GIANTS RESPECT. I'M GOING TO NEED TO GET A LITTLE BIGGER.
NO, YOUR MAJESTY!
LIKE AN AVENGER. (YOU KNOW THE ONE.)
DRRF! WHAT ARE YOU DOING?! I'M CASTING A SPELL TO SAVE US, YOU SUICIDAL SNOW MONKEY!
PLEASE, NO MORE! NO MORE BLOOD!

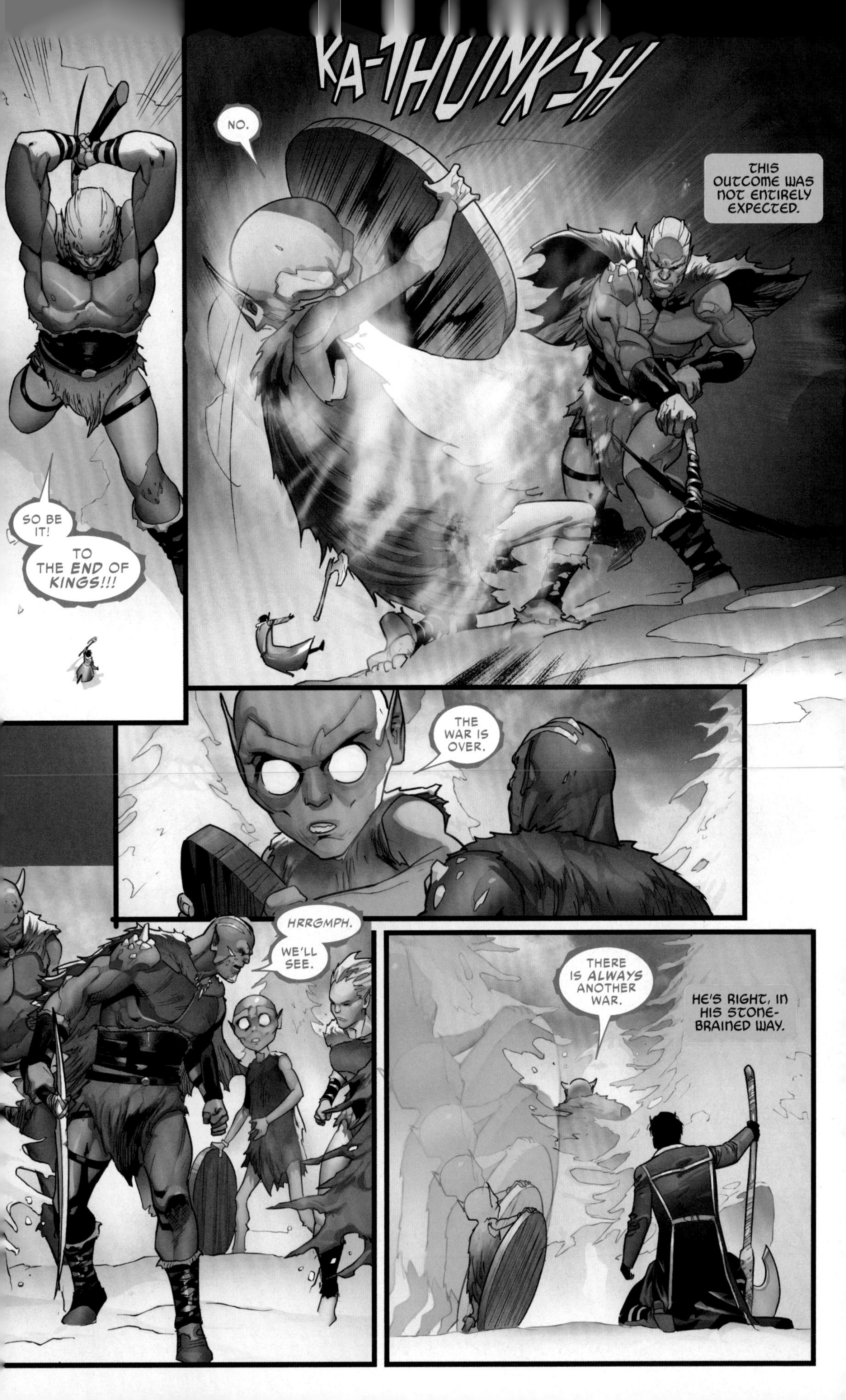

SO BE IT!
TO THE END OF KINGS!!!
KA-THUNKSH
NO.
THIS OUTCOME WAS NOT ENTIRELY EXPECTED.
THE WAR IS OVER.
HRRGMPH.
WE'LL SEE.
THERE IS ALWAYS ANOTHER WAR.
HE'S RIGHT, IN HIS STONE-BRAINED WAY.

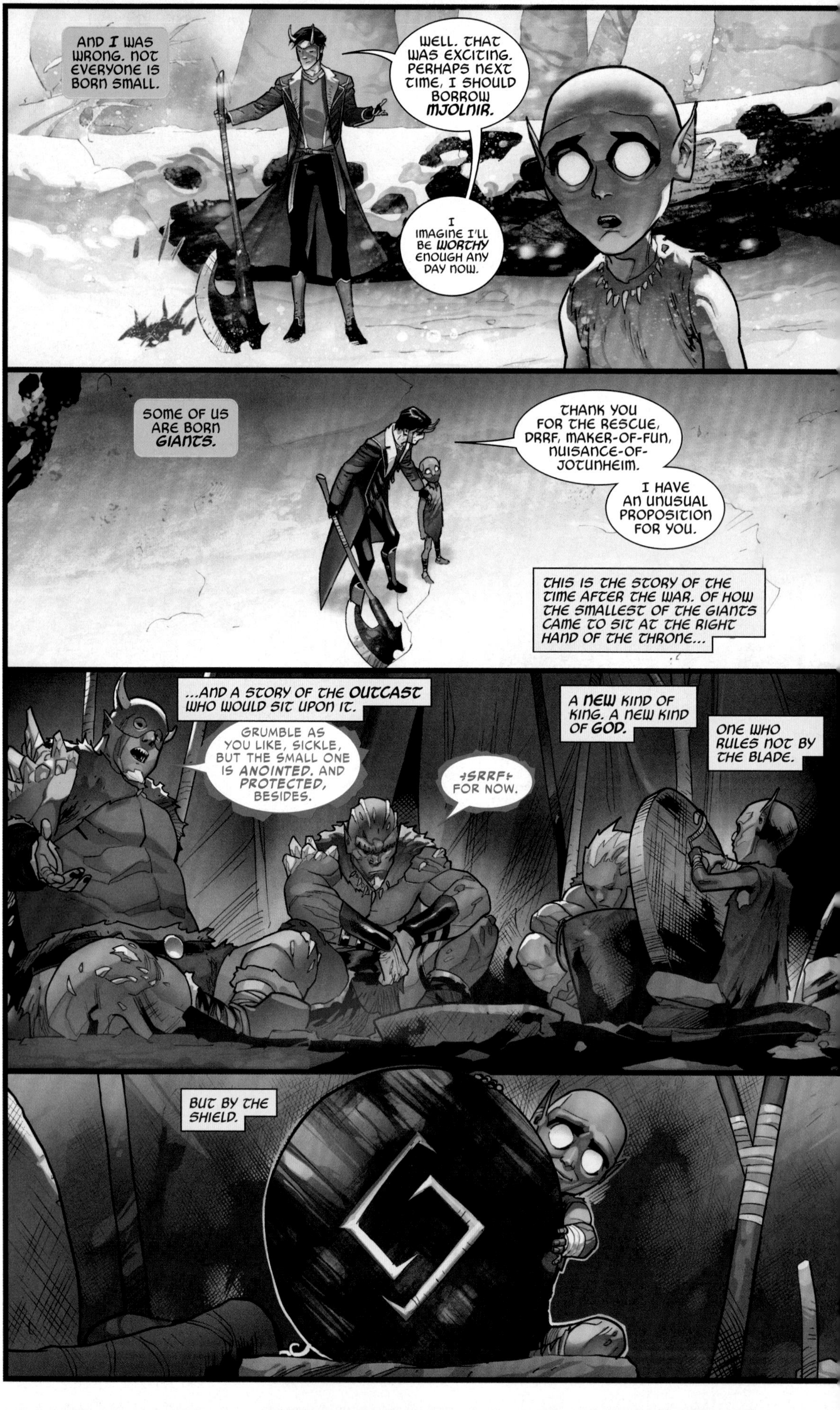
AND I WAS WRONG. NOT EVERYONE IS BORN SMALL.
WELL. THAT WAS EXCITING. PERHAPS NEXT TIME, I SHOULD BORROW MJOLNIR.
I IMAGINE I'LL BE WORTHY ENOUGH ANY DAY NOW.
SOME OF US ARE BORN GIANTS.
THANK YOU FOR THE RESCUE, DRRF, MAKER-OF-FUN, NUISANCE-OF-JOTUNHEIM.
I HAVE AN UNUSUAL PROPOSITION FOR YOU.
THIS IS THE STORY OF THE TIME AFTER THE WAR. OF HOW THE SMALLEST OF THE GIANTS CAME TO SIT AT THE RIGHT HAND OF THE THRONE...
...AND A STORY OF THE OUTCAST WHO WOULD SIT UPON IT.
GRUMBLE AS YOU LIKE, SICKLE, BUT THE SMALL ONE IS ANOINTED. AND PROTECTED, BESIDES.
SRRF FOR NOW.
A NEW KIND OF KING. A NEW KIND OF GOD.
ONE WHO RULES NOT BY THE BLADE.
BUT BY THE SHIELD.

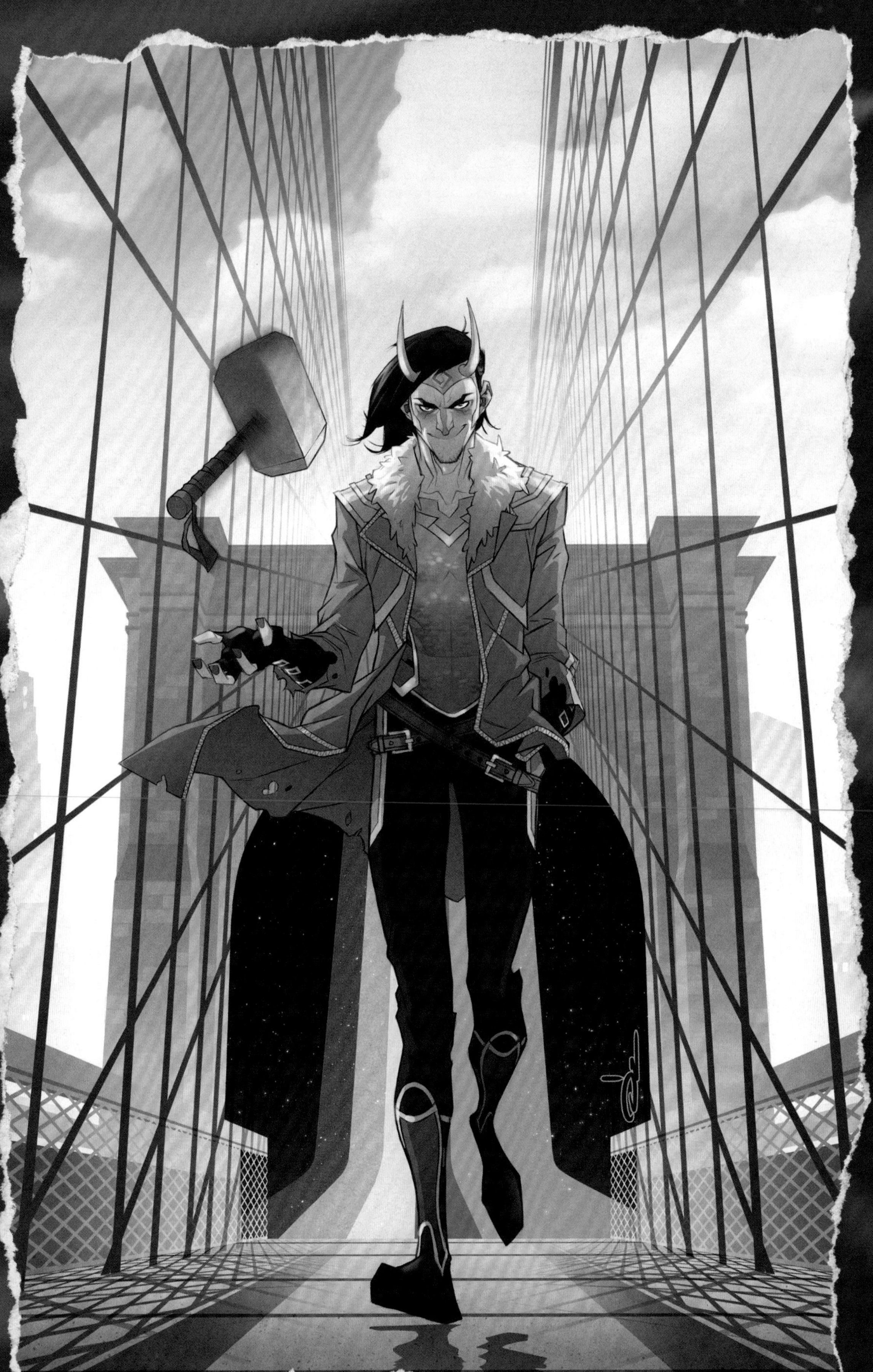

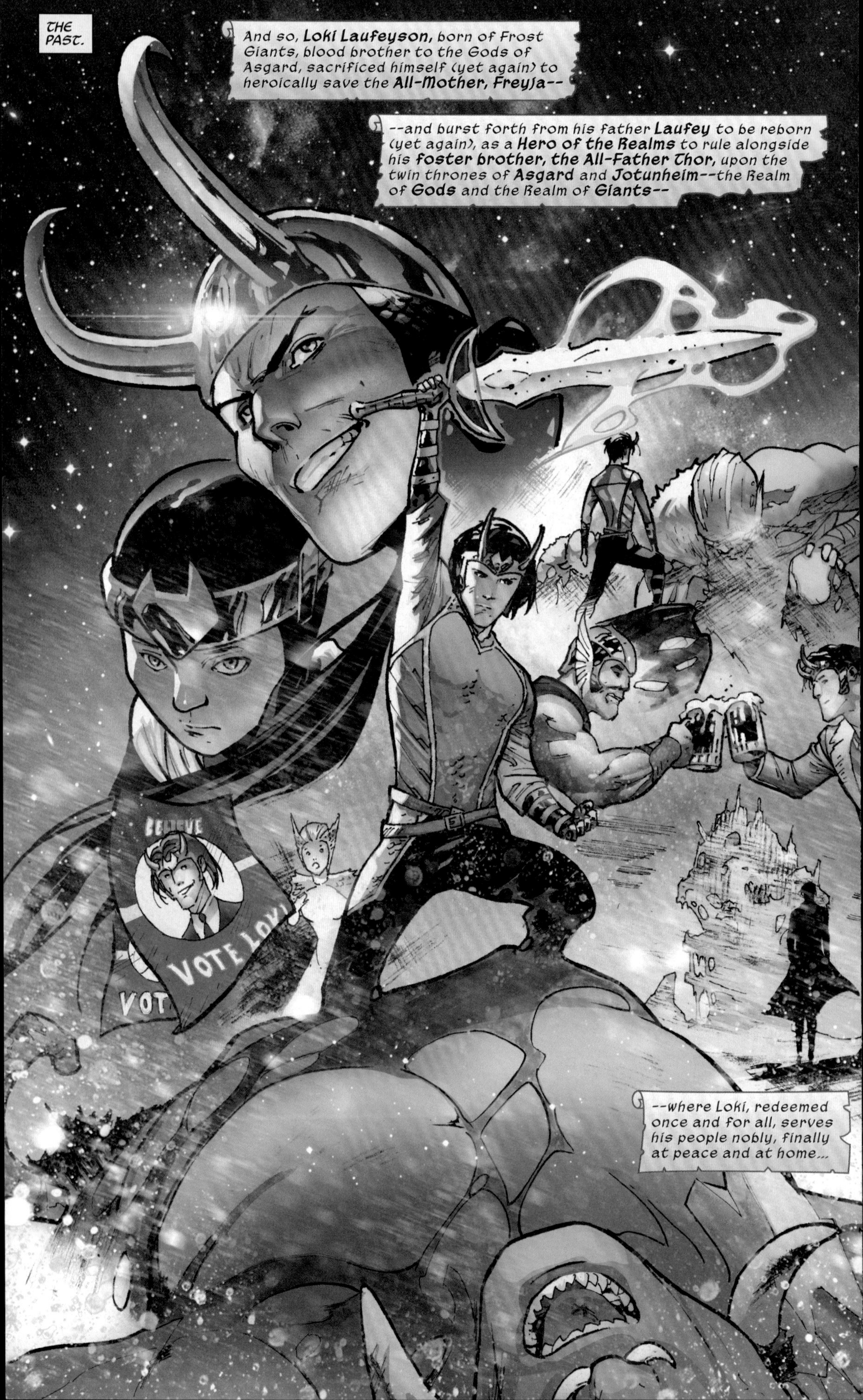
THE PAST.
And so, Loki Laufeyson, born of Frost Giants, blood brother to the Gods of Asgard, sacrificed himself (yet again) to heroically save the All-Mother, Freyja--
--and burst forth from his father Laufey to be reborn (yet again), as a Hero of the Realms to rule alongside his foster brother, the All-Father Thor, upon the twin thrones of Asgard and Jotunheim--the Realm of Gods and the Realm of Giants--
BELIEVE
VOTE LOKI
--where Loki, redeemed once and for all, serves his people nobly, finally at peace and at home...

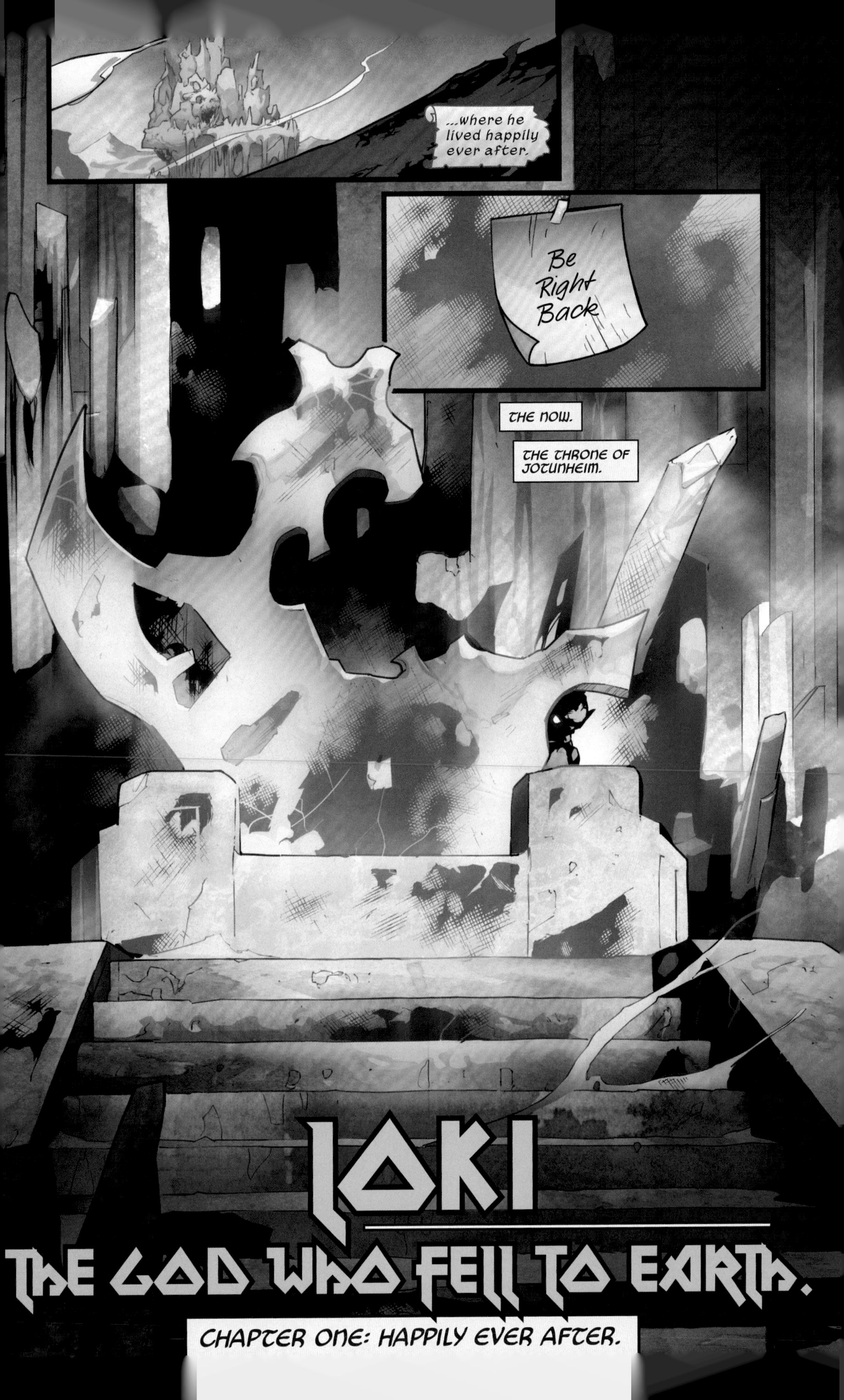
...where he lived happily ever after.
Be Right Back
THE NOW.
THE THRONE OF JOTUNHEIM.
LOKI
THE GOD WHO FELL TO EARTH.
CHAPTER ONE: HAPPILY EVER AFTER.

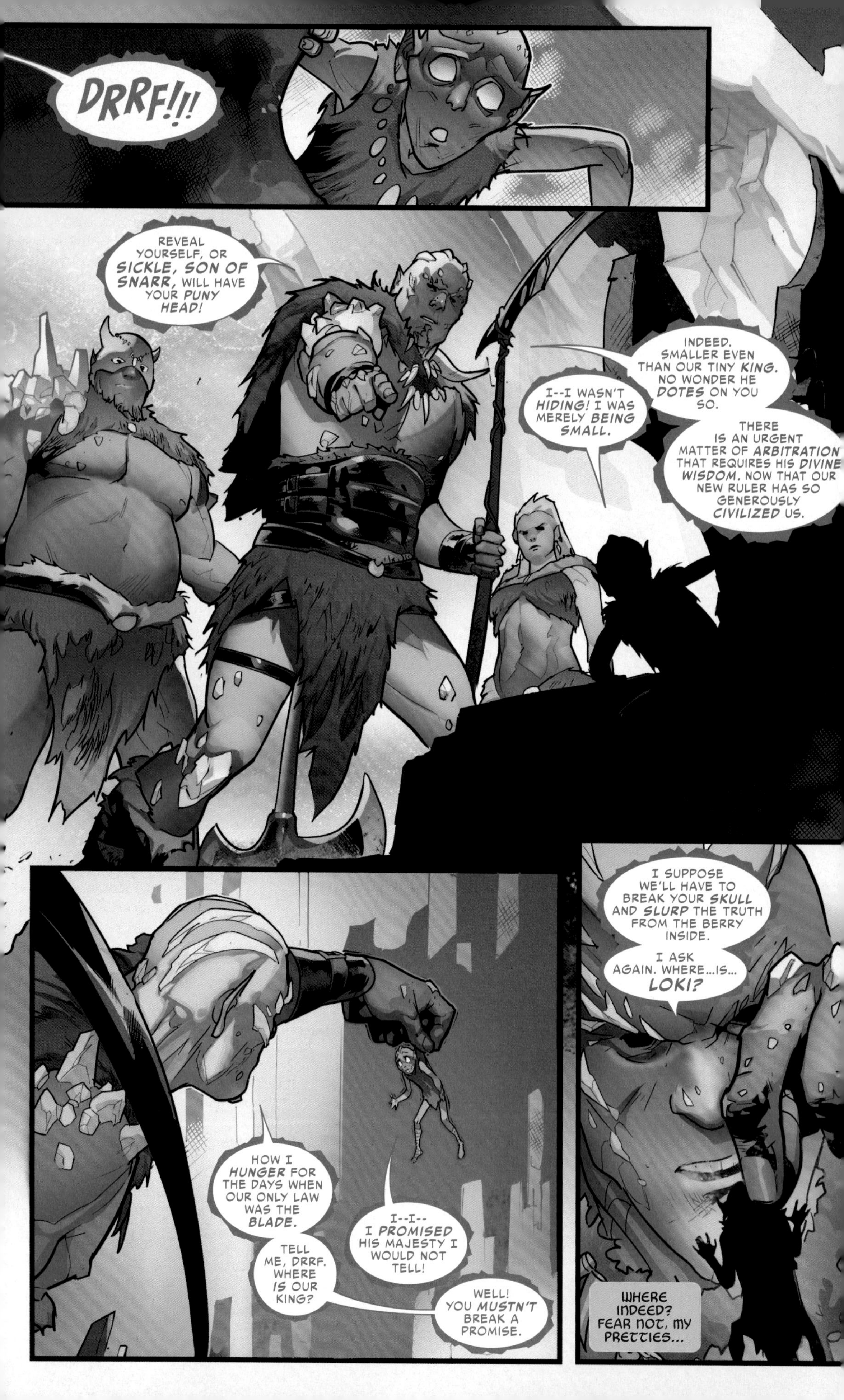
DRRF!!!
REVEAL YOURSELF, OR SICKLE, SON OF SNARR, WILL HAVE YOUR PUNY HEAD!
I--I WASN'T HIDING! I WAS MERELY BEING SMALL.
INDEED. SMALLER EVEN THAN OUR TINY KING. NO WONDER HE DOTES ON YOU SO.
THERE IS AN URGENT MATTER OF ARBITRATION THAT REQUIRES HIS DIVINE WISDOM. NOW THAT OUR NEW RULER HAS SO GENEROUSLY CIVILIZED US.
HOW I HUNGER FOR THE DAYS WHEN OUR ONLY LAW WAS THE BLADE.
TELL ME, DRRF. WHERE IS OUR KING?
I--I-- I PROMISED HIS MAJESTY I WOULD NOT TELL!
WELL! YOU MUSTN'T BREAK A PROMISE.
I SUPPOSE WE'LL HAVE TO BREAK YOUR SKULL AND SLURP THE TRUTH FROM THE BERRY INSIDE.
I ASK AGAIN. WHERE...IS... LOKI?
WHERE INDEED? FEAR NOT, MY PRETTIES...

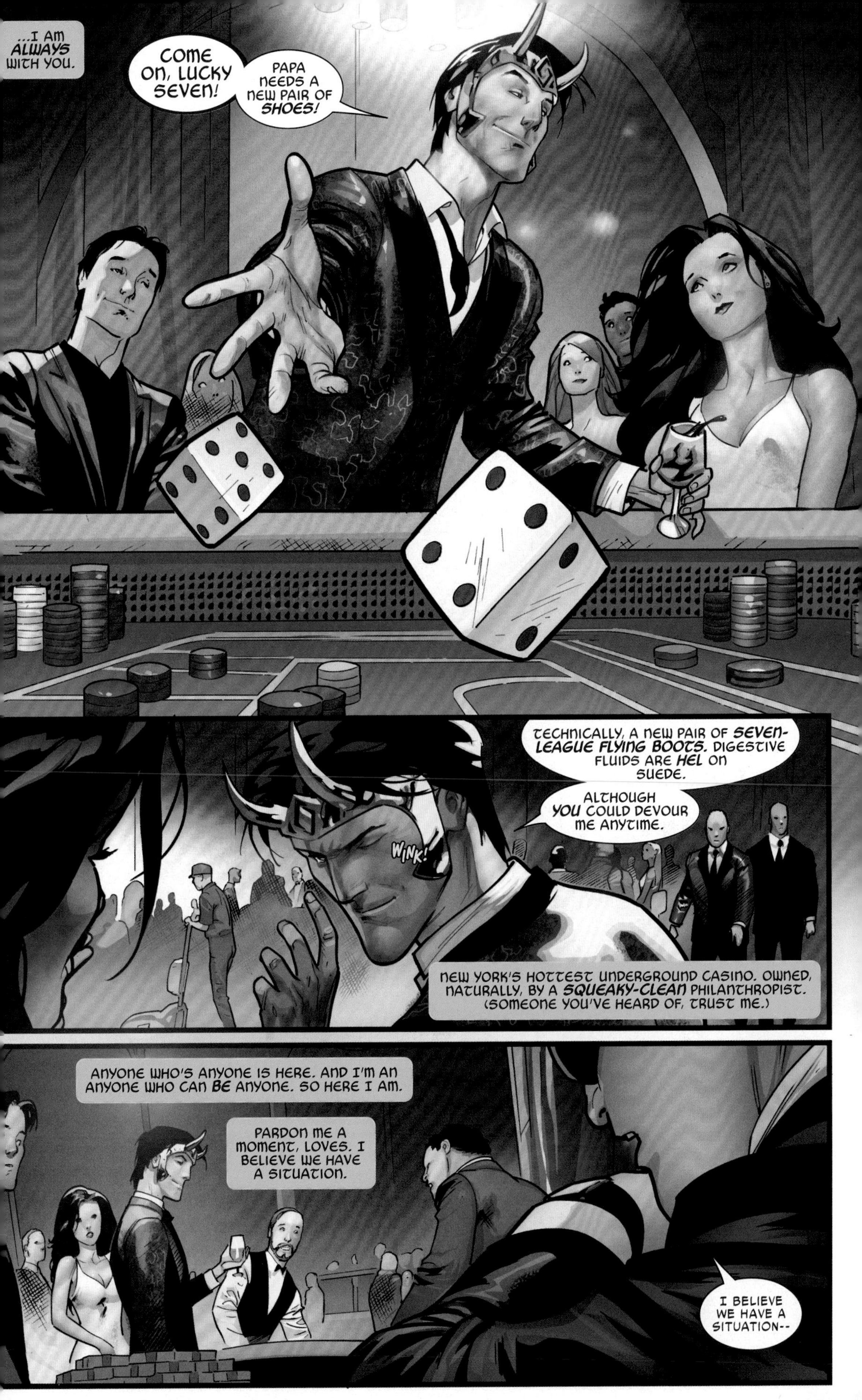

...I AM ALWAYS WITH YOU.
COME ON, LUCKY SEVEN!
PAPA NEEDS A NEW PAIR OF SHOES!
TECHNICALLY, A NEW PAIR OF SEVEN-LEAGUE FLYING BOOTS. DIGESTIVE FLUIDS ARE HEL ON SUEDE.
ALTHOUGH YOU COULD DEVOUR ME ANYTIME.
WINK!
NEW YORK'S HOTTEST UNDERGROUND CASINO. OWNED, NATURALLY, BY A SQUEAKY-CLEAN PHILANTHROPIST. (SOMEONE YOU'VE HEARD OF, TRUST ME.)
ANYONE WHO'S ANYONE IS HERE. AND I'M AN ANYONE WHO CAN BE ANYONE. SO HERE I AM.
PARDON ME A MOMENT, LOVES. I BELIEVE WE HAVE A SITUATION.
I BELIEVE WE HAVE A SITUATION--

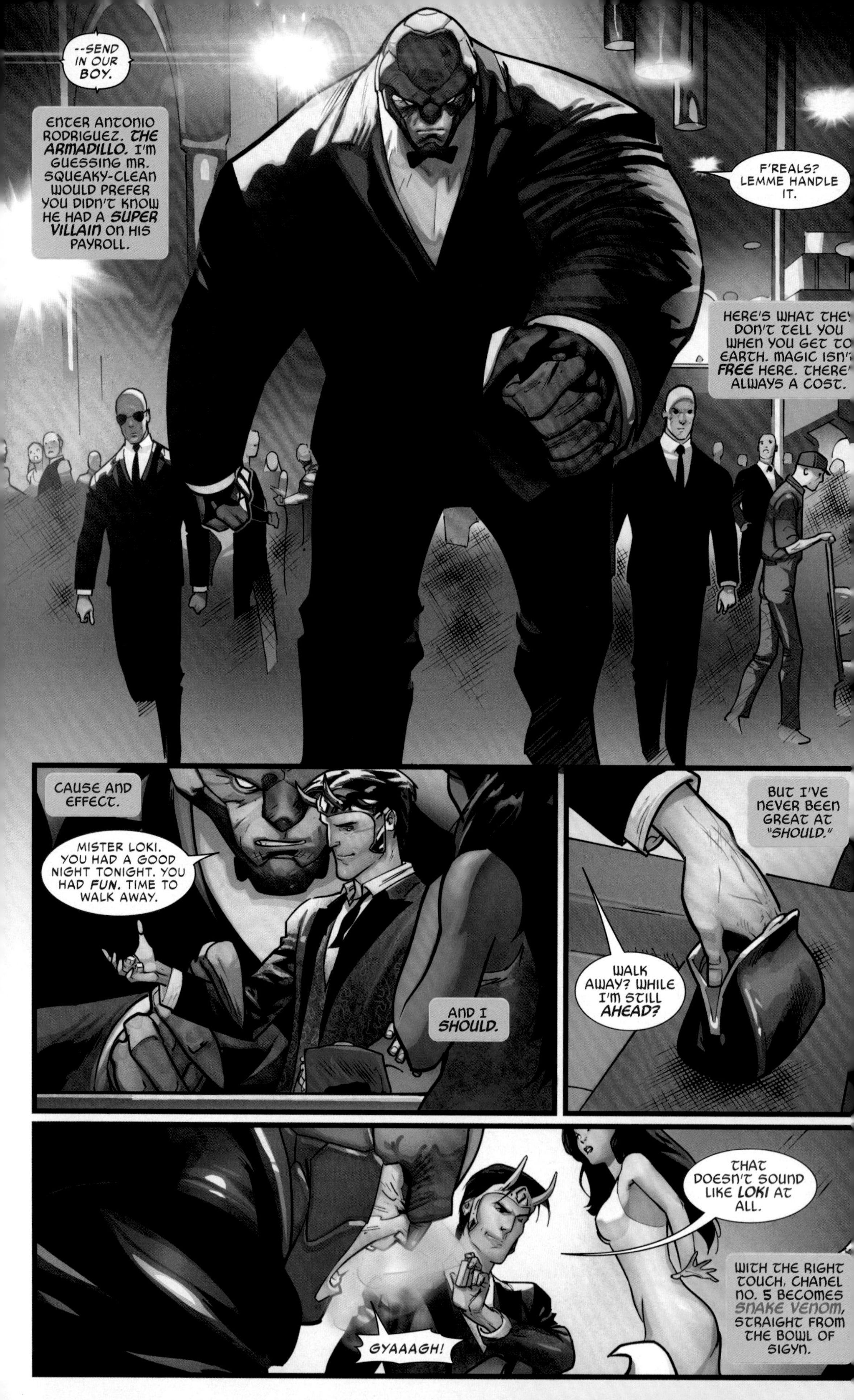
--SEND IN OUR BOY.
ENTER ANTONIO RODRIGUEZ. THE ARMADILLO. I'M GUESSING MR. SQUEAKY-CLEAN WOULD PREFER YOU DIDN'T KNOW HE HAD A SUPER VILLAIN ON HIS PAYROLL.
F'REALS? LEMME HANDLE IT.
HERE'S WHAT THEY DON'T TELL YOU WHEN YOU GET TO EARTH. MAGIC ISN'T FREE HERE. THERE'S ALWAYS A COST.
CAUSE AND EFFECT.
MISTER LOKI. YOU HAD A GOOD NIGHT TONIGHT. YOU HAD FUN. TIME TO WALK AWAY.
AND I SHOULD.
BUT I'VE NEVER BEEN GREAT AT "SHOULD."
WALK AWAY? WHILE I'M STILL AHEAD?
THAT DOESN'T SOUND LIKE LOKI AT ALL.
WITH THE RIGHT TOUCH, CHANEL NO. 5 BECOMES SNAKE VENOM, STRAIGHT FROM THE BOWL OF SIGYN.
GYAAAGH!

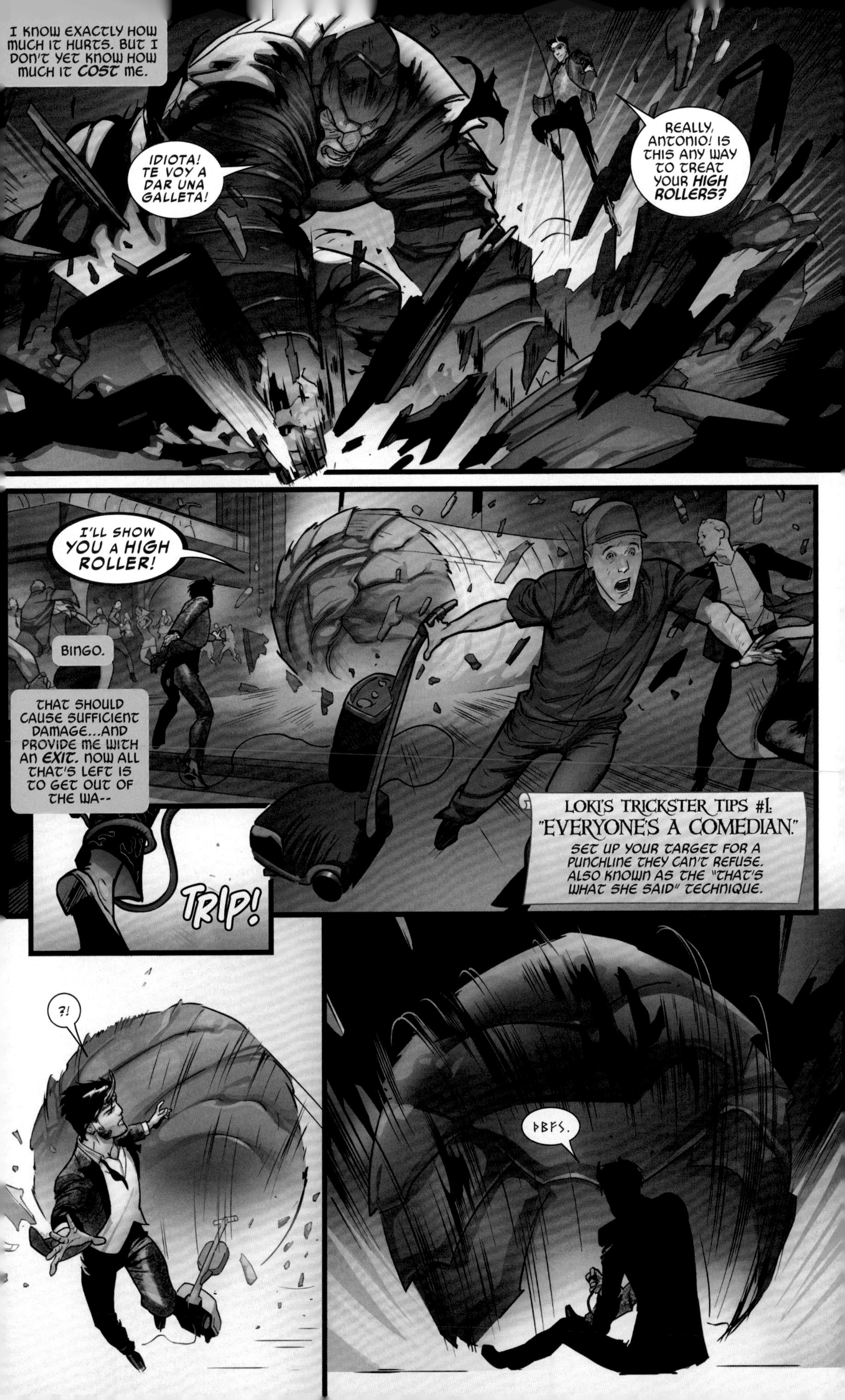
I KNOW EXACTLY HOW MUCH IT HURTS. BUT I DON'T YET KNOW HOW MUCH IT COST ME.
IDIOTA! TE VOY A DAR UNA GALLETA!
REALLY, ANTONIO! IS THIS ANY WAY TO TREAT YOUR HIGH ROLLERS?
I'LL SHOW YOU A HIGH ROLLER!
BINGO.
THAT SHOULD CAUSE SUFFICIENT DAMAGE...AND PROVIDE ME WITH AN EXIT. NOW ALL THAT'S LEFT IS TO GET OUT OF THE WA--
TRIP!
LOKI'S TRICKSTER TIPS #1: "EVERYONE'S A COMEDIAN."
SET UP YOUR TARGET FOR A PUNCHLINE THEY CAN'T REFUSE. ALSO KNOWN AS THE "THAT'S WHAT SHE SAID" TECHNIQUE.
?!
ᚦᛒᚠᛊ.

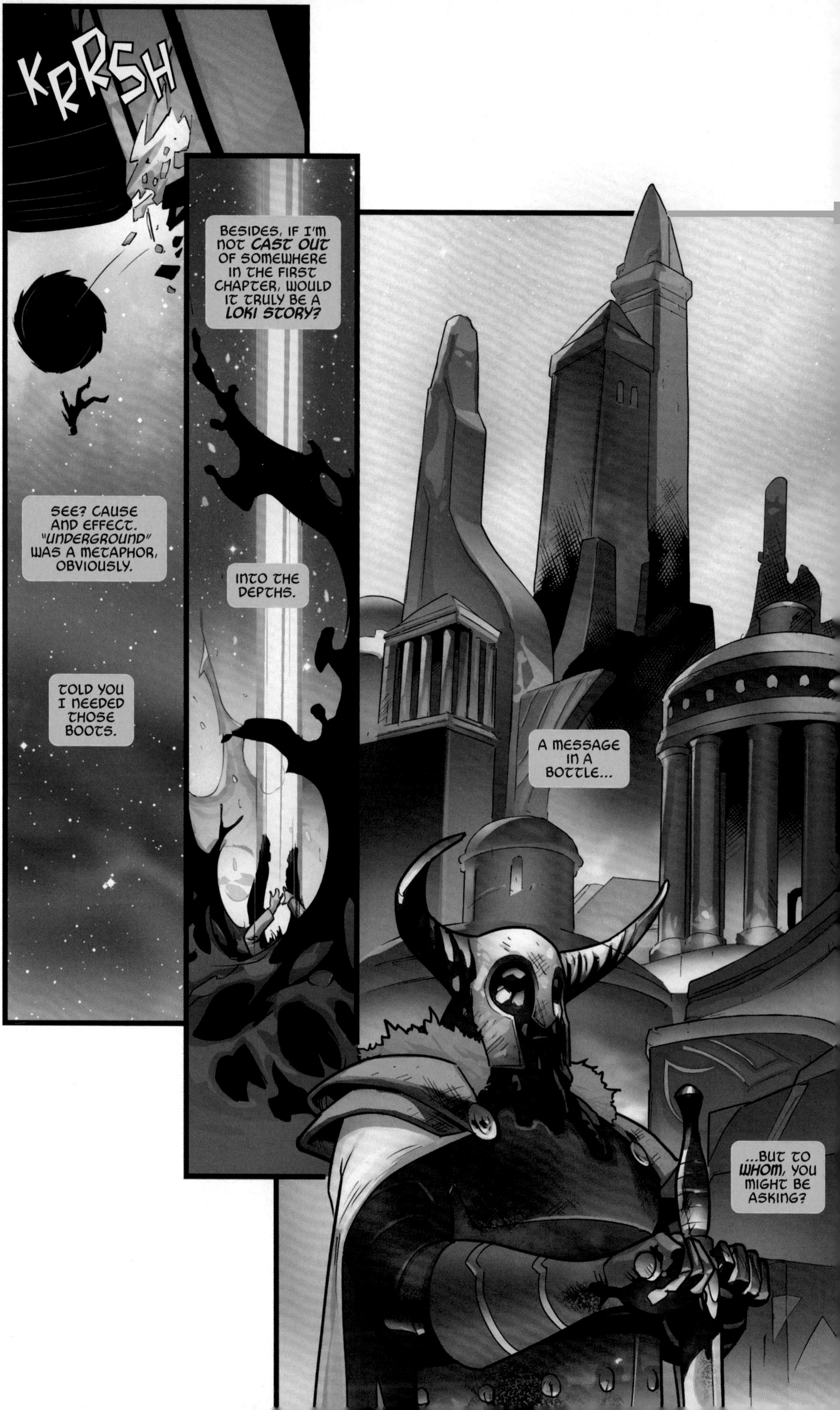

KRRSH
SEE? CAUSE AND EFFECT. "UNDERGROUND" WAS A METAPHOR, OBVIOUSLY.
TOLD YOU I NEEDED THOSE BOOTS.
BESIDES, IF I'M NOT CAST OUT OF SOMEWHERE IN THE FIRST CHAPTER, WOULD IT TRULY BE A LOKI STORY?
INTO THE DEPTHS.
A MESSAGE IN A BOTTLE...
...BUT TO WHOM, YOU MIGHT BE ASKING?

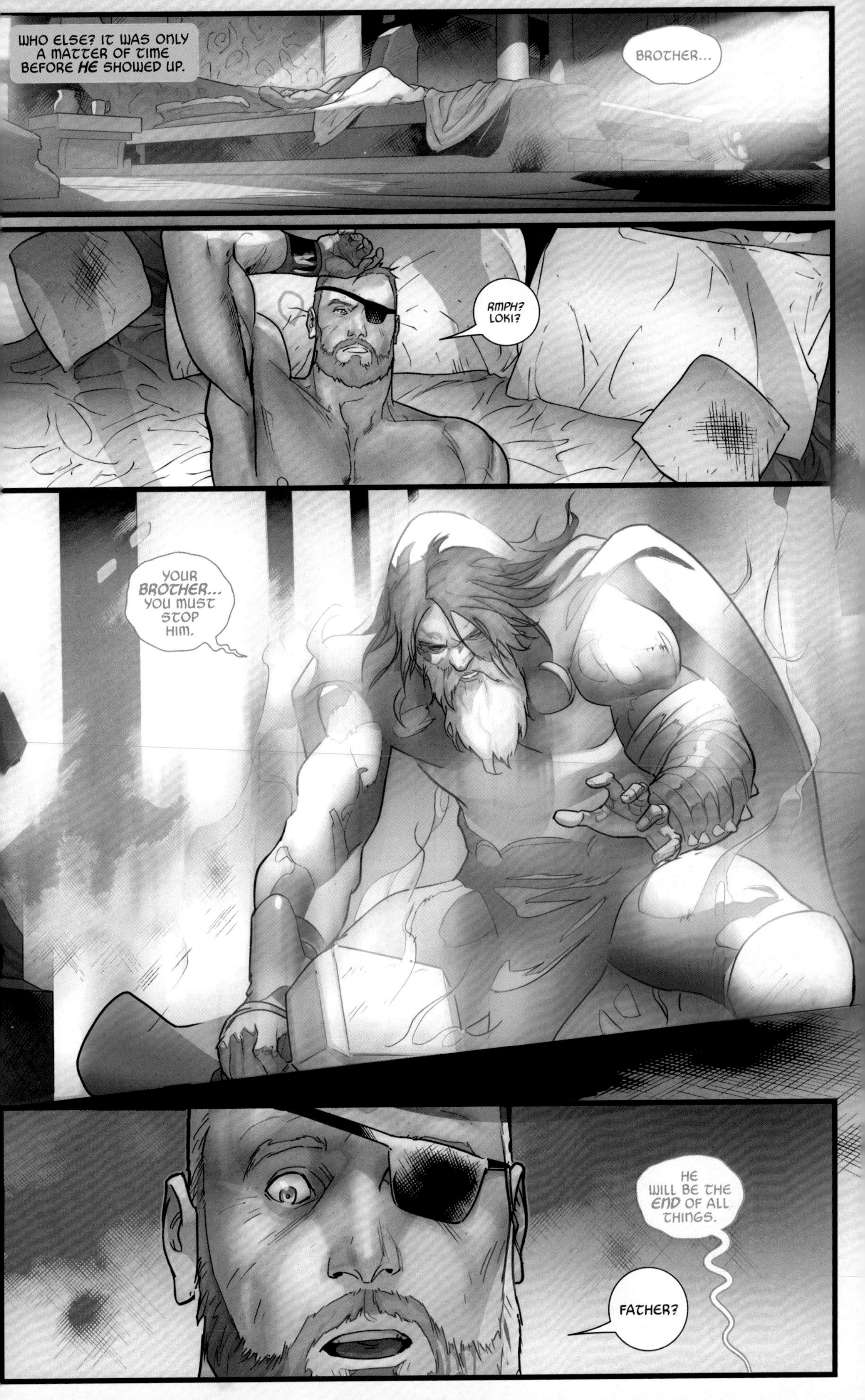
WHO ELSE? IT WAS ONLY A MATTER OF TIME BEFORE HE SHOWED UP.
BROTHER...
RMPH? LOKI?
YOUR BROTHER... YOU MUST STOP HIM.
HE WILL BE THE END OF ALL THINGS.
FATHER?

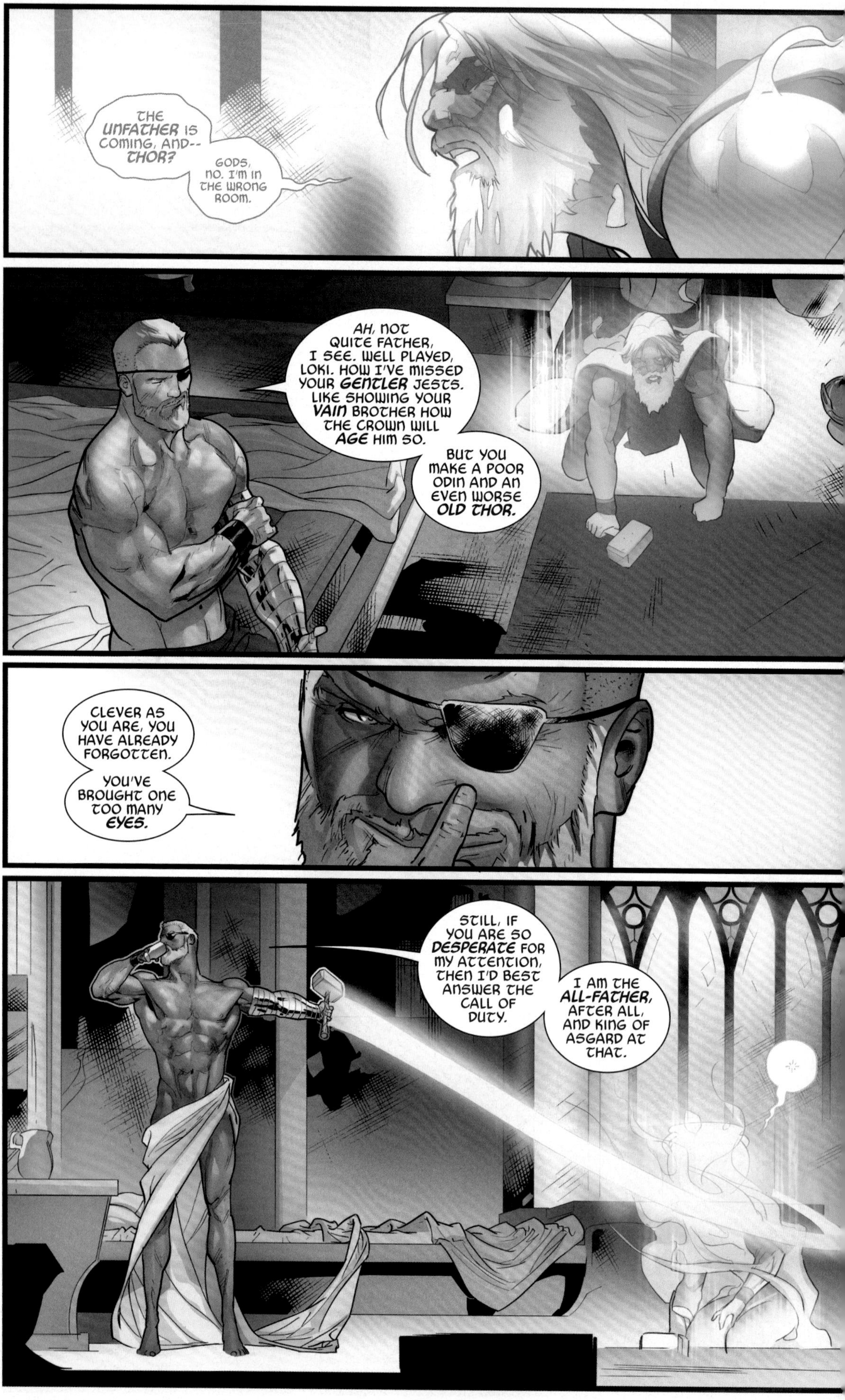
THE UNFATHER IS COMING, AND-- THOR?
GODS, NO. I'M IN THE WRONG ROOM.
AH, NOT QUITE FATHER, I SEE. WELL PLAYED, LOKI. HOW I'VE MISSED YOUR GENTLER JESTS. LIKE SHOWING YOUR VAIN BROTHER HOW THE CROWN WILL AGE HIM SO.
BUT YOU MAKE A POOR ODIN AND AN EVEN WORSE OLD THOR.
CLEVER AS YOU ARE, YOU HAVE ALREADY FORGOTTEN.
YOU'VE BROUGHT ONE TOO MANY EYES.
STILL, IF YOU ARE SO DESPERATE FOR MY ATTENTION, THEN I'D BEST ANSWER THE CALL OF DUTY.
I AM THE ALL-FATHER, AFTER ALL, AND KING OF ASGARD AT THAT.

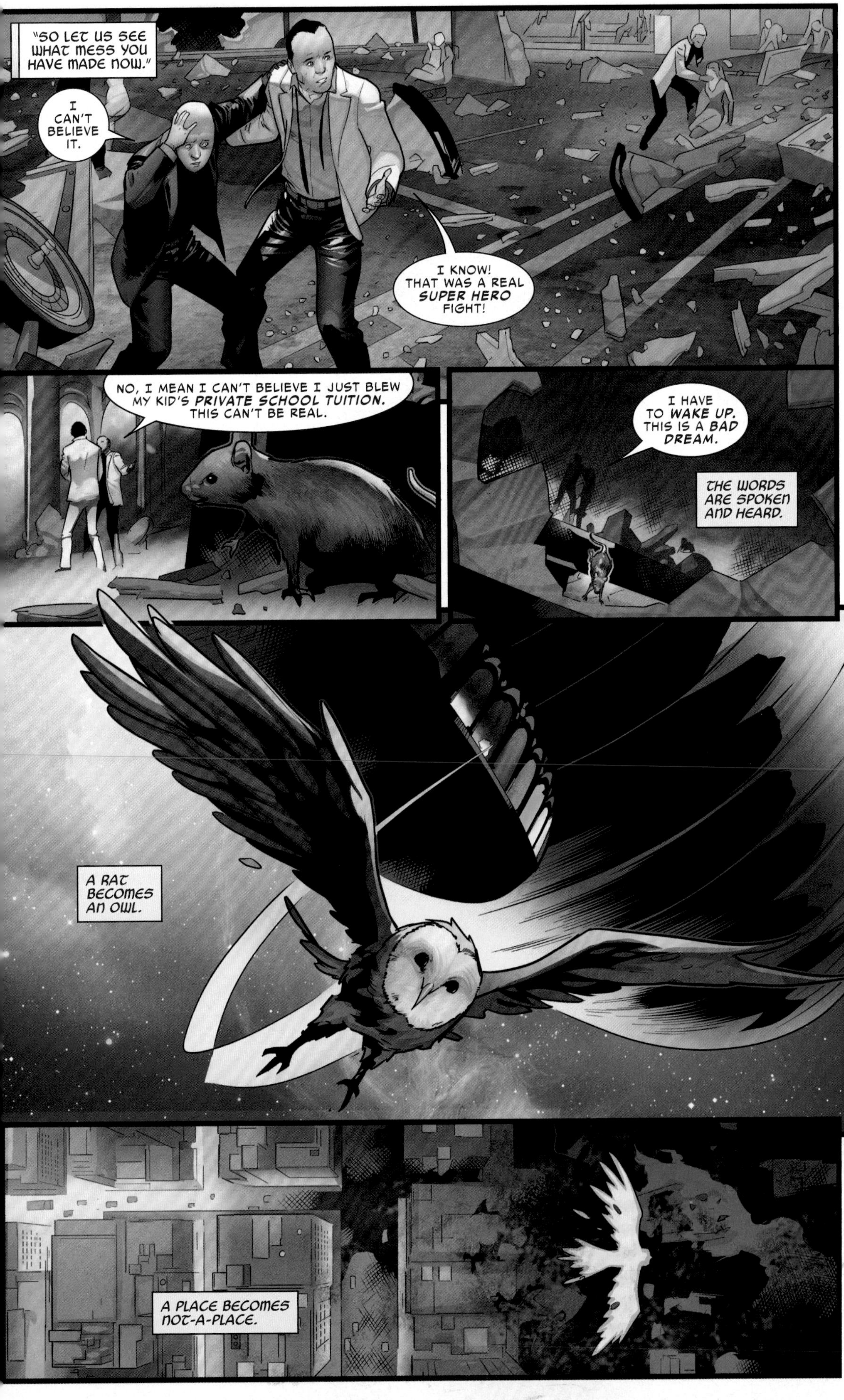
"SO LET US SEE WHAT MESS YOU HAVE MADE NOW."
I CAN'T BELIEVE IT.
I KNOW! THAT WAS A REAL SUPER HERO FIGHT!
NO, I MEAN I CAN'T BELIEVE I JUST BLEW MY KID'S PRIVATE SCHOOL TUITION. THIS CAN'T BE REAL.
I HAVE TO WAKE UP. THIS IS A BAD DREAM.
THE WORDS ARE SPOKEN AND HEARD.
A RAT BECOMES AN OWL.
A PLACE BECOMES NOT-A-PLACE.

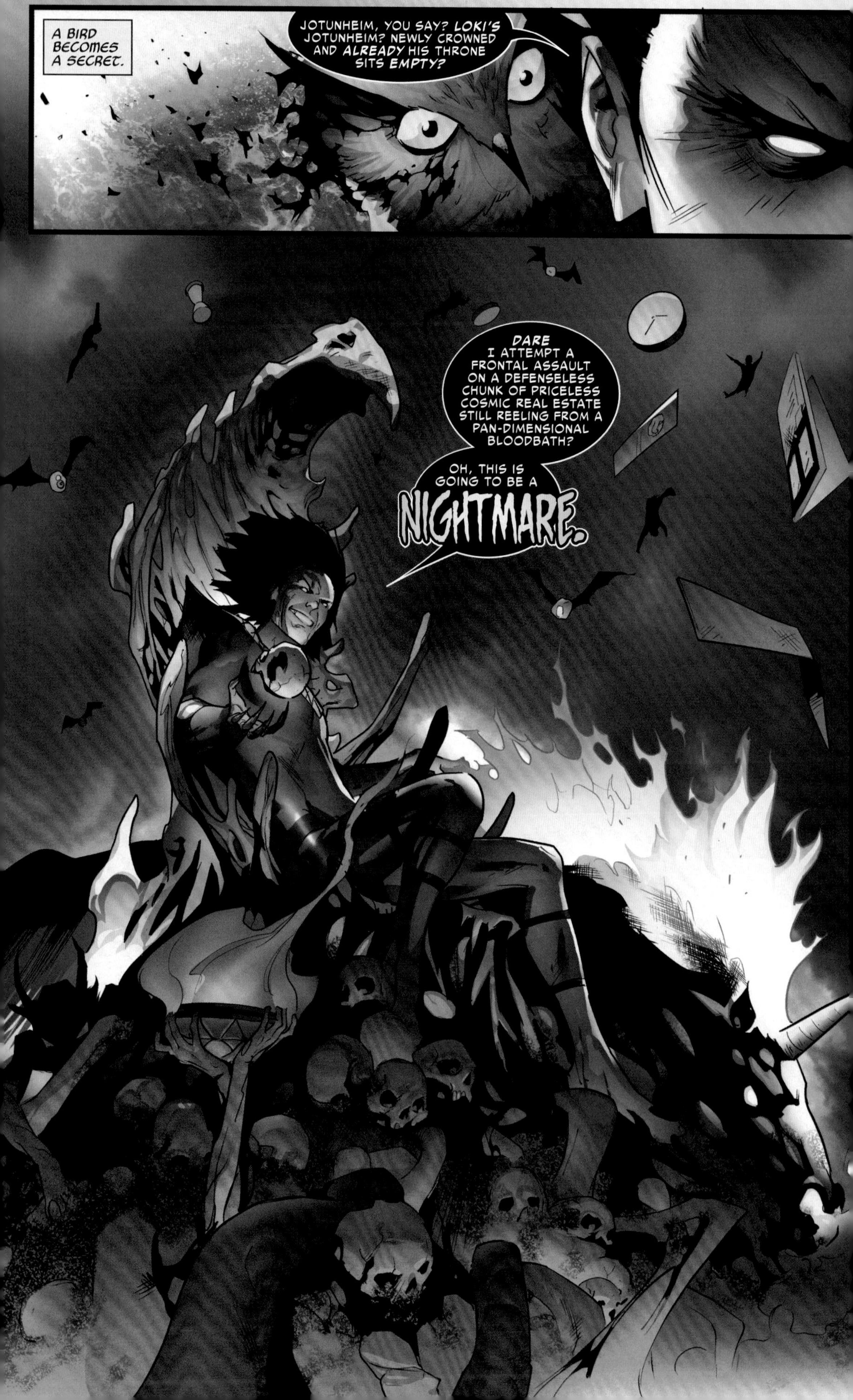
A BIRD BECOMES A SECRET.
JOTUNHEIM, YOU SAY? LOKI'S JOTUNHEIM? NEWLY CROWNED AND ALREADY HIS THRONE SITS EMPTY?
DARE I ATTEMPT A FRONTAL ASSAULT ON A DEFENSELESS CHUNK OF PRICELESS COSMIC REAL ESTATE STILL REELING FROM A PAN-DIMENSIONAL BLOODBATH?
OH, THIS IS GOING TO BE A NIGHTMARE.

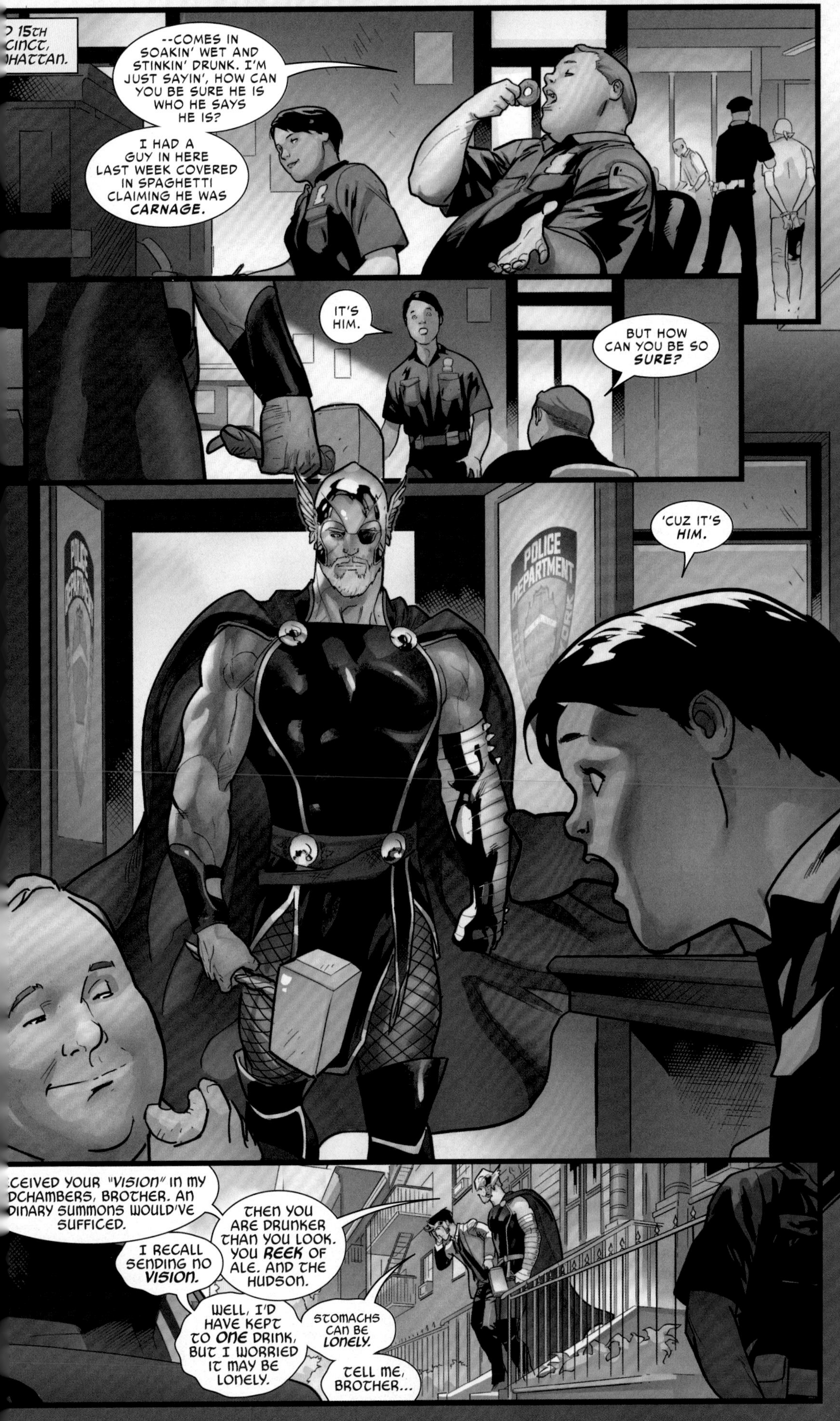

D 15TH
CINCT,
HATTAN.
--COMES IN SOAKIN' WET AND STINKIN' DRUNK. I'M JUST SAYIN', HOW CAN YOU BE SURE HE IS WHO HE SAYS HE IS?
I HAD A GUY IN HERE LAST WEEK COVERED IN SPAGHETTI CLAIMING HE WAS CARNAGE.
IT'S HIM.
BUT HOW CAN YOU BE SO SURE?
'CUZ IT'S HIM.
CEIVED YOUR "VISION" IN MY DCHAMBERS, BROTHER. AN DINARY SUMMONS WOULD'VE SUFFICED.
I RECALL SENDING NO VISION.
THEN YOU ARE DRUNKER THAN YOU LOOK. YOU REEK OF ALE. AND THE HUDSON.
WELL, I'D HAVE KEPT TO ONE DRINK, BUT I WORRIED IT MAY BE LONELY.
STOMACHS CAN BE LONELY.
TELL ME, BROTHER...

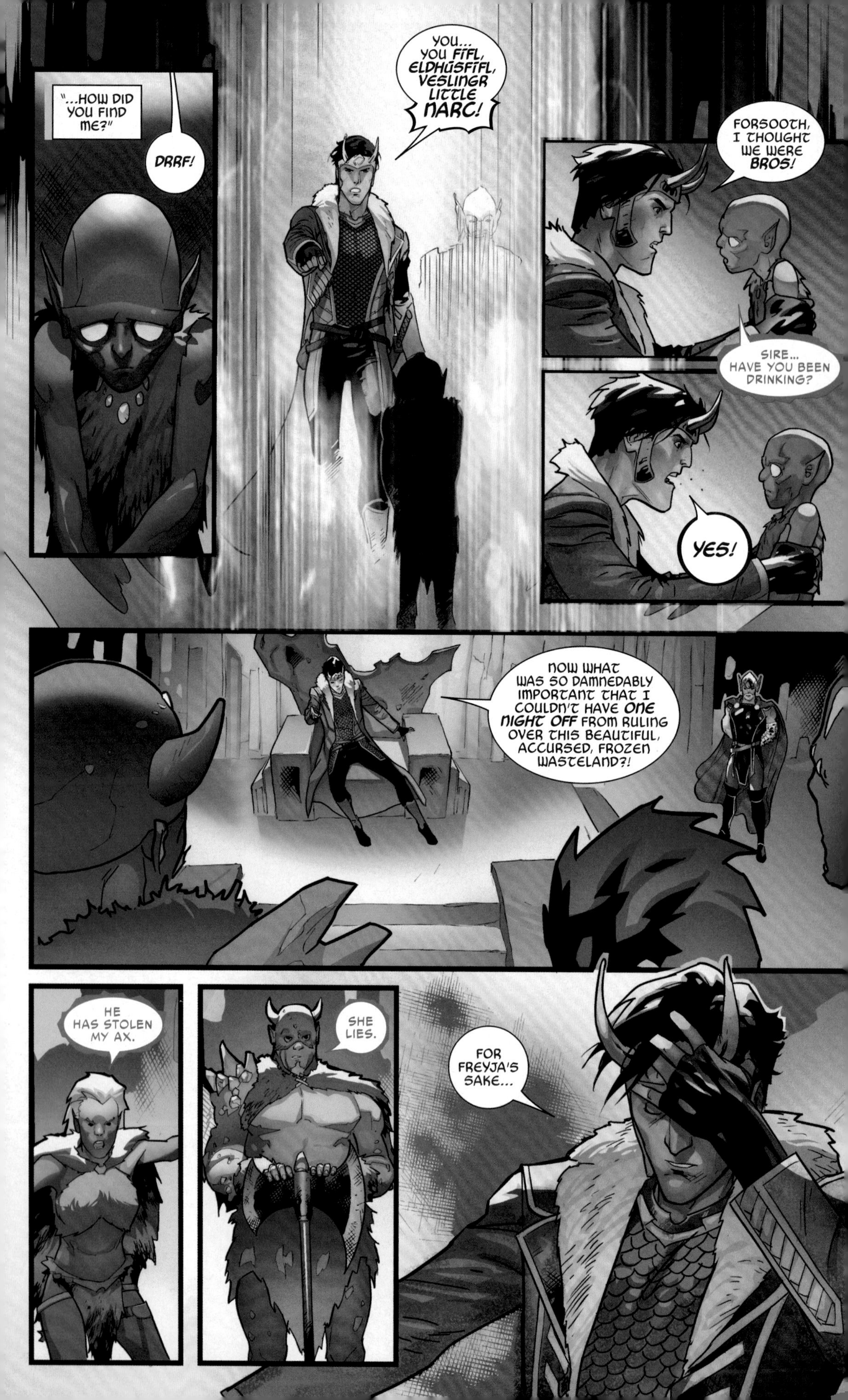
"...HOW DID YOU FIND ME?"
DRRF!
YOU... YOU FÍFL, ELDHÚSFÍFL, VESLINGR LITTLE NARC!
FORSOOTH, I THOUGHT WE WERE BROS!
SIRE... HAVE YOU BEEN DRINKING?
YES!
NOW WHAT WAS SO DAMNEDABLY IMPORTANT THAT I COULDN'T HAVE ONE NIGHT OFF FROM RULING OVER THIS BEAUTIFUL, ACCURSED, FROZEN WASTELAND?!
HE HAS STOLEN MY AX.
SHE LIES.
FOR FREYJA'S SAKE...

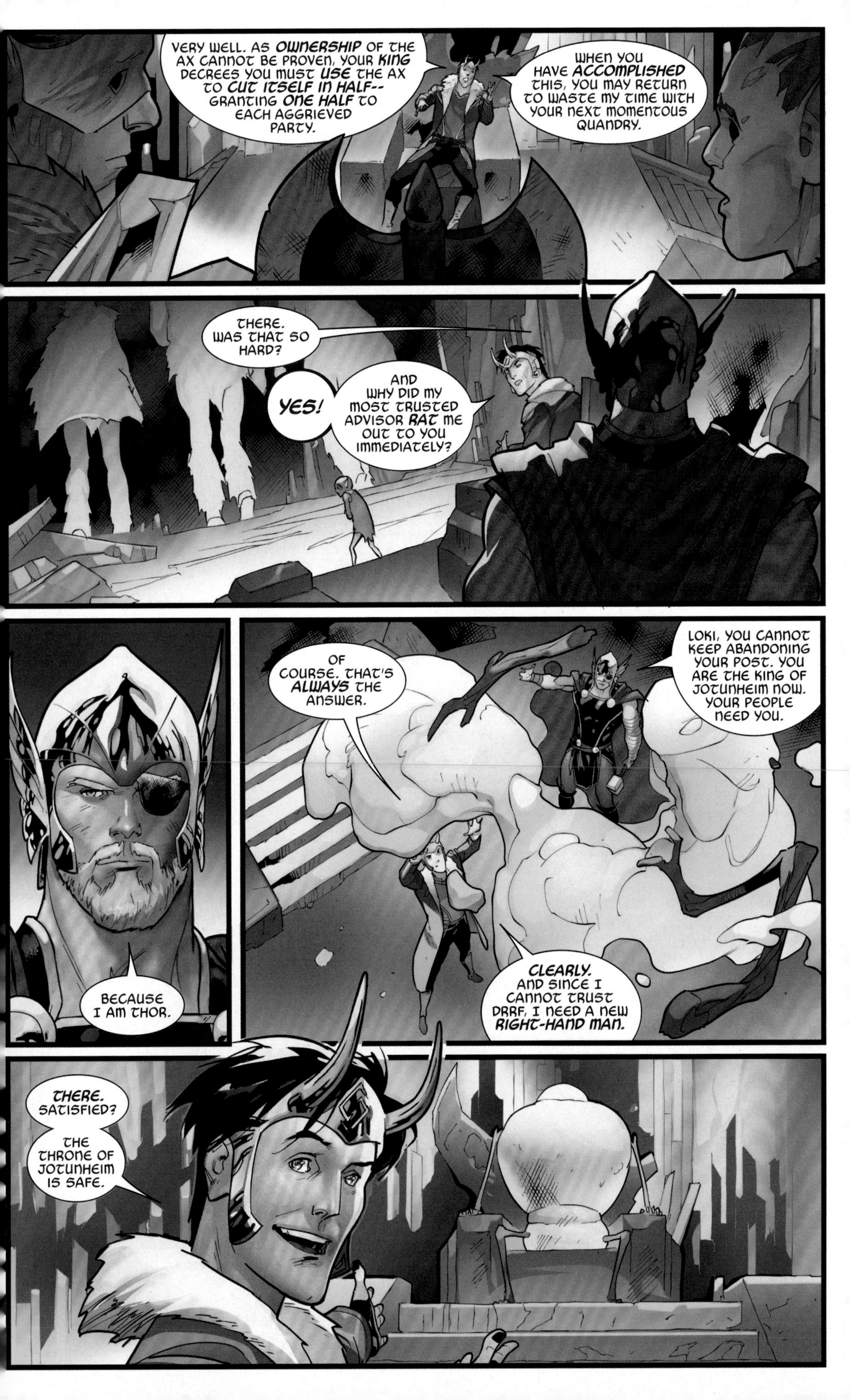
VERY WELL. AS OWNERSHIP OF THE AX CANNOT BE PROVEN, YOUR KING DECREES YOU MUST USE THE AX TO CUT ITSELF IN HALF-- GRANTING ONE HALF TO EACH AGGRIEVED PARTY.
WHEN YOU HAVE ACCOMPLISHED THIS, YOU MAY RETURN TO WASTE MY TIME WITH YOUR NEXT MOMENTOUS QUANDRY.
THERE. WAS THAT SO HARD?
YES!
AND WHY DID MY MOST TRUSTED ADVISOR RAT ME OUT TO YOU IMMEDIATELY?
BECAUSE I AM THOR.
OF COURSE. THAT'S ALWAYS THE ANSWER.
LOKI, YOU CANNOT KEEP ABANDONING YOUR POST. YOU ARE THE KING OF JOTUNHEIM NOW. YOUR PEOPLE NEED YOU.
CLEARLY. AND SINCE I CANNOT TRUST DRRF, I NEED A NEW RIGHT-HAND MAN.
THERE. SATISFIED?
THE THRONE OF JOTUNHEIM IS SAFE.

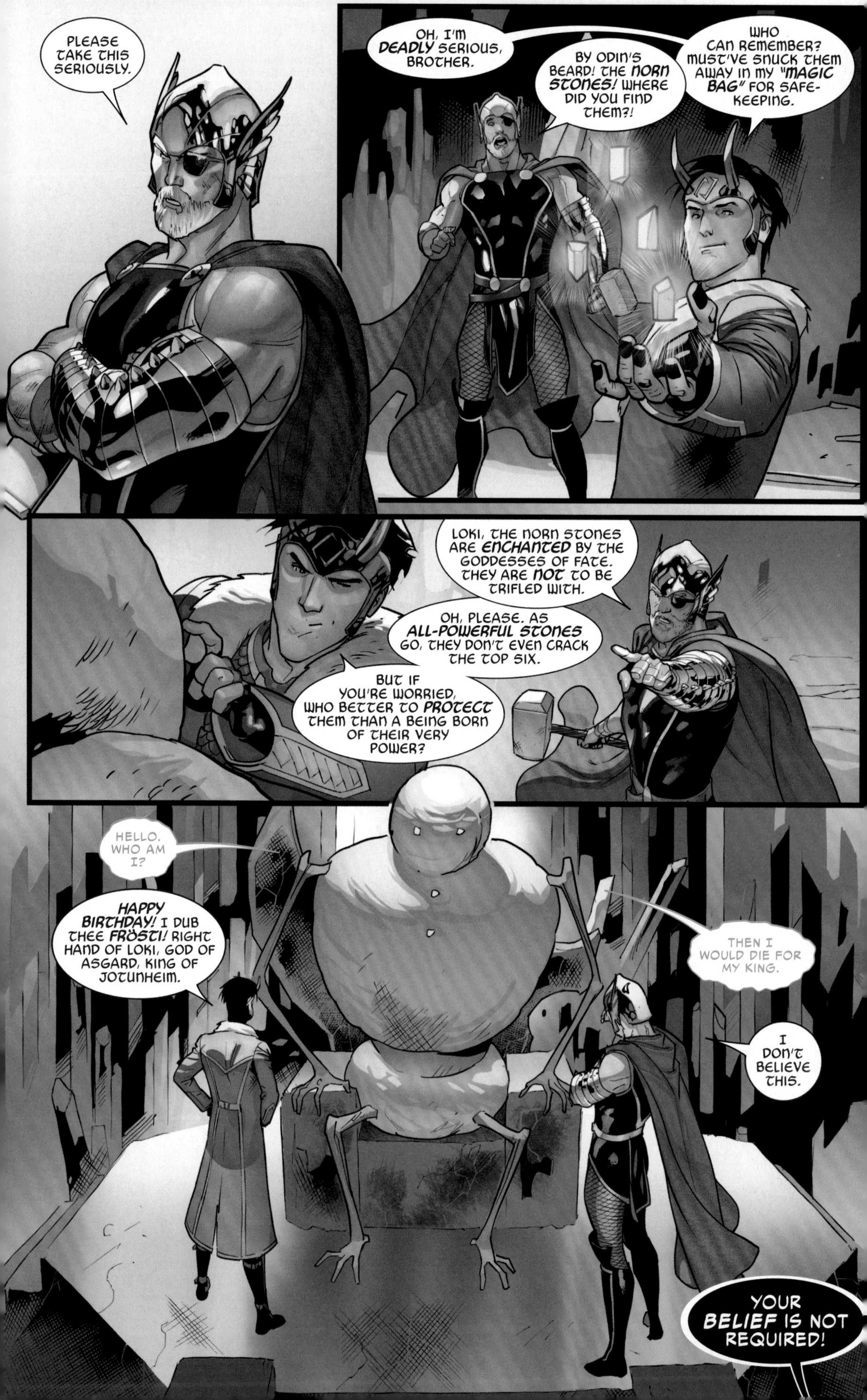
PLEASE TAKE THIS SERIOUSLY.
OH, I'M DEADLY SERIOUS, BROTHER.
BY ODIN'S BEARD! THE NORN STONES! WHERE DID YOU FIND THEM?!
WHO CAN REMEMBER? MUST'VE SNUCK THEM AWAY IN MY "MAGIC BAG" FOR SAFE-KEEPING.
LOKI, THE NORN STONES ARE ENCHANTED BY THE GODDESSES OF FATE. THEY ARE NOT TO BE TRIFLED WITH.
OH, PLEASE. AS ALL-POWERFUL STONES GO, THEY DON'T EVEN CRACK THE TOP SIX.
BUT IF YOU'RE WORRIED, WHO BETTER TO PROTECT THEM THAN A BEING BORN OF THEIR VERY POWER?
HELLO. WHO AM I?
HAPPY BIRTHDAY! I DUB THEE FRÖSTI! RIGHT HAND OF LOKI, GOD OF ASGARD, KING OF JOTUNHEIM.
THEN I WOULD DIE FOR MY KING.
I DON'T BELIEVE THIS.
YOUR BELIEF IS NOT REQUIRED!

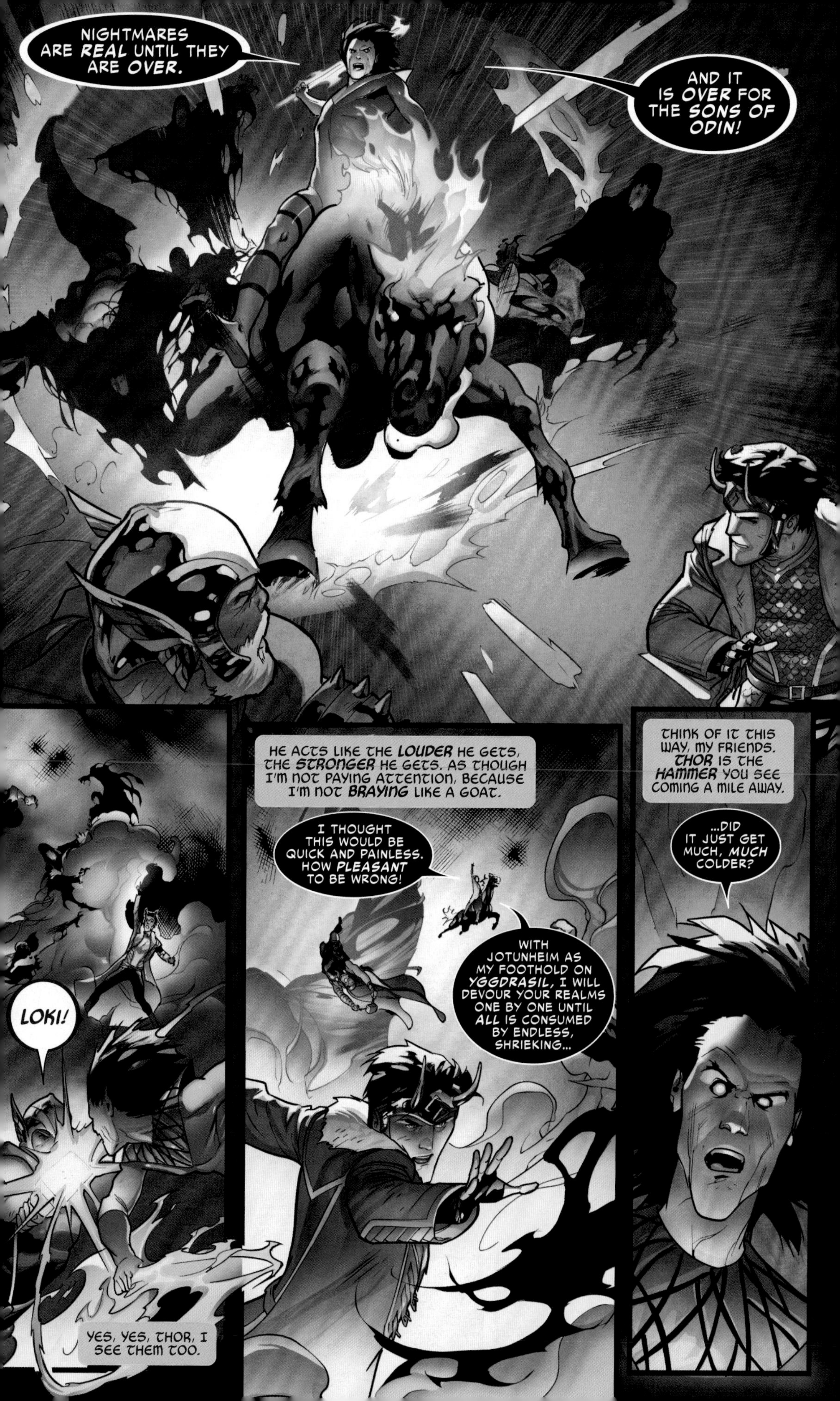

NIGHTMARES ARE REAL UNTIL THEY ARE OVER.
AND IT IS OVER FOR THE SONS OF ODIN!
LOKI!
YES, YES, THOR, I SEE THEM TOO.
HE ACTS LIKE THE LOUDER HE GETS, THE STRONGER HE GETS. AS THOUGH I'M NOT PAYING ATTENTION, BECAUSE I'M NOT BRAYING LIKE A GOAT.
I THOUGHT THIS WOULD BE QUICK AND PAINLESS. HOW PLEASANT TO BE WRONG!
WITH JOTUNHEIM AS MY FOOTHOLD ON YGGDRASIL, I WILL DEVOUR YOUR REALMS ONE BY ONE UNTIL ALL IS CONSUMED BY ENDLESS, SHRIEKING...
THINK OF IT THIS WAY, MY FRIENDS. THOR IS THE HAMMER YOU SEE COMING A MILE AWAY.
...DID IT JUST GET MUCH, MUCH COLDER?

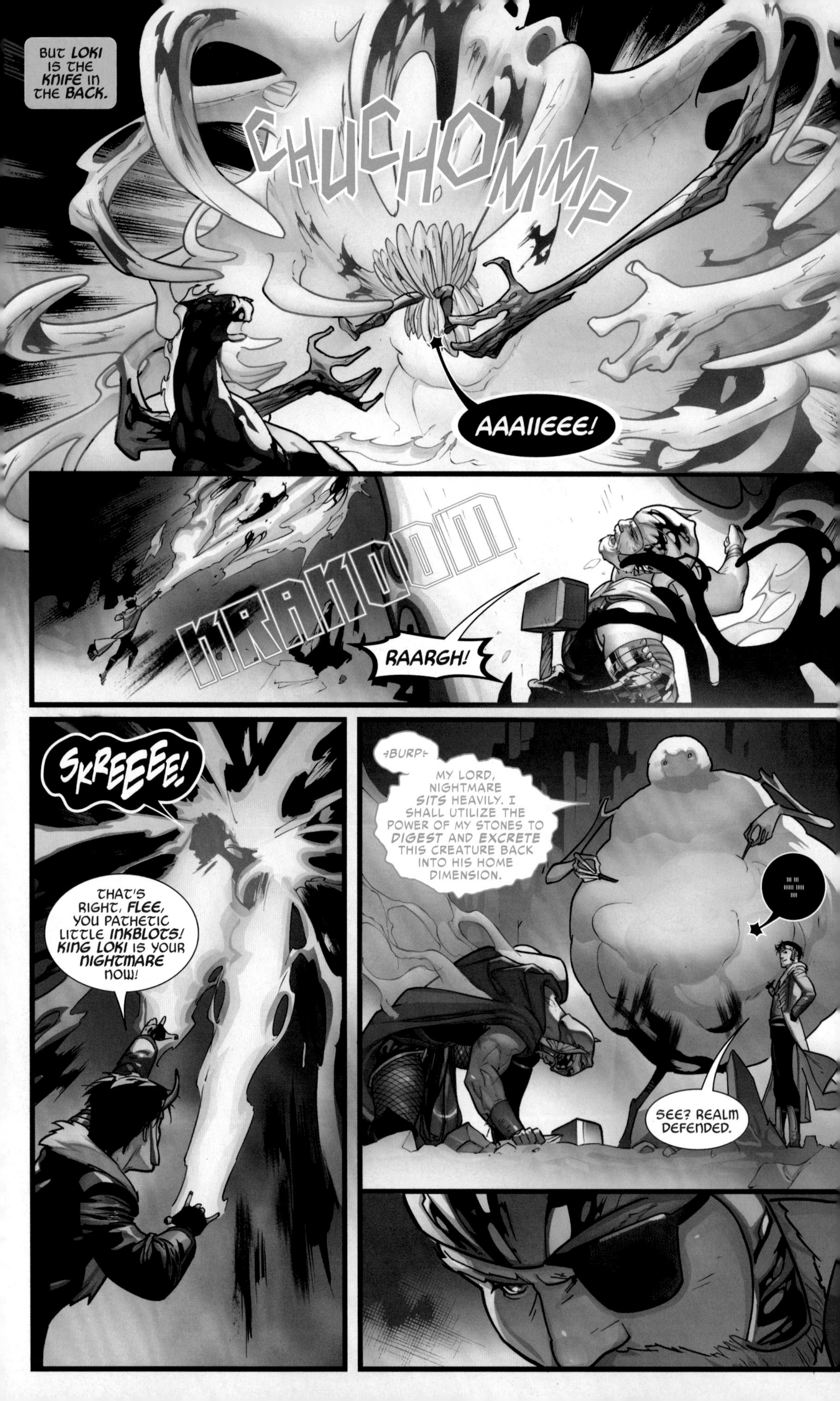

BUT LOKI IS THE KNIFE IN THE BACK.
CHUCHOMMP
AAAIIEEE!
KRAKOOM
RAARGH!
SKREEEE!
THAT'S RIGHT, FLEE, YOU PATHETIC LITTLE INKBLOTS! KING LOKI IS YOUR NIGHTMARE NOW!
BURP
MY LORD, NIGHTMARE SITS HEAVILY. I SHALL UTILIZE THE POWER OF MY STONES TO DIGEST AND EXCRETE THIS CREATURE BACK INTO HIS HOME DIMENSION.
SEE? REALM DEFENDED.

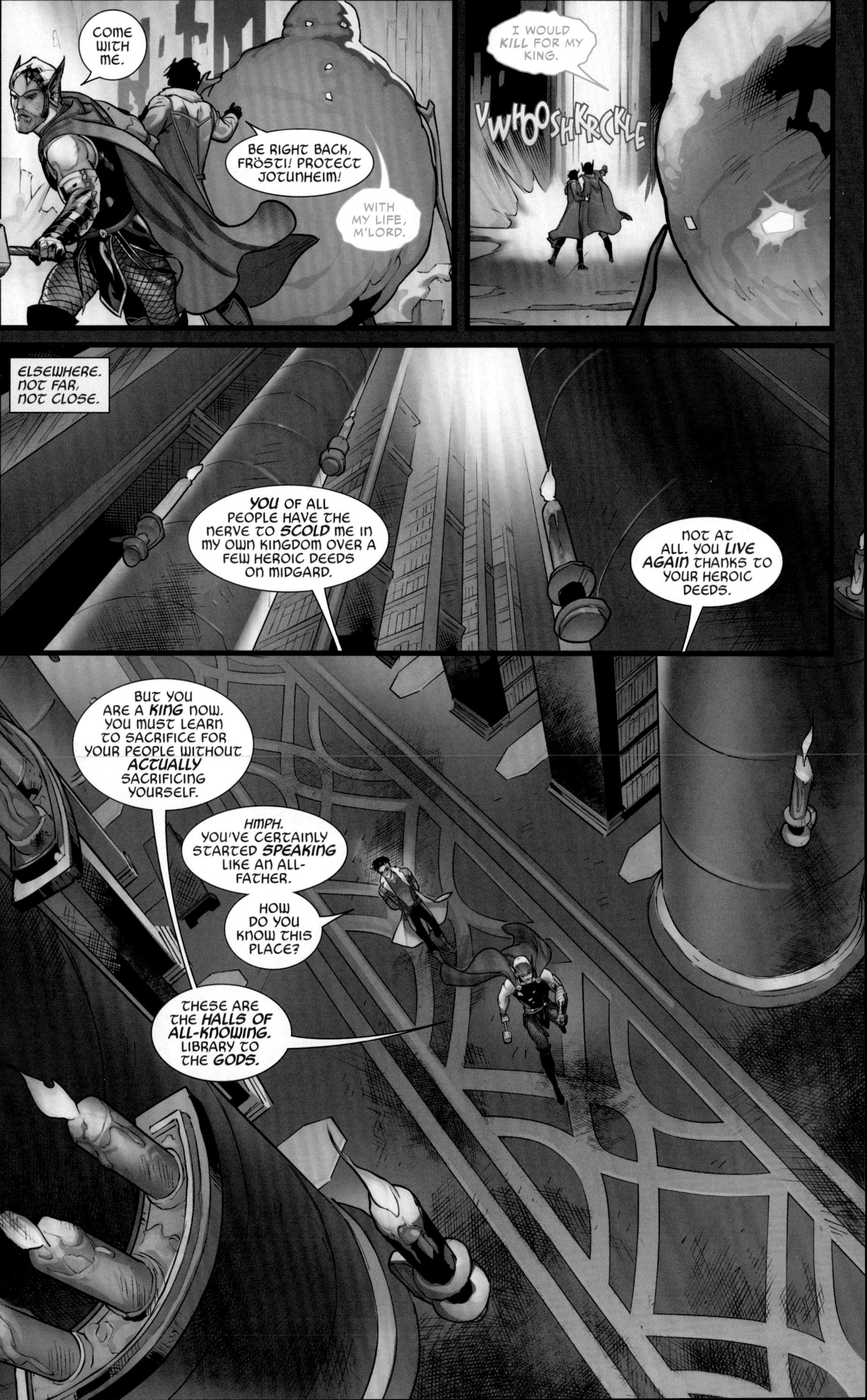
COME WITH ME.
BE RIGHT BACK, FRÖSTI! PROTECT JOTUNHEIM!
WITH MY LIFE, M'LORD.
I WOULD KILL FOR MY KING.
VWHOOSHKRCKLE
ELSEWHERE. NOT FAR, NOT CLOSE.
YOU OF ALL PEOPLE HAVE THE NERVE TO SCOLD ME IN MY OWN KINGDOM OVER A FEW HEROIC DEEDS ON MIDGARD.
NOT AT ALL. YOU LIVE AGAIN THANKS TO YOUR HEROIC DEEDS.
BUT YOU ARE A KING NOW. YOU MUST LEARN TO SACRIFICE FOR YOUR PEOPLE WITHOUT ACTUALLY SACRIFICING YOURSELF.
HMPH. YOU'VE CERTAINLY STARTED SPEAKING LIKE AN ALL-FATHER.
HOW DO YOU KNOW THIS PLACE?
THESE ARE THE HALLS OF ALL-KNOWING. LIBRARY TO THE GODS.

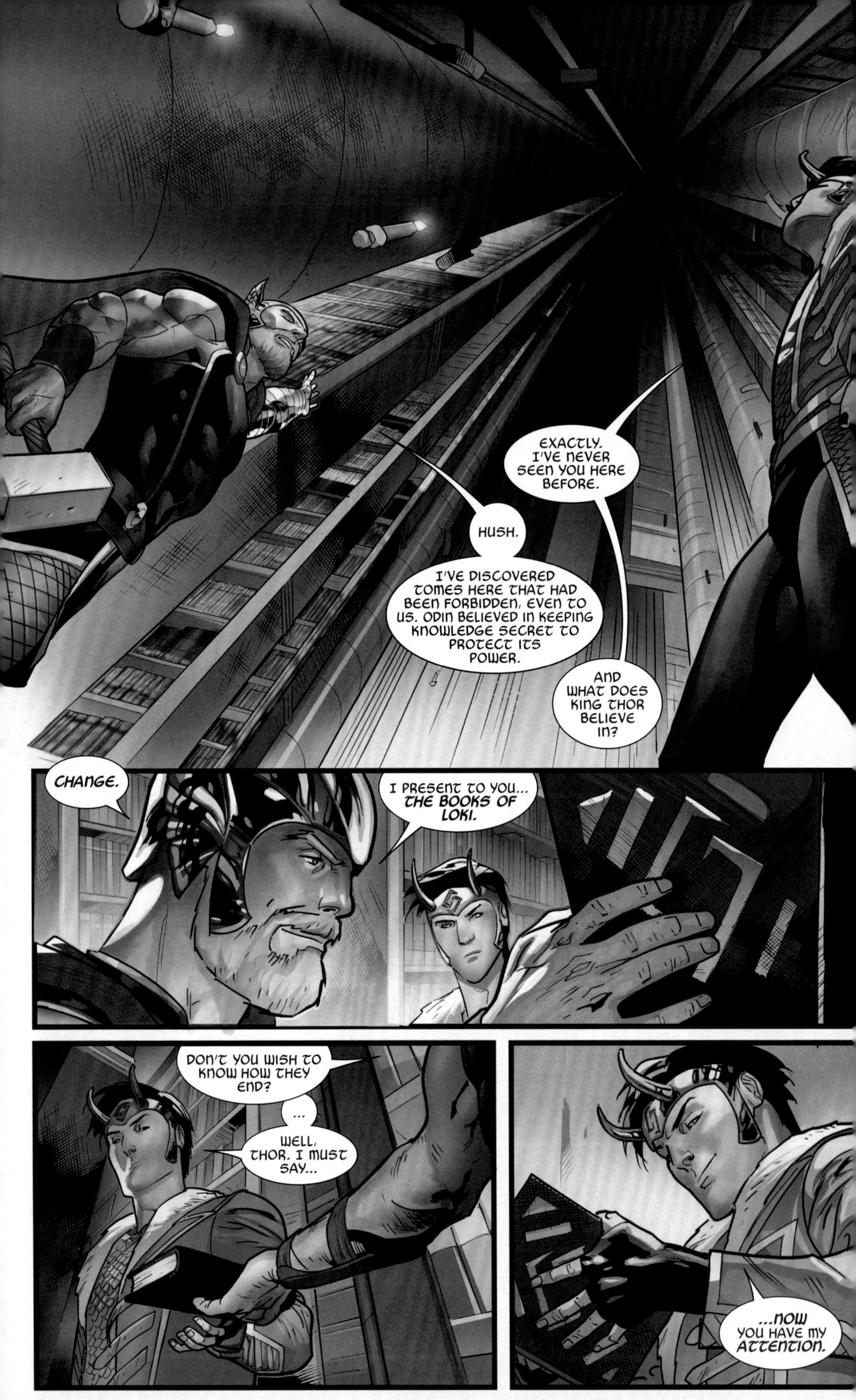
EXACTLY. I'VE NEVER SEEN YOU HERE BEFORE.
HUSH.
I'VE DISCOVERED TOMES HERE THAT HAD BEEN FORBIDDEN, EVEN TO US. ODIN BELIEVED IN KEEPING KNOWLEDGE SECRET TO PROTECT ITS POWER.
AND WHAT DOES KING THOR BELIEVE IN?
CHANGE.
I PRESENT TO YOU... THE BOOKS OF LOKI.
DON'T YOU WISH TO KNOW HOW THEY END?
...
WELL, THOR. I MUST SAY...
...NOW YOU HAVE MY ATTENTION.

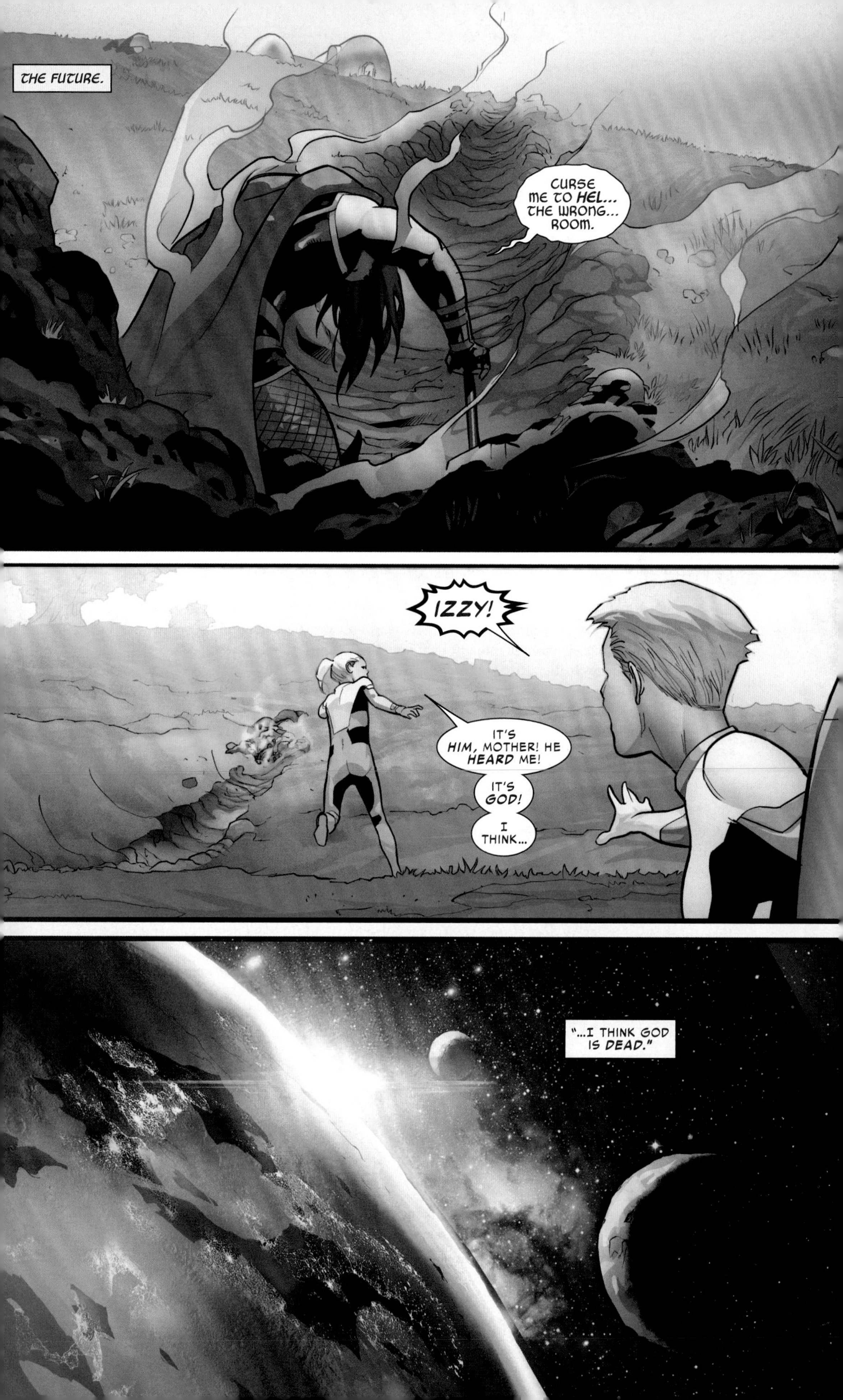
THE FUTURE.
CURSE ME TO HEL... THE WRONG... ROOM.
IZZY!
IT'S HIM, MOTHER! HE HEARD ME!
IT'S GOD!
I THINK...
"...I THINK GOD IS DEAD."

"Here I am destined to remain until my plight causes someone to shed a tear!"

So spoken by Loki in his first appearance, in *Journey Into Mystery #85*. He's stuck in a tree (sure) and gets free (obviously) on a technicality (of course). For who could ever shed a "real" tear for the God of Mischief? Or Chaos? Or, dare I say, "Evil"?

The phrase "too clever for their own good" is very revealing. It equates intelligence with destructiveness and ignorance with safety. It reeks of unearned authority, which is to say, almost all authority.

When I was in eighth grade, Mrs. L., the language arts teacher, and Mr. A., the vice-principal, had just wrapped up some kind of forgettable grade-wide assembly to a room of 200+ agitated pubescents who wanted nothing more than to mash each other's faces together and/or play *Mortal Kombat*. So after we were done learning about the dangers of stealing stop signs or whatever, they asked us, "Any questions?"

I don't remember deciding to raise my hand: "Why are you dressed the same?"

The room erupted with laughter. You see, Mrs. L. and Mr. A. had come to work that day in identical outfits of a salmon-colored collared shirt beneath a navy sweater and pale gray khakis. It was so uncanny that I genuinely thought they might have done it on purpose, still mistakenly projecting wisdom on to the actions of adults. It wasn't even a JOKE, it was just an accurate observation. Lesson One: Some people don't know the difference, and they assume the joke is on them.

Lesson Two: This will not go unpunished. They dismissed everyone but me and then asked a question I was not prepared for: "Why did you do that?"

WHY? In the words of our one true god, "How the Hel should I know?" The circumstances presented themselves, and once you notice something, you can't un-notice it. I made them feel vulnerable, so they made me feel villainous.

Loki is a story about — and "for," and honestly "by" — the kids who really try to do everything right and still get punished for it. Those who can't shut off their minds, who don't think before they speak, who try every door just to see if it's unlocked — and then the next door behind it.

For the first time in his nearly 60-year history in the Marvel Universe (and the many thousands of years before that), Loki is operating in the black. He's got the benefit of the doubt and a little goodwill to burn. After half-heartedly vying for the throne of Asgard for so long, he's now ruler of his own kingdom! He's an undisputed hero who finally got everything he ever wanted! Right?

But that's not much of a story for the God of Stories. Or Mischief. Or Chaos. Or Evil. Maybe there's a reason none of these titles seem to stick. Maybe Loki has always been the God of Something Else Entirely...

Now let us pray.

-Daniel Kibblesmith

P.S. Next time, this will be a letter column, so name suggestions appreciated. Perhaps said prayers will be answered. Write us at MHEROES@marvel.com (and mark "Okay to print").

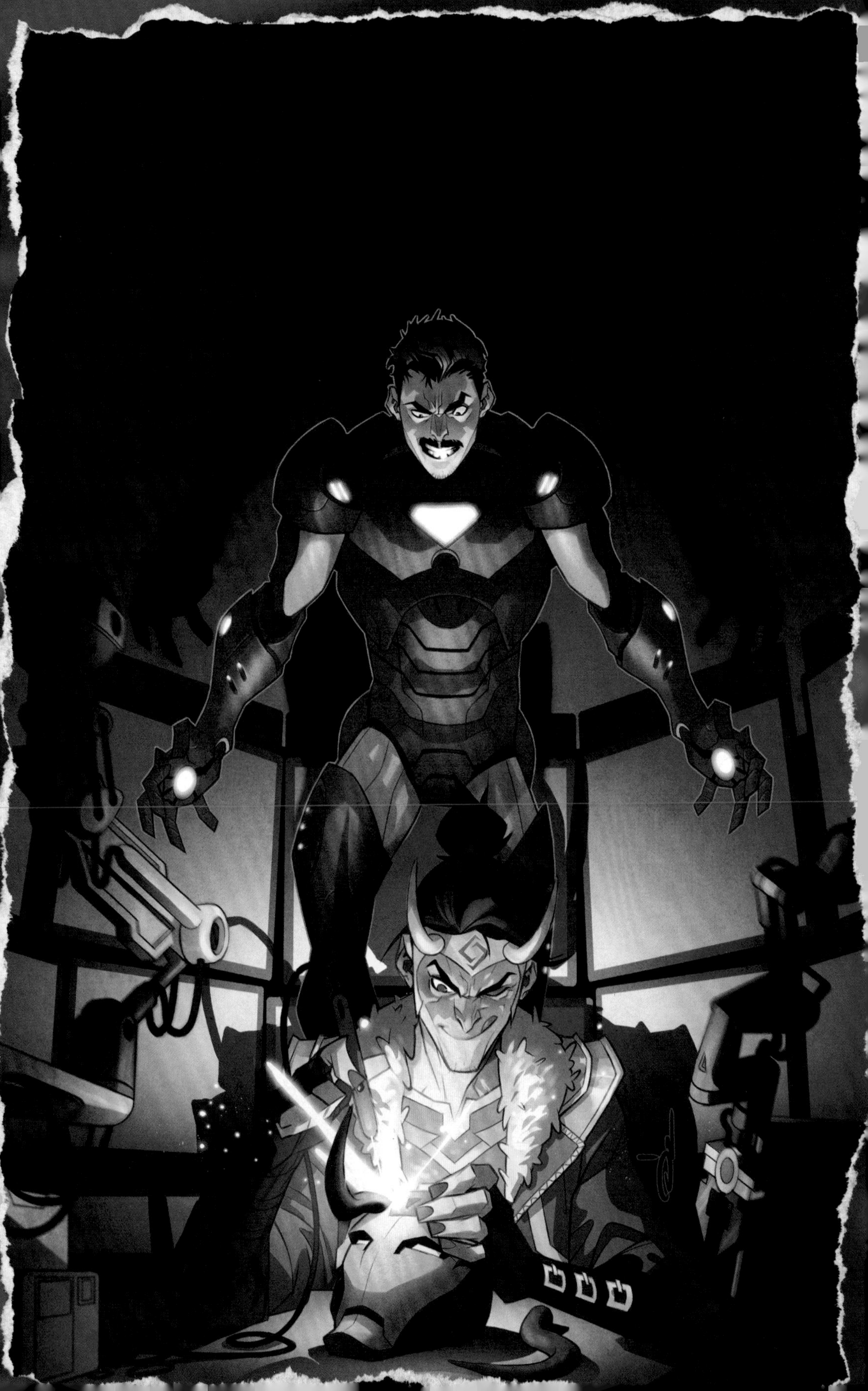

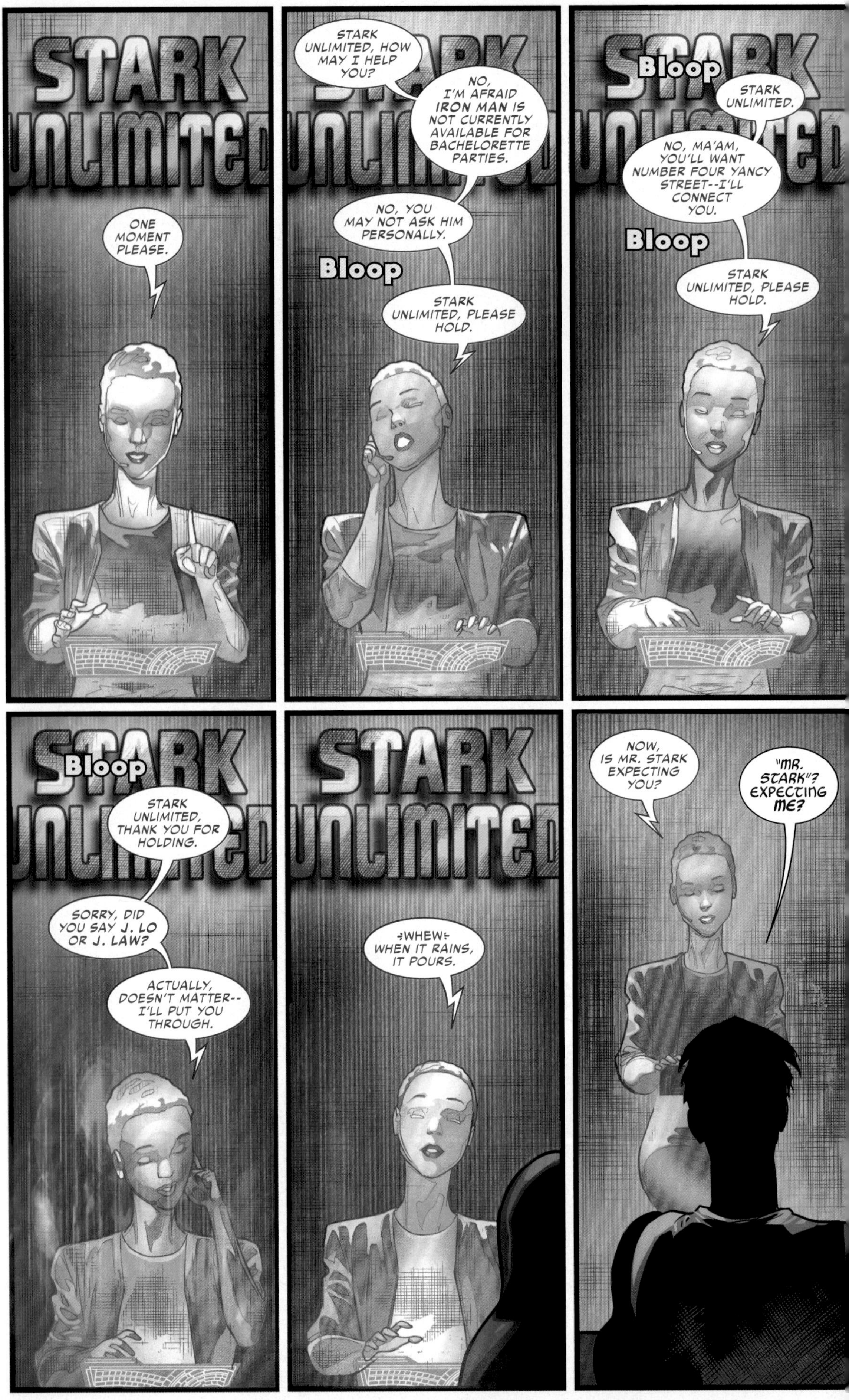
STARK UNLIMITED
ONE MOMENT PLEASE.
STARK UNLIMITED, HOW MAY I HELP YOU?
NO, I'M AFRAID IRON MAN IS NOT CURRENTLY AVAILABLE FOR BACHELORETTE PARTIES.
NO, YOU MAY NOT ASK HIM PERSONALLY.
Bloop
STARK UNLIMITED, PLEASE HOLD.
Bloop
STARK UNLIMITED.
NO, MA'AM, YOU'LL WANT NUMBER FOUR YANCY STREET--I'LL CONNECT YOU.
Bloop
STARK UNLIMITED, PLEASE HOLD.
Bloop
STARK UNLIMITED, THANK YOU FOR HOLDING.
SORRY, DID YOU SAY J. LO OR J. LAW?
ACTUALLY, DOESN'T MATTER--I'LL PUT YOU THROUGH.
STARK UNLIMITED
WHEW WHEN IT RAINS, IT POURS.
NOW, IS MR. STARK EXPECTING YOU?
"MR. STARK"? EXPECTING ME?

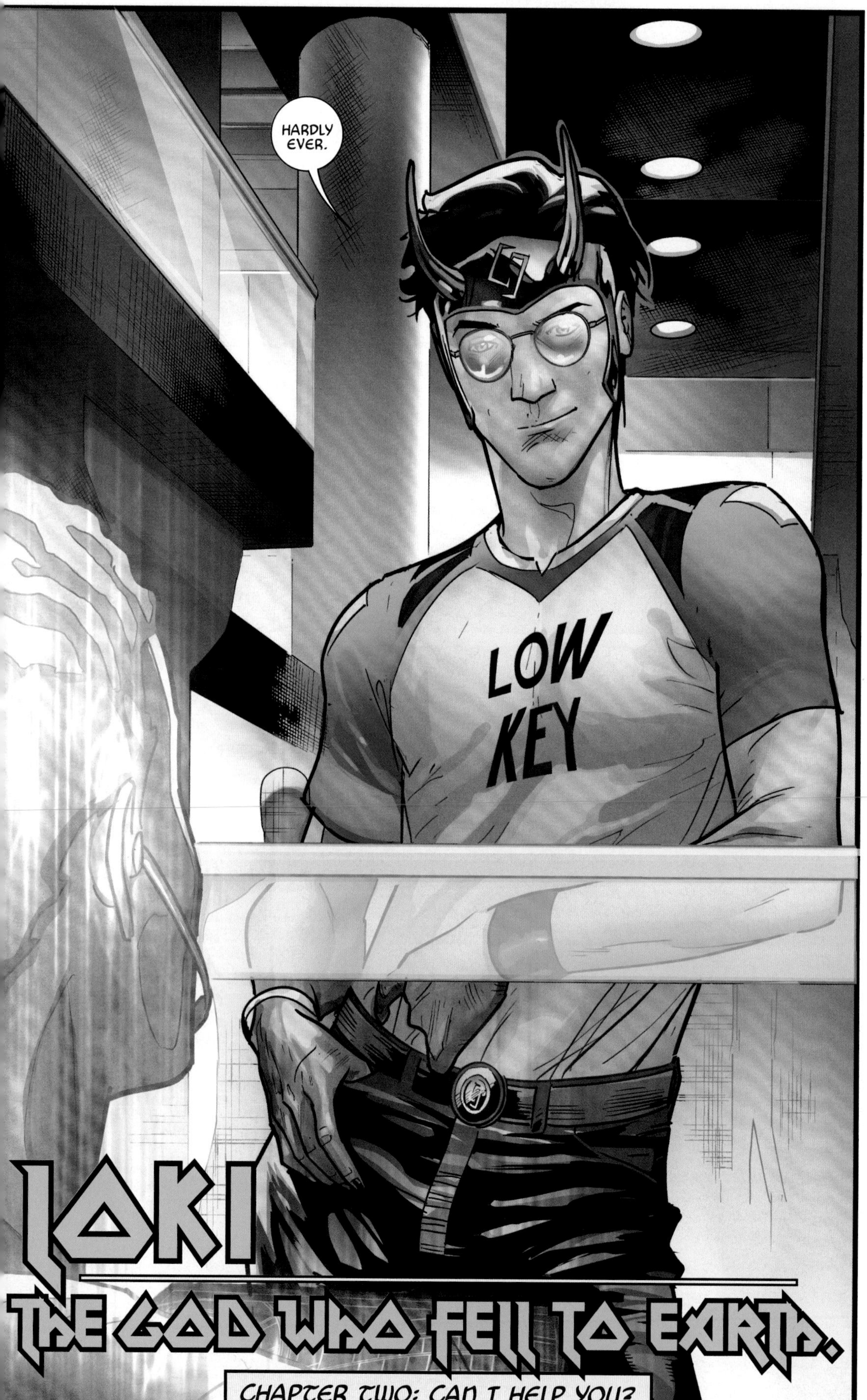

HARDLY EVER.
LOW KEY
LOKI
THE GOD WHO FELL TO EARTH.
CHAPTER TWO: CAN I HELP YOU?

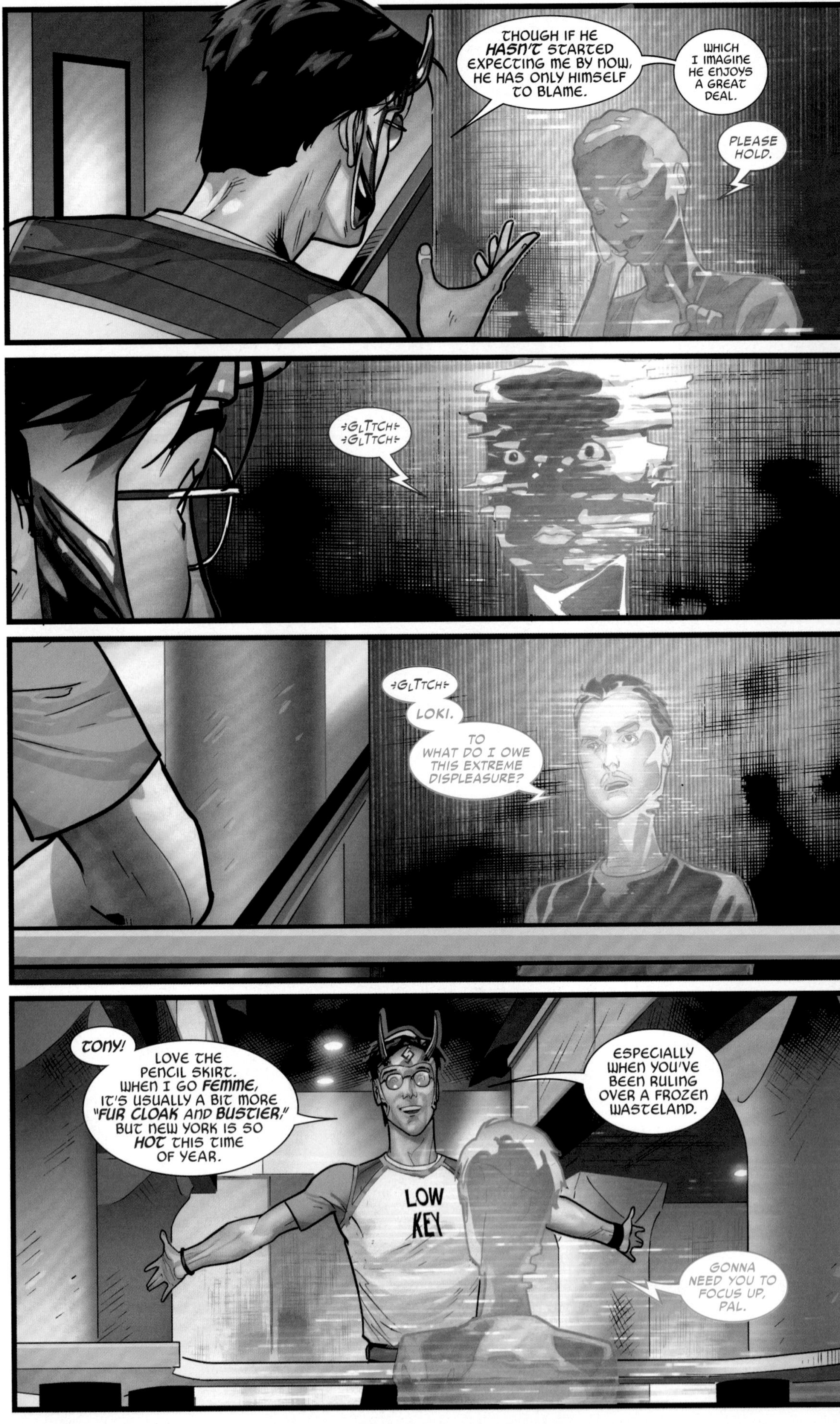
THOUGH IF HE HASN'T STARTED EXPECTING ME BY NOW, HE HAS ONLY HIMSELF TO BLAME.
WHICH I IMAGINE HE ENJOYS A GREAT DEAL.
PLEASE HOLD.
GLTTCH GLTTCH
GLTTCH
LOKI.
TO WHAT DO I OWE THIS EXTREME DISPLEASURE?
TONY!
LOVE THE PENCIL SKIRT. WHEN I GO FEMME, IT'S USUALLY A BIT MORE "FUR CLOAK AND BUSTIER," BUT NEW YORK IS SO HOT THIS TIME OF YEAR.
ESPECIALLY WHEN YOU'VE BEEN RULING OVER A FROZEN WASTELAND.
LOW KEY
GONNA NEED YOU TO FOCUS UP, PAL.

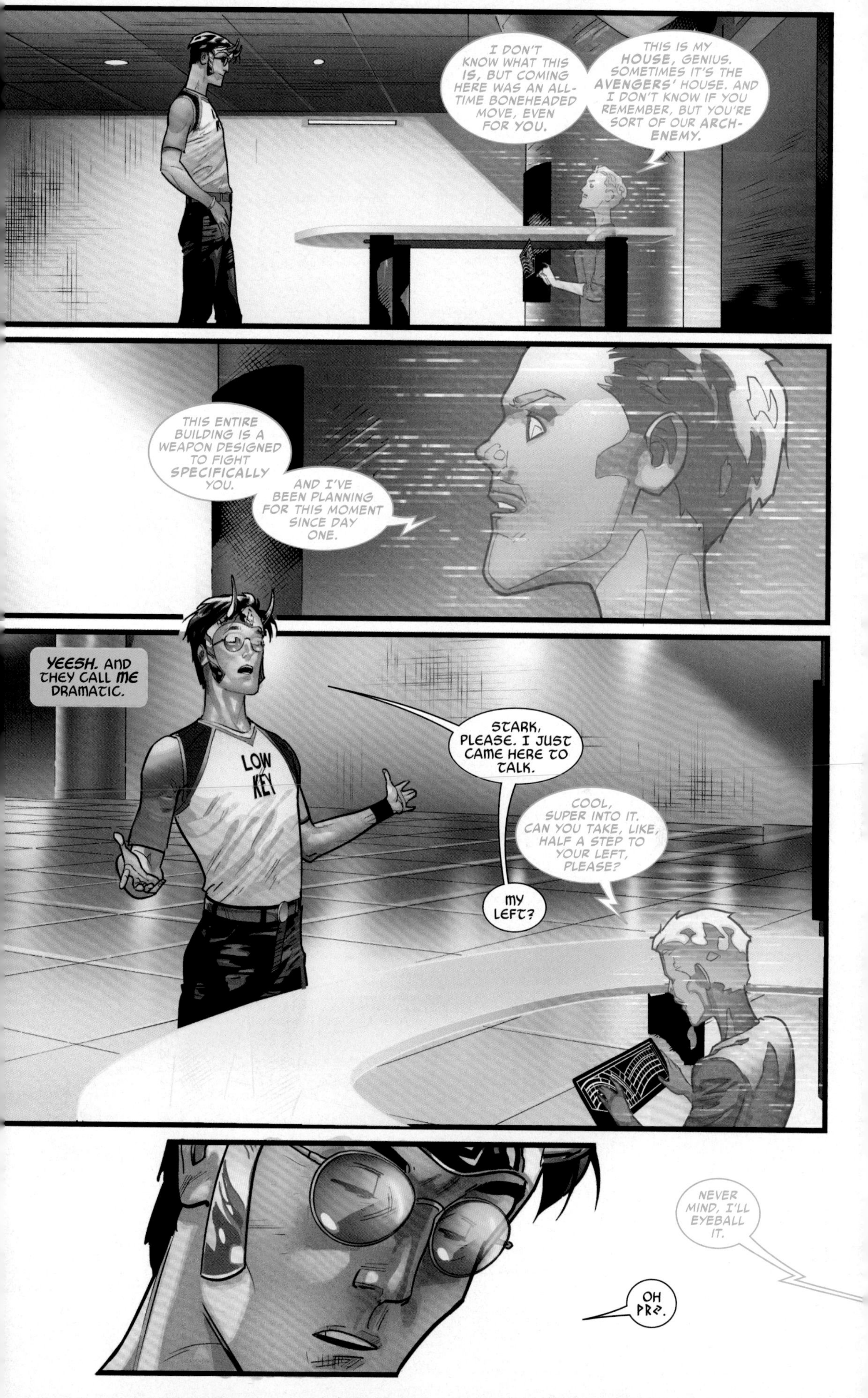
I DON'T KNOW WHAT THIS IS, BUT COMING HERE WAS AN ALL-TIME BONEHEADED MOVE, EVEN FOR YOU.
THIS IS MY HOUSE, GENIUS. SOMETIMES IT'S THE AVENGERS' HOUSE. AND I DON'T KNOW IF YOU REMEMBER, BUT YOU'RE SORT OF OUR ARCH-ENEMY.
THIS ENTIRE BUILDING IS A WEAPON DESIGNED TO FIGHT SPECIFICALLY YOU.
AND I'VE BEEN PLANNING FOR THIS MOMENT SINCE DAY ONE.
YEESH. AND THEY CALL ME DRAMATIC.
STARK, PLEASE. I JUST CAME HERE TO TALK.
COOL, SUPER INTO IT. CAN YOU TAKE, LIKE, HALF A STEP TO YOUR LEFT, PLEASE?
MY LEFT?
LOW KEY
NEVER MIND, I'LL EYEBALL IT.
OH PRE.

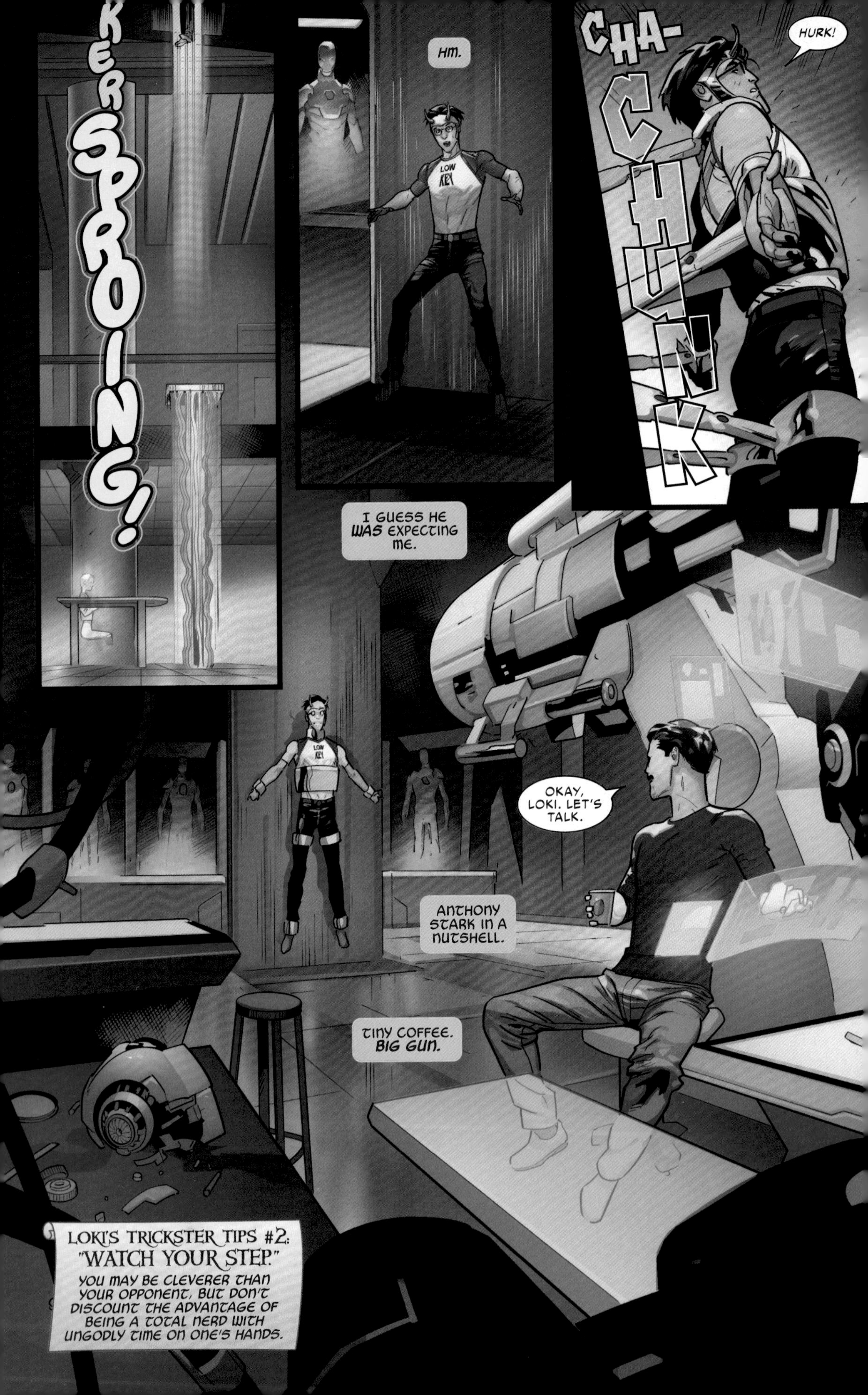
KER-SPROING!
HM.
CHA-CHUNK
HURK!
I GUESS HE WAS EXPECTING ME.
OKAY, LOKI. LET'S TALK.
ANTHONY STARK IN A NUTSHELL.
TINY COFFEE. BIG GUN.
LOKI'S TRICKSTER TIPS #2: "WATCH YOUR STEP."
YOU MAY BE CLEVERER THAN YOUR OPPONENT, BUT DON'T DISCOUNT THE ADVANTAGE OF BEING A TOTAL NERD WITH UNGODLY TIME ON ONE'S HANDS.

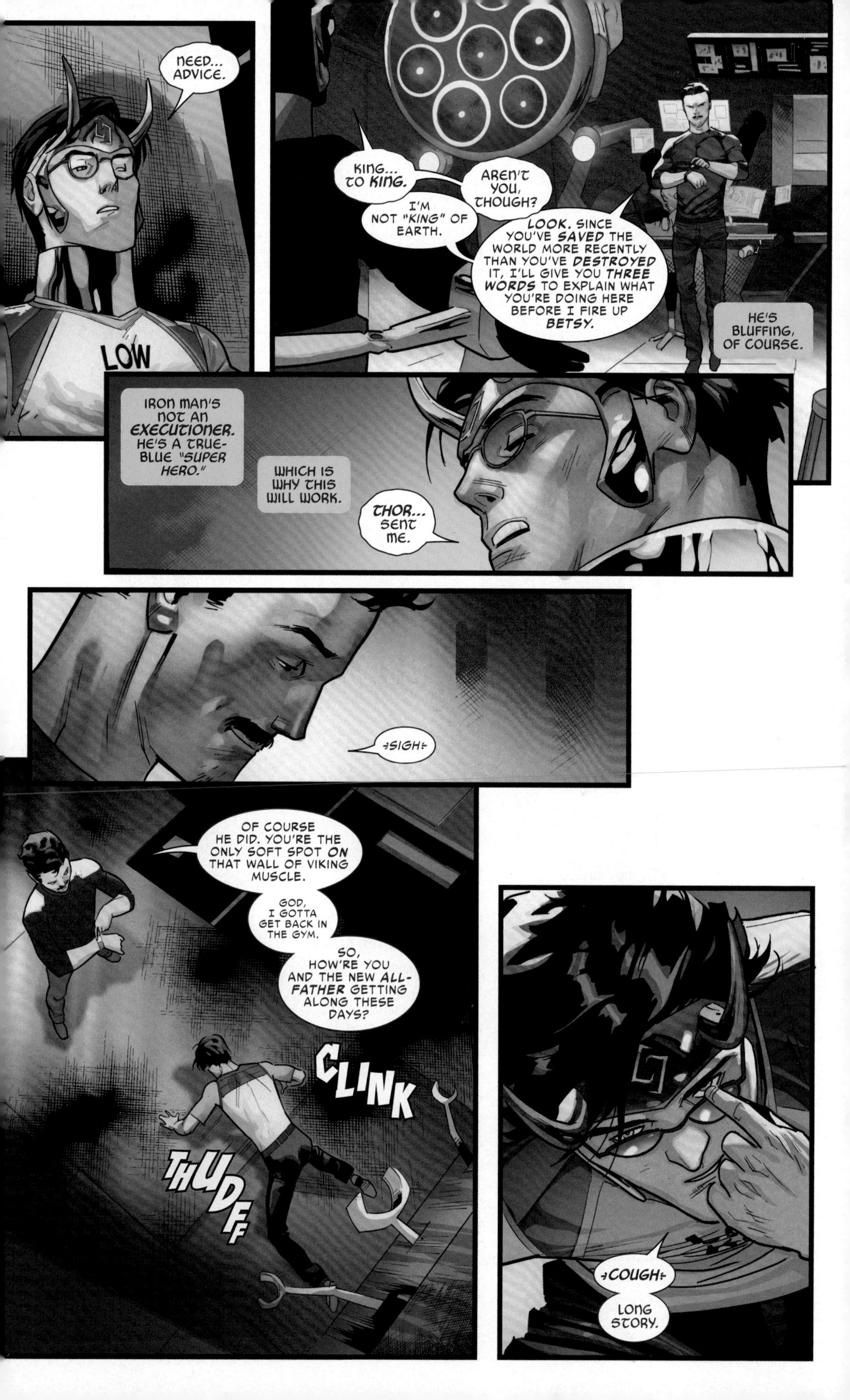
NEED... ADVICE.
KING... TO KING.
I'M NOT "KING" OF EARTH.
AREN'T YOU, THOUGH?
LOOK. SINCE YOU'VE SAVED THE WORLD MORE RECENTLY THAN YOU'VE DESTROYED IT, I'LL GIVE YOU THREE WORDS TO EXPLAIN WHAT YOU'RE DOING HERE BEFORE I FIRE UP BETSY.
HE'S BLUFFING, OF COURSE.
IRON MAN'S NOT AN EXECUTIONER. HE'S A TRUE-BLUE "SUPER HERO."
WHICH IS WHY THIS WILL WORK.
THOR... SENT ME.
SIGH
OF COURSE HE DID. YOU'RE THE ONLY SOFT SPOT ON THAT WALL OF VIKING MUSCLE.
GOD, I GOTTA GET BACK IN THE GYM.
SO, HOW'RE YOU AND THE NEW ALL-FATHER GETTING ALONG THESE DAYS?
CLINK
THUDFF
COUGH
LONG STORY.

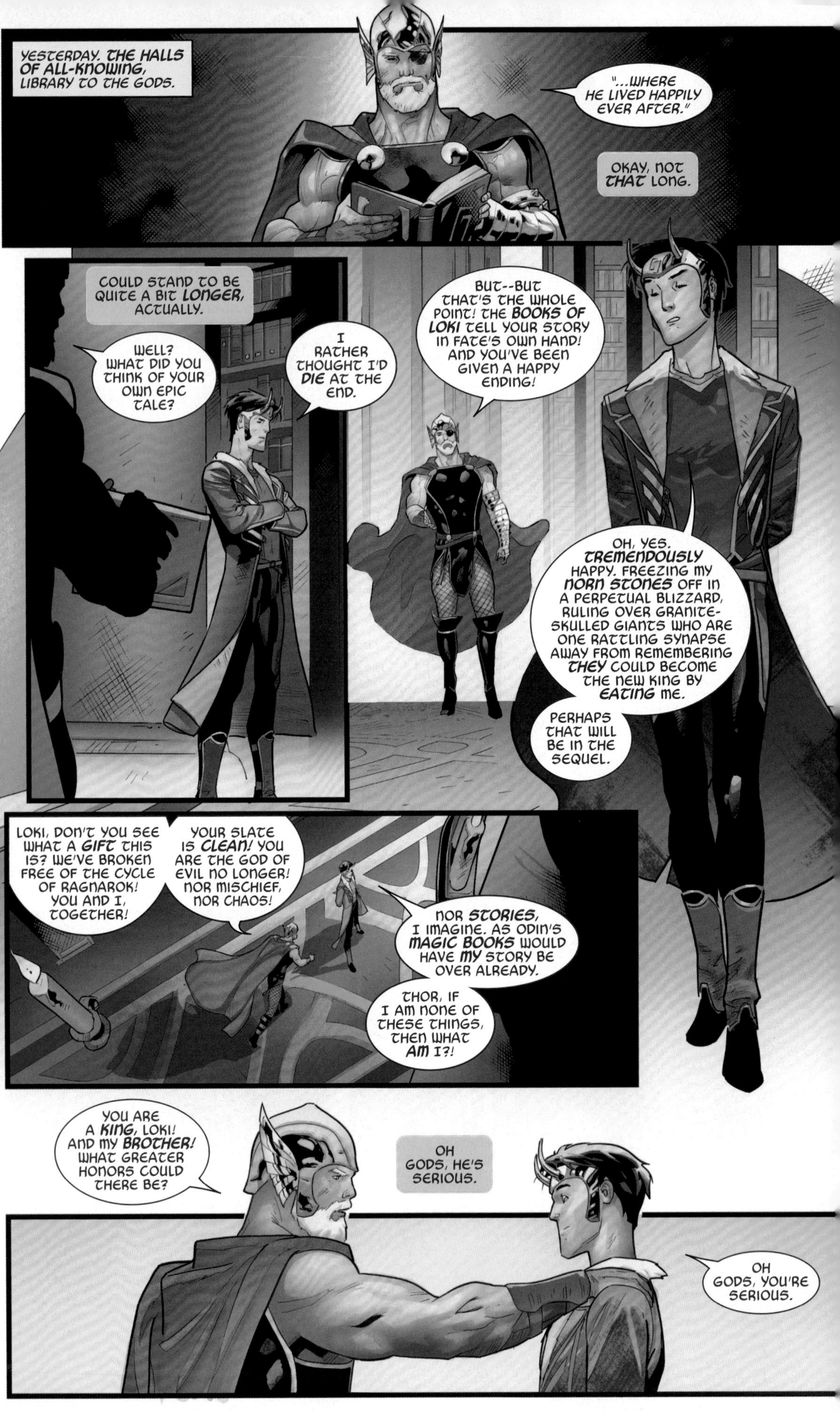

YESTERDAY. THE HALLS OF ALL-KNOWING, LIBRARY TO THE GODS.
"...WHERE HE LIVED HAPPILY EVER AFTER."
OKAY, NOT THAT LONG.
COULD STAND TO BE QUITE A BIT LONGER, ACTUALLY.
WELL? WHAT DID YOU THINK OF YOUR OWN EPIC TALE?
I RATHER THOUGHT I'D DIE AT THE END.
BUT--BUT THAT'S THE WHOLE POINT! THE BOOKS OF LOKI TELL YOUR STORY IN FATE'S OWN HAND! AND YOU'VE BEEN GIVEN A HAPPY ENDING!
OH, YES. TREMENDOUSLY HAPPY. FREEZING MY NORN STONES OFF IN A PERPETUAL BLIZZARD, RULING OVER GRANITE-SKULLED GIANTS WHO ARE ONE RATTLING SYNAPSE AWAY FROM REMEMBERING THEY COULD BECOME THE NEW KING BY EATING ME.
PERHAPS THAT WILL BE IN THE SEQUEL.
LOKI, DON'T YOU SEE WHAT A GIFT THIS IS? WE'VE BROKEN FREE OF THE CYCLE OF RAGNAROK! YOU AND I, TOGETHER!
YOUR SLATE IS CLEAN! YOU ARE THE GOD OF EVIL NO LONGER! NOR MISCHIEF, NOR CHAOS!
NOR STORIES, I IMAGINE. AS ODIN'S MAGIC BOOKS WOULD HAVE MY STORY BE OVER ALREADY.
THOR, IF I AM NONE OF THESE THINGS, THEN WHAT AM I?!
YOU ARE A KING, LOKI! AND MY BROTHER! WHAT GREATER HONORS COULD THERE BE?
OH GODS, HE'S SERIOUS.
OH GODS, YOU'RE SERIOUS.

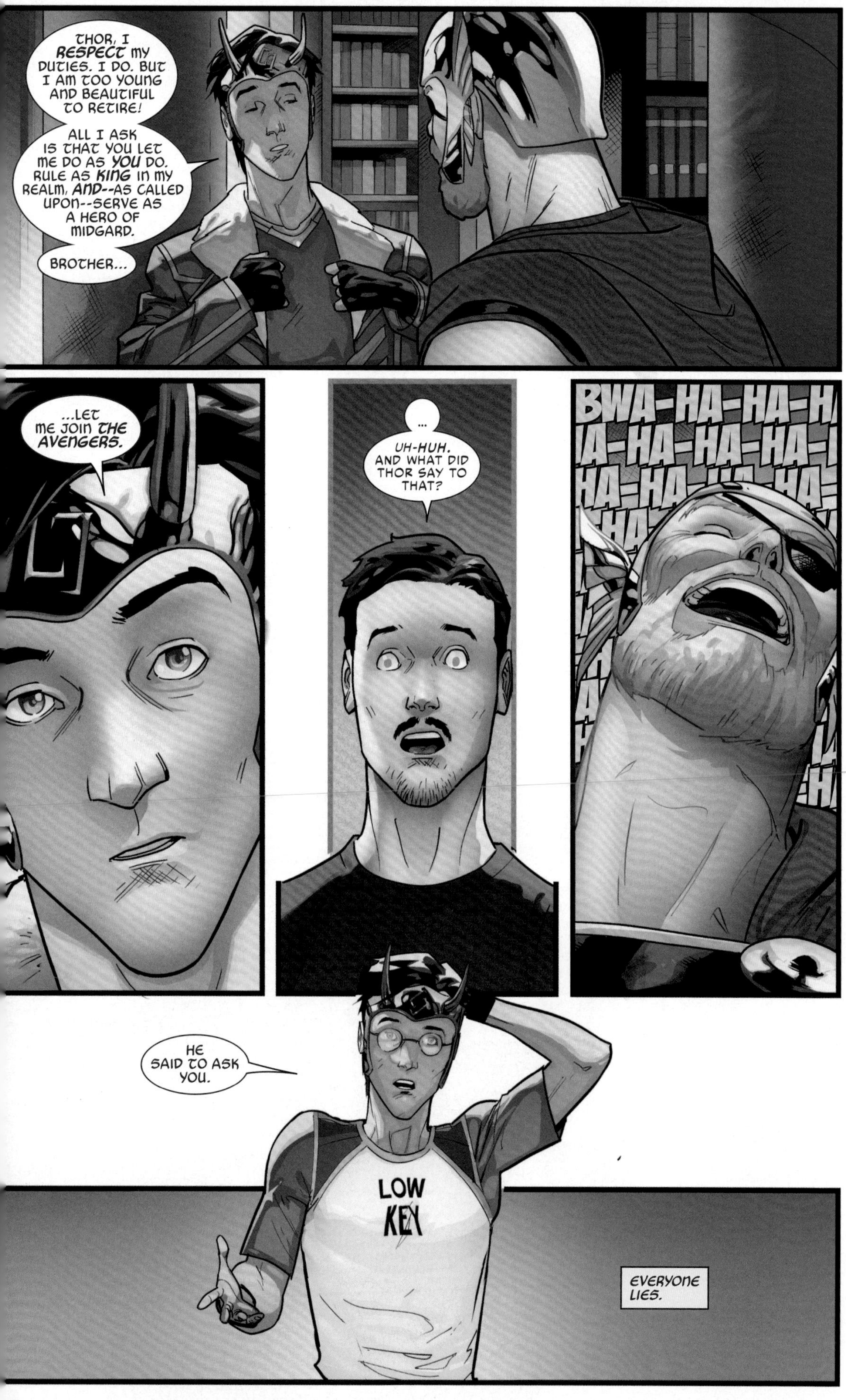

THOR, I *RESPECT* MY DUTIES. I DO. BUT I AM TOO YOUNG AND BEAUTIFUL TO RETIRE!
ALL I ASK IS THAT YOU LET ME DO AS *YOU* DO. RULE AS *KING* IN MY REALM, *AND*--AS CALLED UPON--SERVE AS A HERO OF MIDGARD.
BROTHER...
...LET ME JOIN *THE AVENGERS.*
...
UH-HUH. AND WHAT DID THOR SAY TO THAT?
BWA-HA-HA-HA-HA-HA-HA-HA-HA-HA-HA-HA-HA-HA
HE SAID TO ASK YOU.
LOW KEY
EVERYONE LIES.

EXAMPLE--EVERY DAY, YOU GET UP IN THE MORNING, PRETENDING TO BE A FUNCTIONING PERSON.

WHEN YOU'VE JUST SPENT ROUGHLY EIGHT HOURS IN HELL.

AS FAR AS YOUR MIND AND BODY KNOW WHILE IT'S HAPPENING, A NIGHTMARE IS FULLY REAL. YOU FALL. YOU FLEE. YOU DIE.

ERROR: EMPLOYEE FAILURE EMPLOYEE FAILURE EMPLOYEE FAILURE EMPLOYEE FAILURE

THEN YOU'RE MEANT TO SHOWER IT OFF, HAVE A CUP OF COFFEE AND ACT LIKE IT DIDN'T HAPPEN. EVERY. SINGLE. DAY.

HOW ARE YOU GOING TO LAND THE HENDERSON ACCOUNT IF YOUR FILES KEEP TURNING INTO SNAKES?

I'M SORRY! I DON'T KNOW WHAT'S--

AND WE WONDER WHY PEOPLE SUDDENLY SNAP.

GOORSH!

SIR?! WHAT'S--

I'M GOING TO KILL THAT SNOWMAN.*

OH. I GET IT NOW. I'M DREAMING.

*HE MEANS FRÖSTI--KING LOKI'S NEW NORN STONE-POWERED SNOWMAN AND RIGHT HAND TO THE THRONE OF JOTUNHEIM--WHO "ATE" NIGHTMARE LAST ISSUE. --WAXIN' WIL

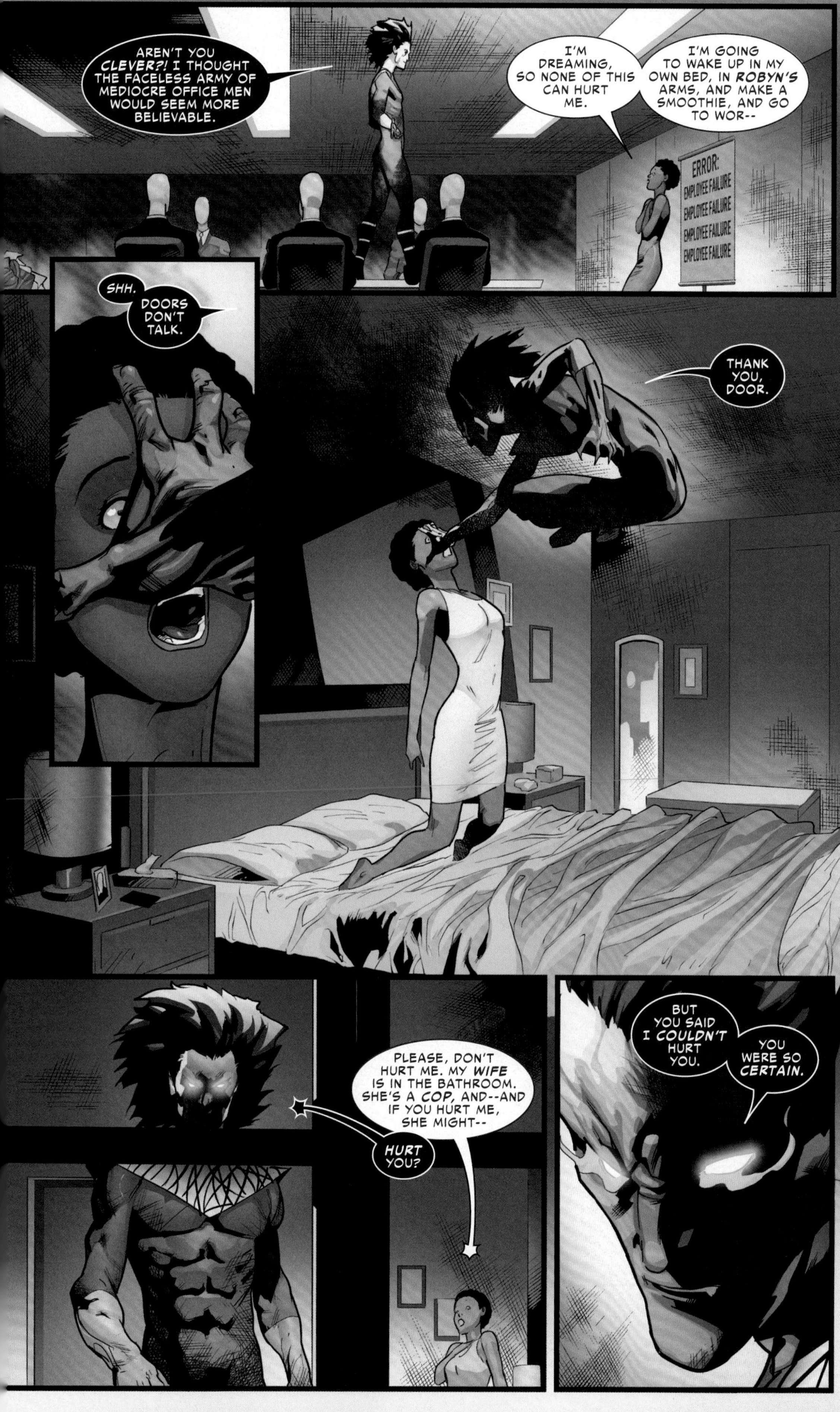
AREN'T YOU CLEVER?! I THOUGHT THE FACELESS ARMY OF MEDIOCRE OFFICE MEN WOULD SEEM MORE BELIEVABLE.
I'M DREAMING, SO NONE OF THIS CAN HURT ME.
I'M GOING TO WAKE UP IN MY OWN BED, IN ROBYN'S ARMS, AND MAKE A SMOOTHIE, AND GO TO WOR--
ERROR: EMPLOYEE FAILURE EMPLOYEE FAILURE EMPLOYEE FAILURE EMPLOYEE FAILURE
SHH.
DOORS DON'T TALK.
THANK YOU, DOOR.
PLEASE, DON'T HURT ME. MY WIFE IS IN THE BATHROOM. SHE'S A COP, AND--AND IF YOU HURT ME, SHE MIGHT--
HURT YOU?
BUT YOU SAID I COULDN'T HURT YOU.
YOU WERE SO CERTAIN.

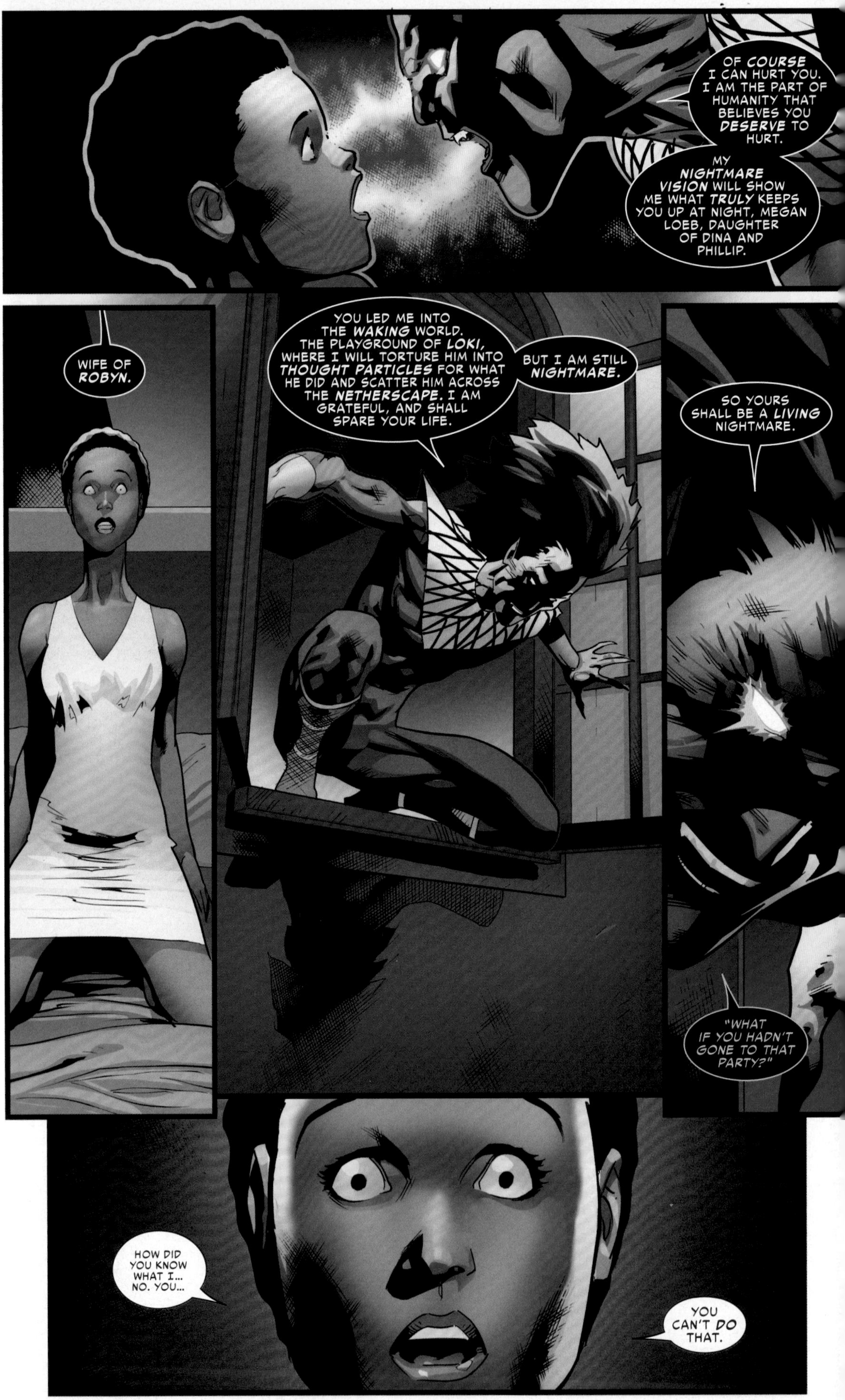
OF COURSE I CAN HURT YOU. I AM THE PART OF HUMANITY THAT BELIEVES YOU DESERVE TO HURT.
MY NIGHTMARE VISION WILL SHOW ME WHAT TRULY KEEPS YOU UP AT NIGHT, MEGAN LOEB, DAUGHTER OF DINA AND PHILLIP.
WIFE OF ROBYN.
YOU LED ME INTO THE WAKING WORLD. THE PLAYGROUND OF LOKI, WHERE I WILL TORTURE HIM INTO THOUGHT PARTICLES FOR WHAT HE DID AND SCATTER HIM ACROSS THE NETHERSCAPE. I AM GRATEFUL, AND SHALL SPARE YOUR LIFE.
BUT I AM STILL NIGHTMARE.
SO YOURS SHALL BE A LIVING NIGHTMARE.
"WHAT IF YOU HADN'T GONE TO THAT PARTY?"
HOW DID YOU KNOW WHAT I... NO. YOU...
YOU CAN'T DO THAT.

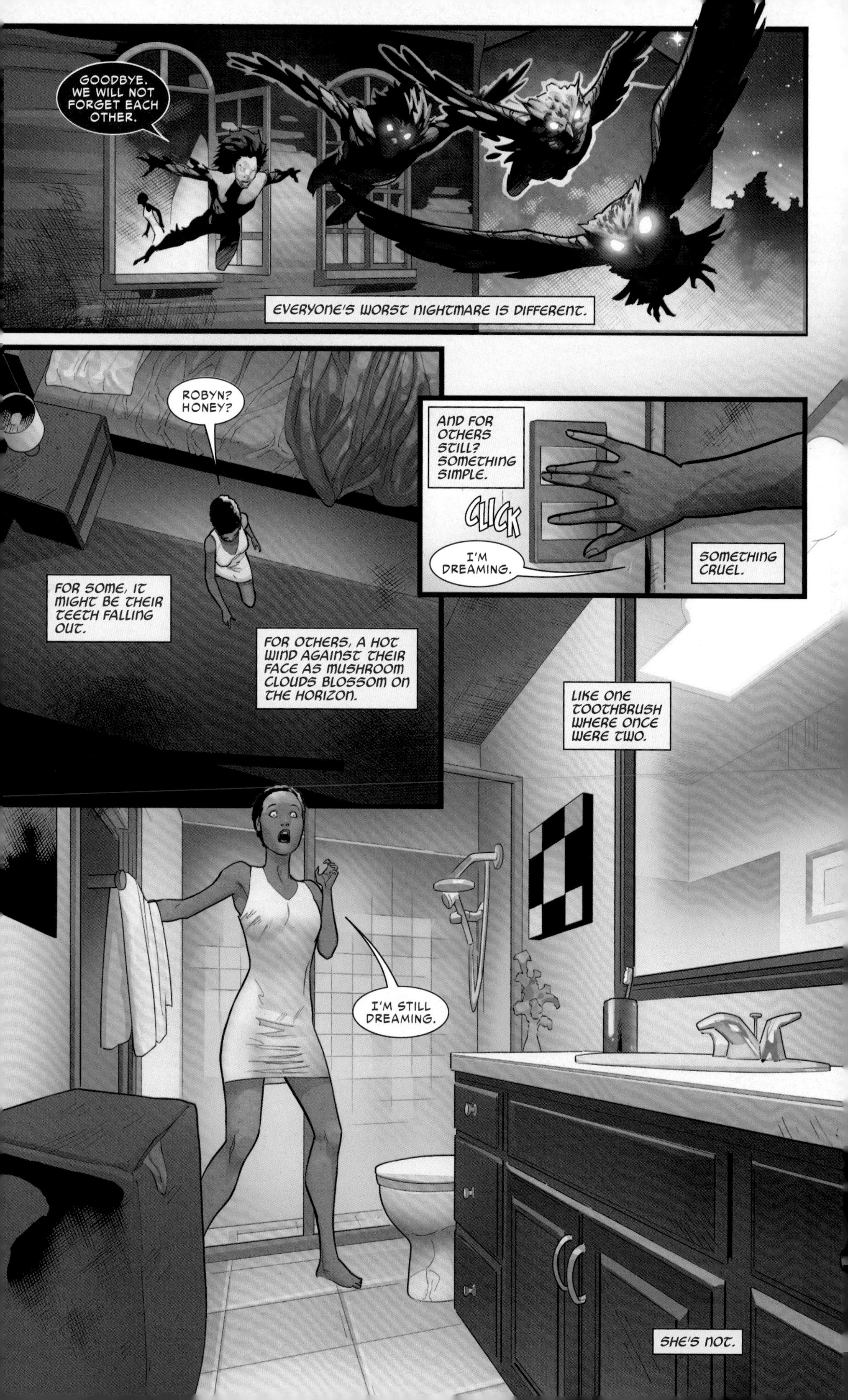
GOODBYE. WE WILL NOT FORGET EACH OTHER.
EVERYONE'S WORST NIGHTMARE IS DIFFERENT.
ROBYN? HONEY?
FOR SOME, IT MIGHT BE THEIR TEETH FALLING OUT.
FOR OTHERS, A HOT WIND AGAINST THEIR FACE AS MUSHROOM CLOUDS BLOSSOM ON THE HORIZON.
AND FOR OTHERS STILL? SOMETHING SIMPLE.
CLICK
I'M DREAMING.
SOMETHING CRUEL.
LIKE ONE TOOTHBRUSH WHERE ONCE WERE TWO.
I'M STILL DREAMING.
SHE'S NOT.

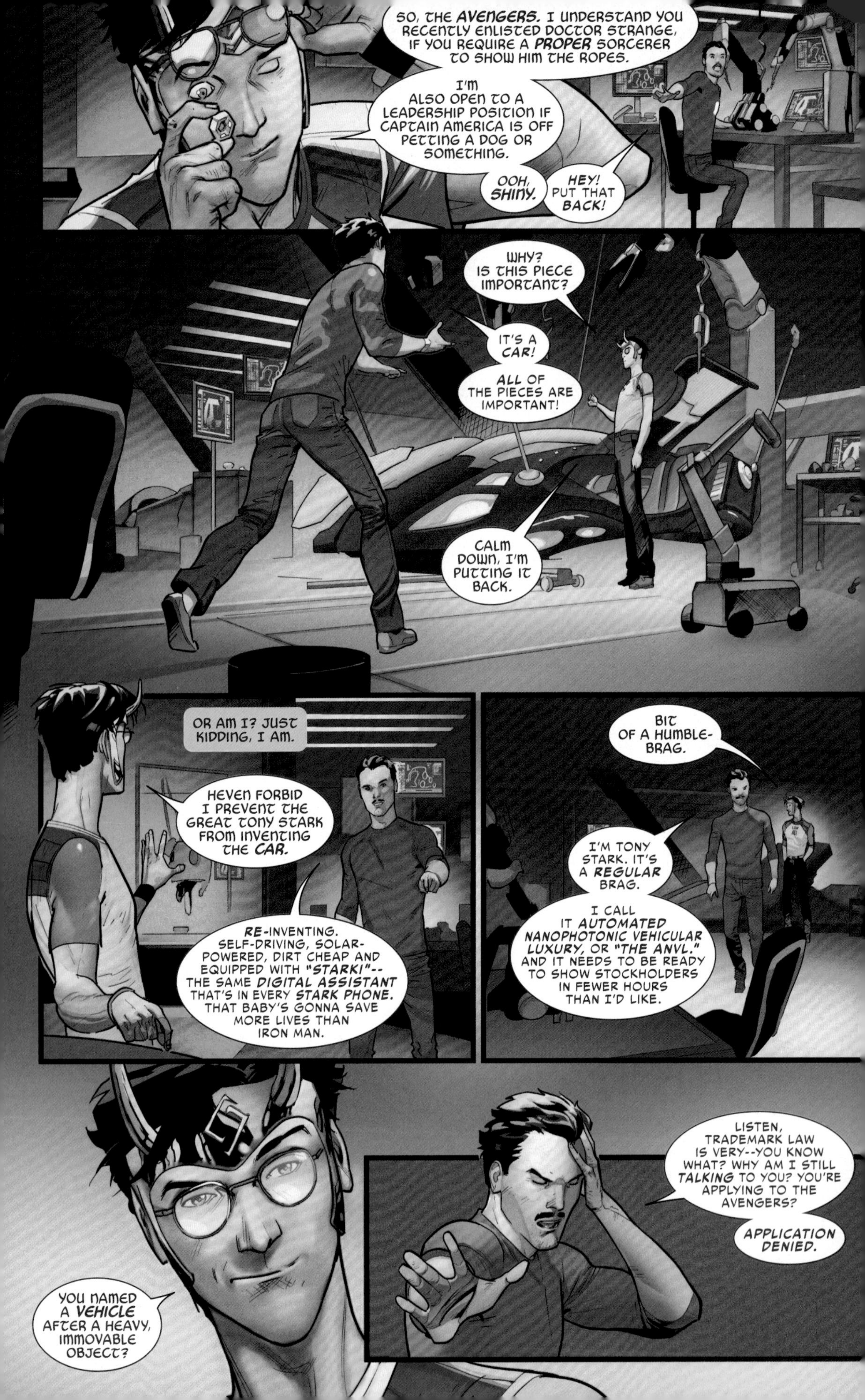
SO, THE AVENGERS. I UNDERSTAND YOU RECENTLY ENLISTED DOCTOR STRANGE, IF YOU REQUIRE A PROPER SORCERER TO SHOW HIM THE ROPES.
I'M ALSO OPEN TO A LEADERSHIP POSITION IF CAPTAIN AMERICA IS OFF PETTING A DOG OR SOMETHING.
OOH, SHINY.
HEY! PUT THAT BACK!
WHY? IS THIS PIECE IMPORTANT?
IT'S A CAR!
ALL OF THE PIECES ARE IMPORTANT!
CALM DOWN, I'M PUTTING IT BACK.
OR AM I? JUST KIDDING, I AM.
HEVEN FORBID I PREVENT THE GREAT TONY STARK FROM INVENTING THE CAR.
RE-INVENTING. SELF-DRIVING, SOLAR-POWERED, DIRT CHEAP AND EQUIPPED WITH "STARKI"--THE SAME DIGITAL ASSISTANT THAT'S IN EVERY STARK PHONE. THAT BABY'S GONNA SAVE MORE LIVES THAN IRON MAN.
BIT OF A HUMBLE-BRAG.
I'M TONY STARK. IT'S A REGULAR BRAG.
I CALL IT AUTOMATED NANOPHOTONIC VEHICULAR LUXURY, OR "THE ANVL." AND IT NEEDS TO BE READY TO SHOW STOCKHOLDERS IN FEWER HOURS THAN I'D LIKE.
YOU NAMED A VEHICLE AFTER A HEAVY, IMMOVABLE OBJECT?
LISTEN, TRADEMARK LAW IS VERY--YOU KNOW WHAT? WHY AM I STILL TALKING TO YOU? YOU'RE APPLYING TO THE AVENGERS?
APPLICATION DENIED.

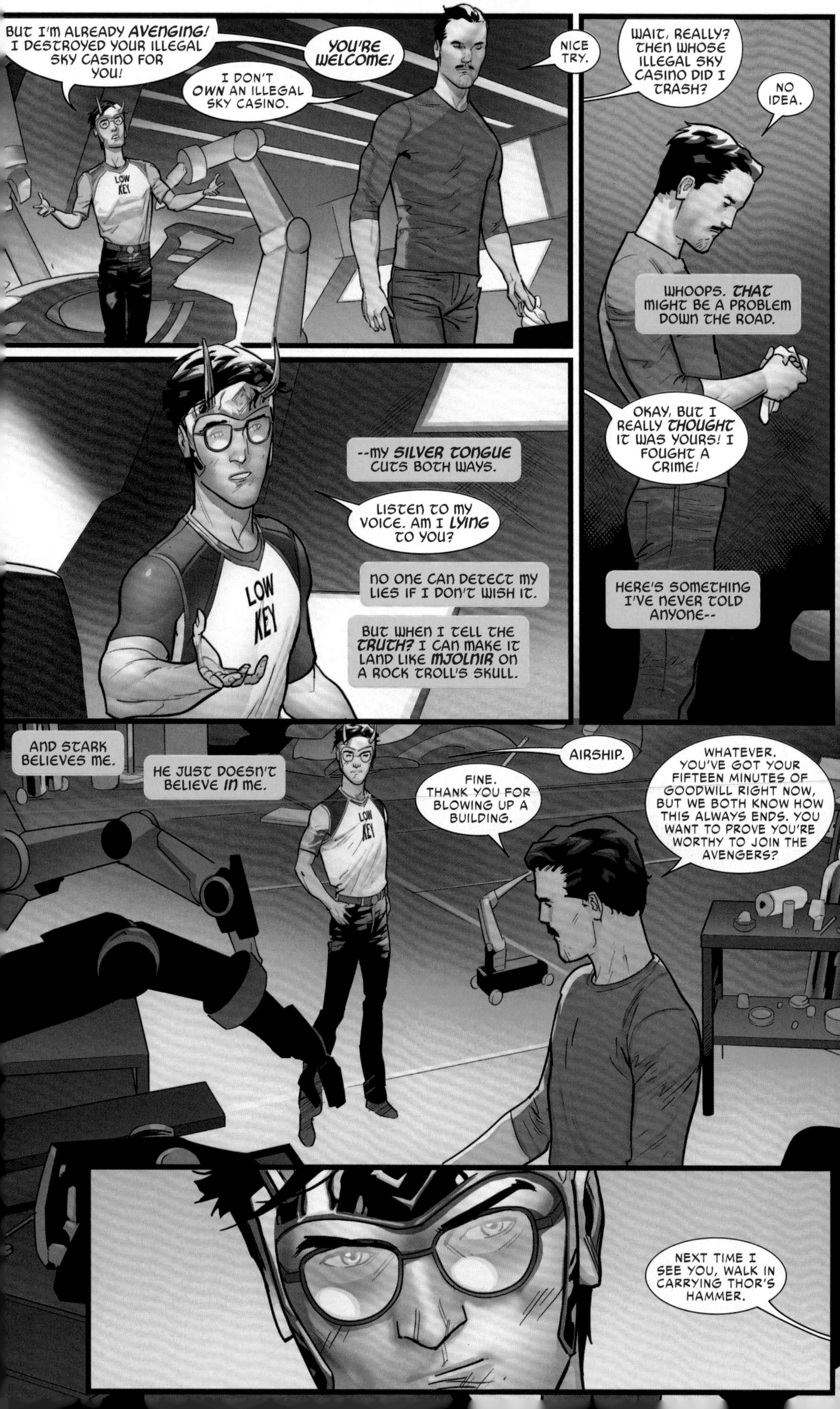
BUT I'M ALREADY AVENGING! I DESTROYED YOUR ILLEGAL SKY CASINO FOR YOU!
YOU'RE WELCOME!
I DON'T OWN AN ILLEGAL SKY CASINO.
NICE TRY.
WAIT, REALLY? THEN WHOSE ILLEGAL SKY CASINO DID I TRASH?
NO IDEA.
WHOOPS. THAT MIGHT BE A PROBLEM DOWN THE ROAD.
OKAY, BUT I REALLY THOUGHT IT WAS YOURS! I FOUGHT A CRIME!
HERE'S SOMETHING I'VE NEVER TOLD ANYONE--
--MY SILVER TONGUE CUTS BOTH WAYS.
LISTEN TO MY VOICE. AM I LYING TO YOU?
NO ONE CAN DETECT MY LIES IF I DON'T WISH IT.
BUT WHEN I TELL THE TRUTH? I CAN MAKE IT LAND LIKE MJOLNIR ON A ROCK TROLL'S SKULL.
AND STARK BELIEVES ME.
HE JUST DOESN'T BELIEVE IN ME.
AIRSHIP.
FINE. THANK YOU FOR BLOWING UP A BUILDING.
WHATEVER. YOU'VE GOT YOUR FIFTEEN MINUTES OF GOODWILL RIGHT NOW, BUT WE BOTH KNOW HOW THIS ALWAYS ENDS. YOU WANT TO PROVE YOU'RE WORTHY TO JOIN THE AVENGERS?
NEXT TIME I SEE YOU, WALK IN CARRYING THOR'S HAMMER.

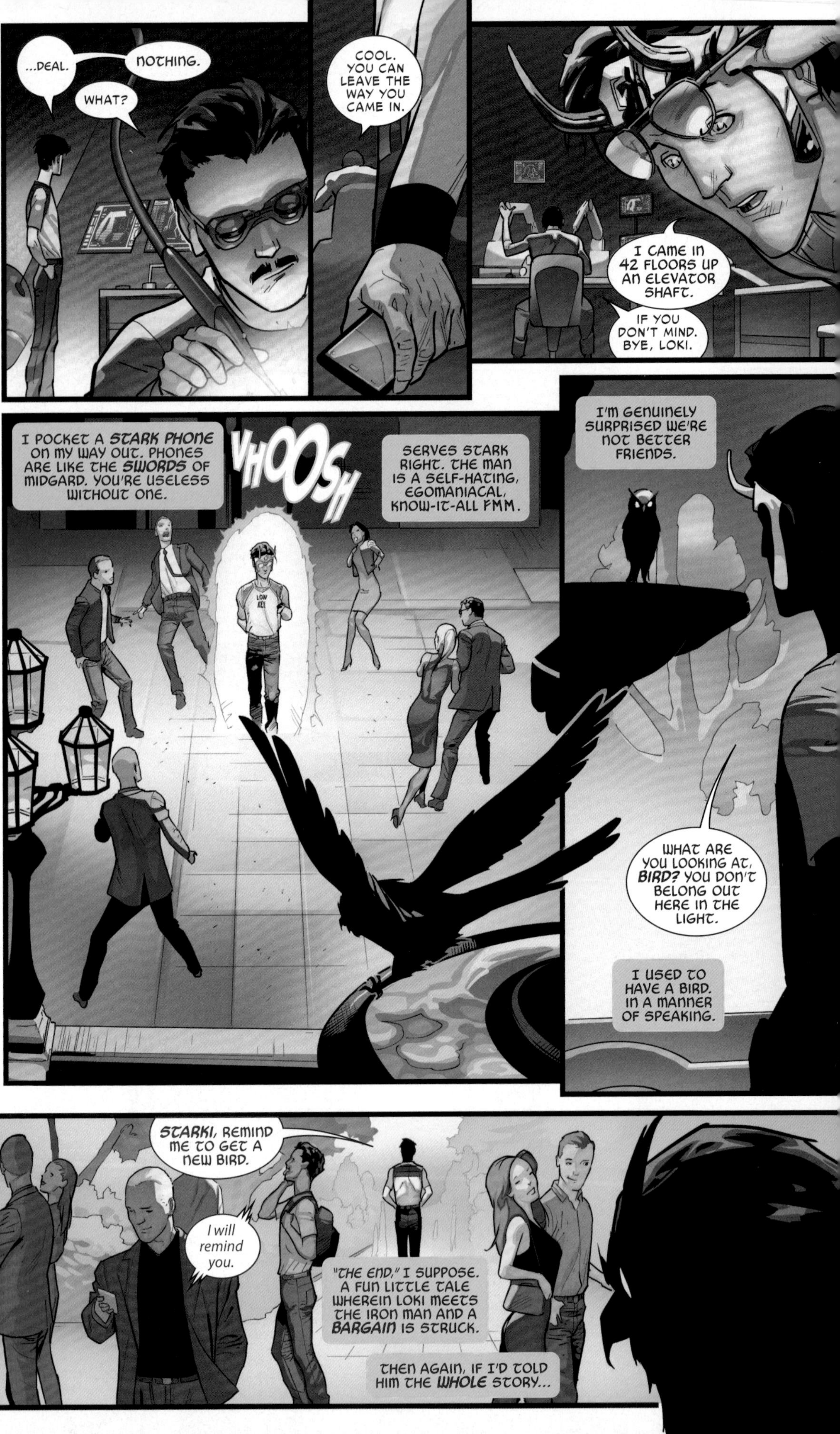

...DEAL.
NOTHING.
WHAT?
COOL. YOU CAN LEAVE THE WAY YOU CAME IN.
I CAME IN 42 FLOORS UP AN ELEVATOR SHAFT.
IF YOU DON'T MIND. BYE, LOKI.
I POCKET A STARK PHONE ON MY WAY OUT. PHONES ARE LIKE THE SWORDS OF MIDGARD. YOU'RE USELESS WITHOUT ONE.
VHOOSH
SERVES STARK RIGHT. THE MAN IS A SELF-HATING, EGOMANIACAL, KNOW-IT-ALL FMM.
I'M GENUINELY SURPRISED WE'RE NOT BETTER FRIENDS.
WHAT ARE YOU LOOKING AT, BIRD? YOU DON'T BELONG OUT HERE IN THE LIGHT.
I USED TO HAVE A BIRD. IN A MANNER OF SPEAKING.
STARKI, REMIND ME TO GET A NEW BIRD.
I will remind you.
"THE END," I SUPPOSE. A FUN LITTLE TALE WHEREIN LOKI MEETS THE IRON MAN AND A BARGAIN IS STRUCK.
THEN AGAIN, IF I'D TOLD HIM THE WHOLE STORY...

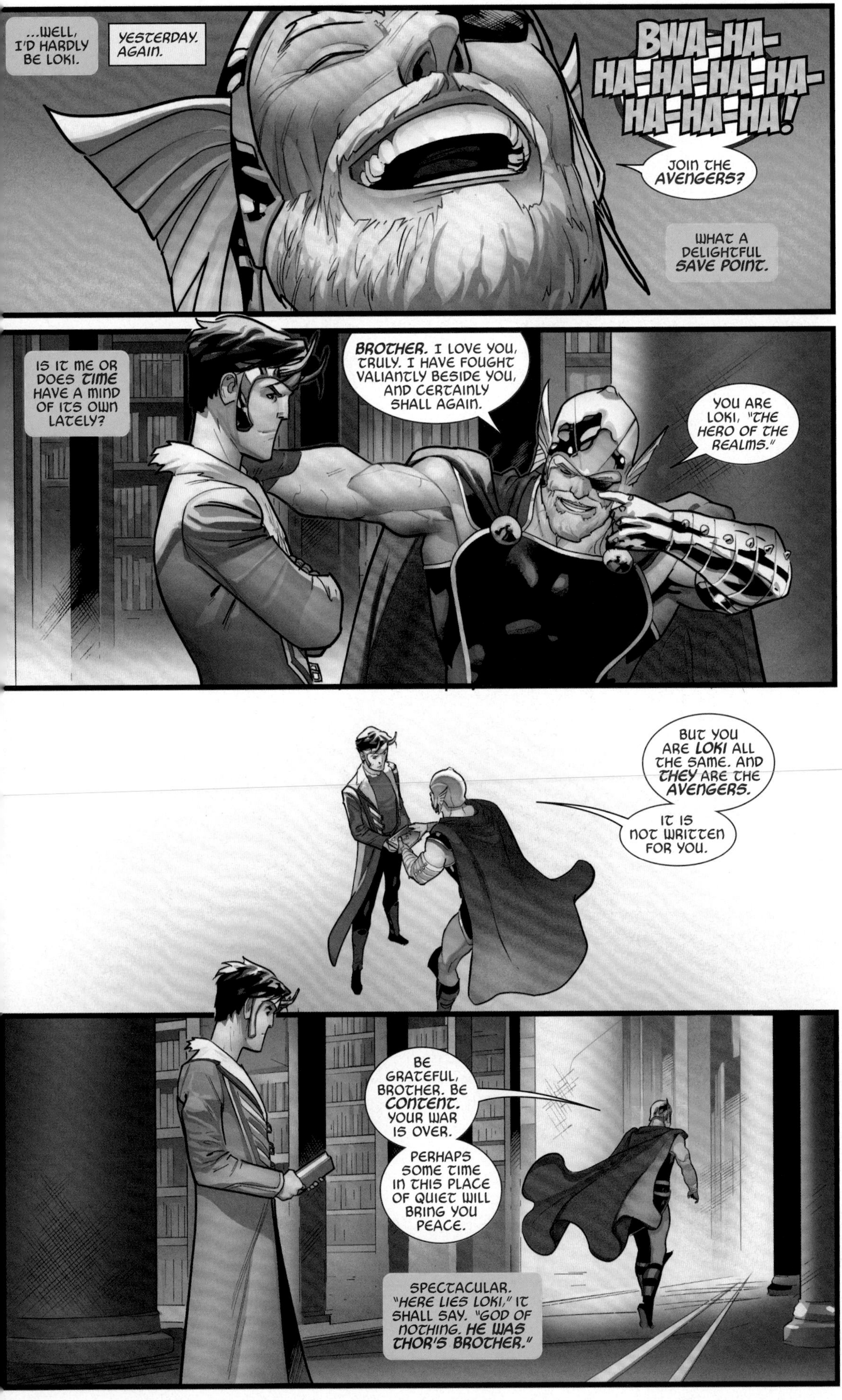
...WELL, I'D HARDLY BE LOKI.
YESTERDAY. AGAIN.
BWA-HA-HA-HA-HA-HA-HA-HA-HA!
JOIN THE AVENGERS?
WHAT A DELIGHTFUL SAVE POINT.
IS IT ME OR DOES TIME HAVE A MIND OF ITS OWN LATELY?
BROTHER. I LOVE YOU, TRULY. I HAVE FOUGHT VALIANTLY BESIDE YOU, AND CERTAINLY SHALL AGAIN.
YOU ARE LOKI, "THE HERO OF THE REALMS."
BUT YOU ARE LOKI ALL THE SAME. AND THEY ARE THE AVENGERS.
IT IS NOT WRITTEN FOR YOU.
BE GRATEFUL, BROTHER. BE CONTENT. YOUR WAR IS OVER.
PERHAPS SOME TIME IN THIS PLACE OF QUIET WILL BRING YOU PEACE.
SPECTACULAR. "HERE LIES LOKI," IT SHALL SAY. "GOD OF NOTHING. HE WAS THOR'S BROTHER."

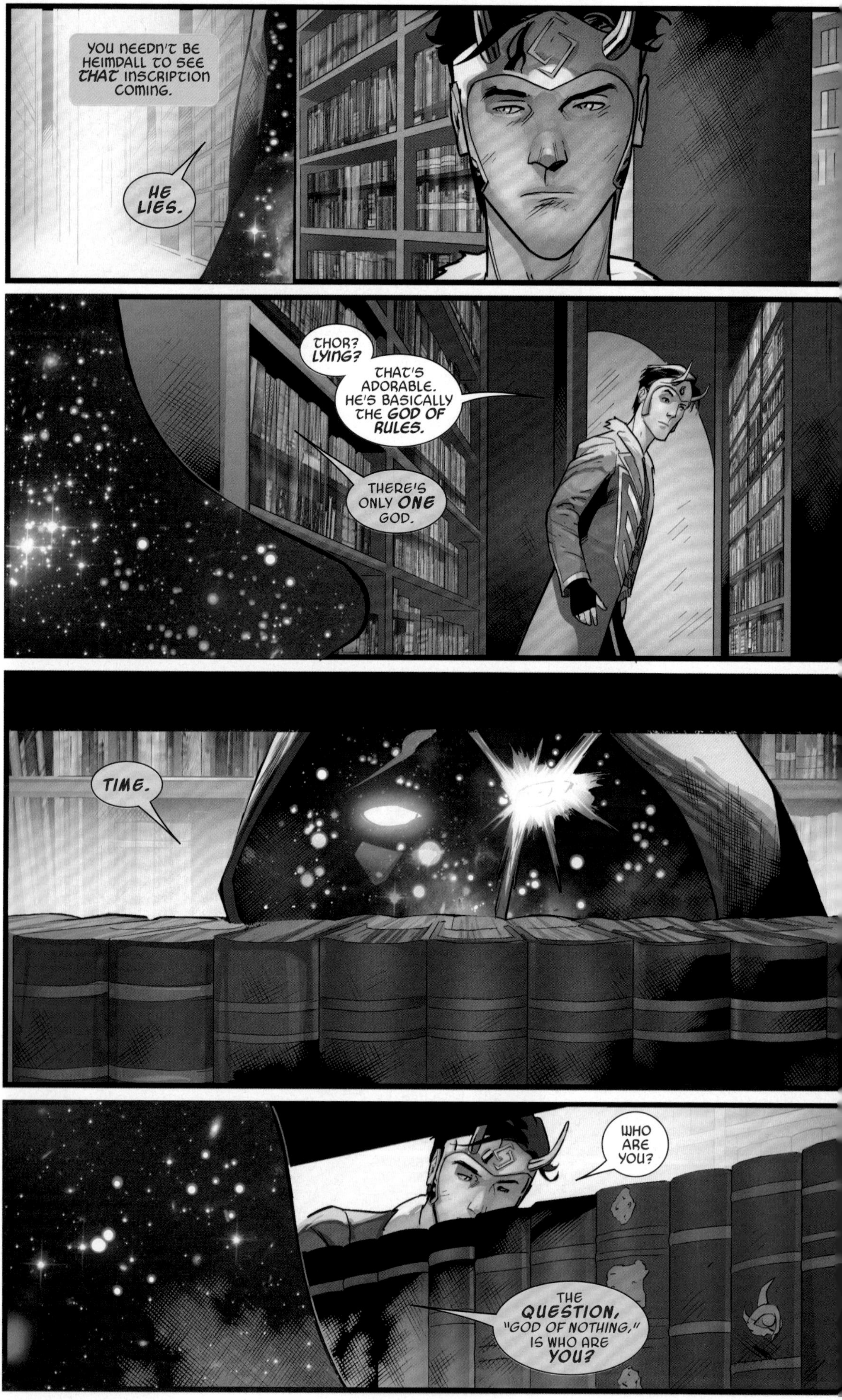

YOU NEEDN'T BE HEIMDALL TO SEE THAT INSCRIPTION COMING.
HE LIES.
THOR? LYING?
THAT'S ADORABLE. HE'S BASICALLY THE GOD OF RULES.
THERE'S ONLY ONE GOD.
TIME.
WHO ARE YOU?
THE QUESTION, "GOD OF NOTHING," IS WHO ARE YOU?

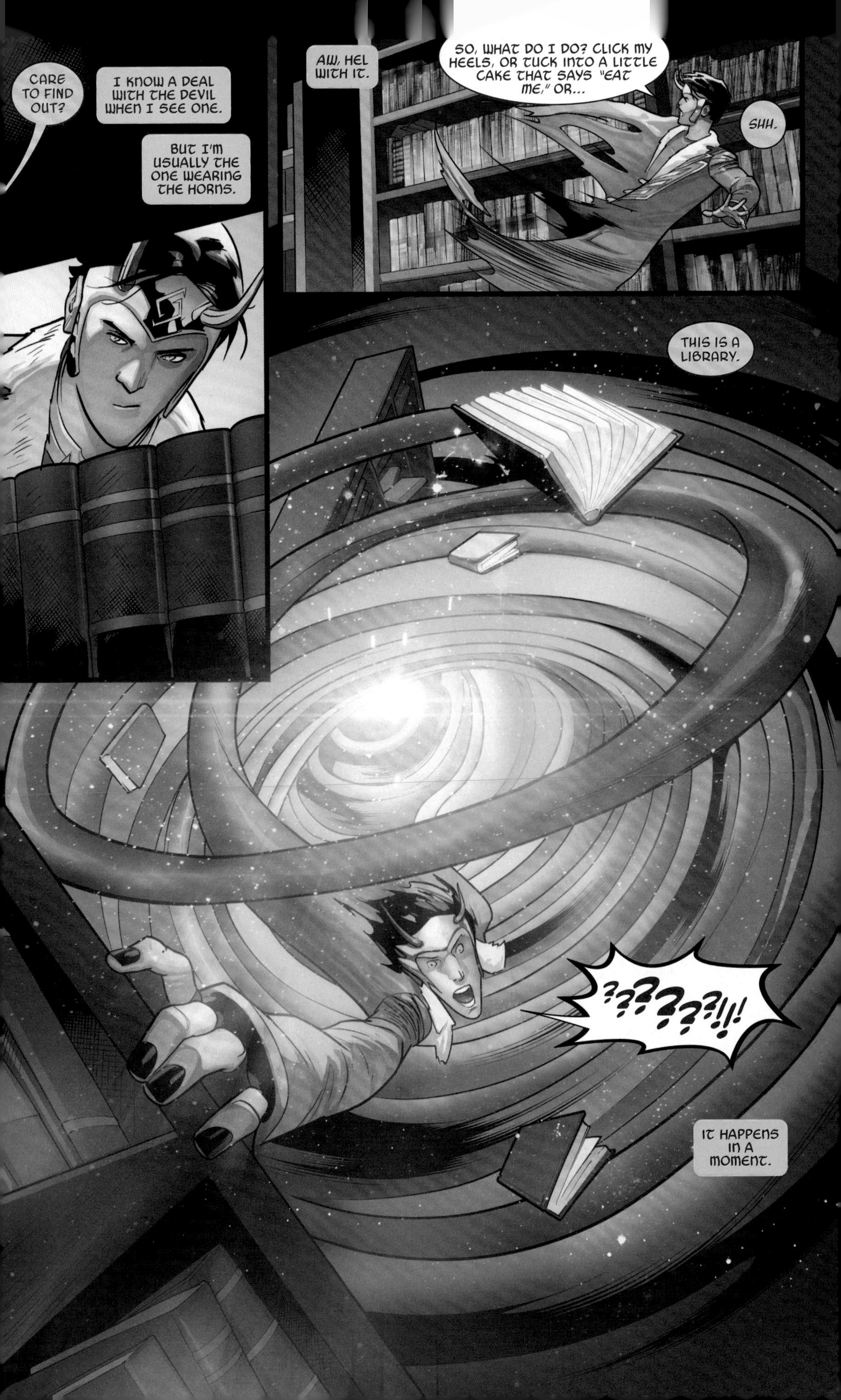
CARE TO FIND OUT?
I KNOW A DEAL WITH THE DEVIL WHEN I SEE ONE.
BUT I'M USUALLY THE ONE WEARING THE HORNS.
AW, HEL WITH IT.
SO, WHAT DO I DO? CLICK MY HEELS, OR TUCK INTO A LITTLE CAKE THAT SAYS "EAT ME," OR...
SHH.
THIS IS A LIBRARY.
?????!!
IT HAPPENS IN A MOMENT.

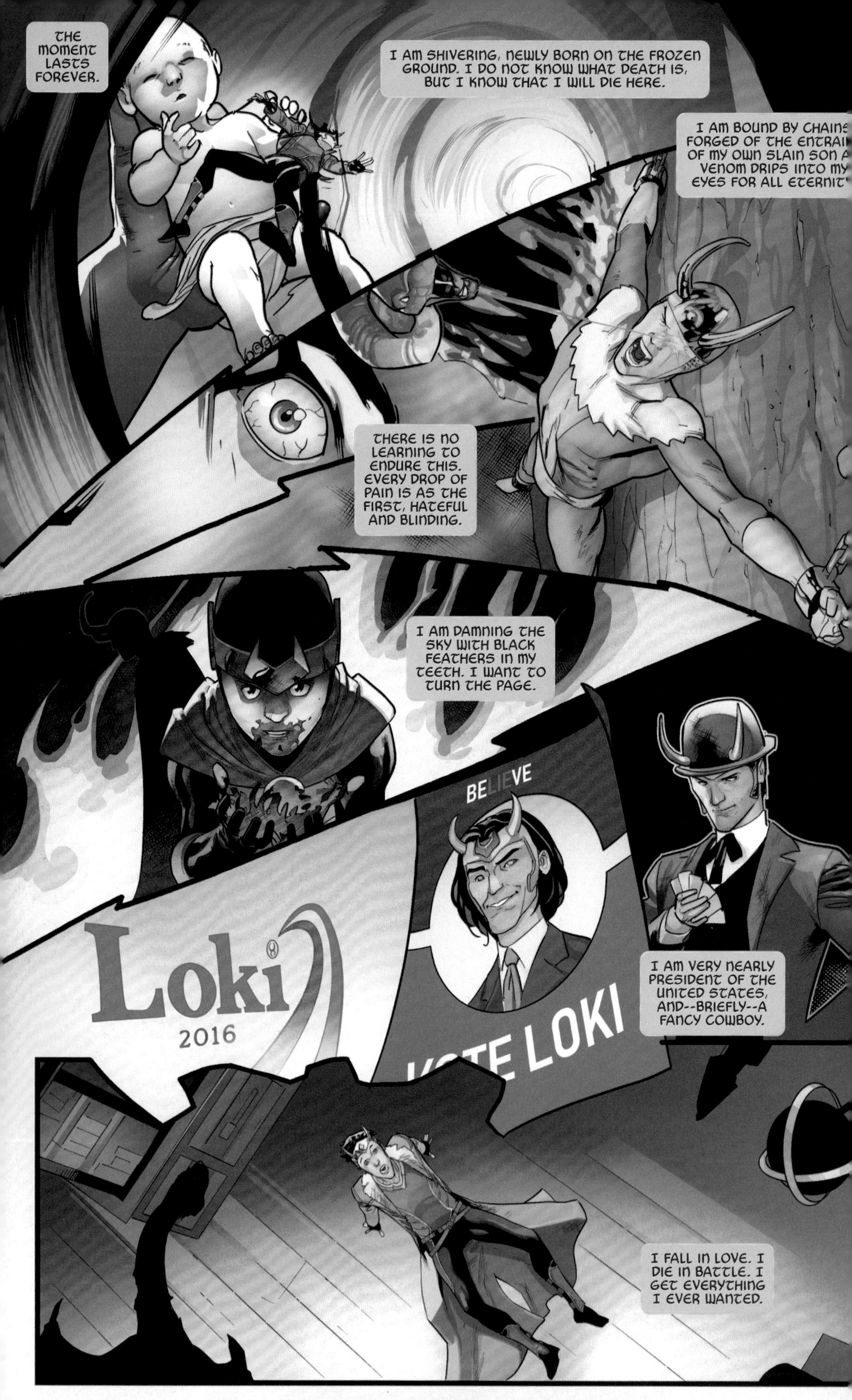
THE MOMENT LASTS FOREVER.
I AM SHIVERING, NEWLY BORN ON THE FROZEN GROUND. I DO NOT KNOW WHAT DEATH IS, BUT I KNOW THAT I WILL DIE HERE.
I AM BOUND BY CHAINS FORGED OF THE ENTRAI OF MY OWN SLAIN SON A VENOM DRIPS INTO MY EYES FOR ALL ETERNIT
THERE IS NO LEARNING TO ENDURE THIS. EVERY DROP OF PAIN IS AS THE FIRST, HATEFUL AND BLINDING.
I AM DAMNING THE SKY WITH BLACK FEATHERS IN MY TEETH. I WANT TO TURN THE PAGE.
BELIEVE
Loki
2016
VOTE LOKI
I AM VERY NEARLY PRESIDENT OF THE UNITED STATES, AND--BRIEFLY--A FANCY COWBOY.
I FALL IN LOVE. I DIE IN BATTLE. I GET EVERYTHING I EVER WANTED.

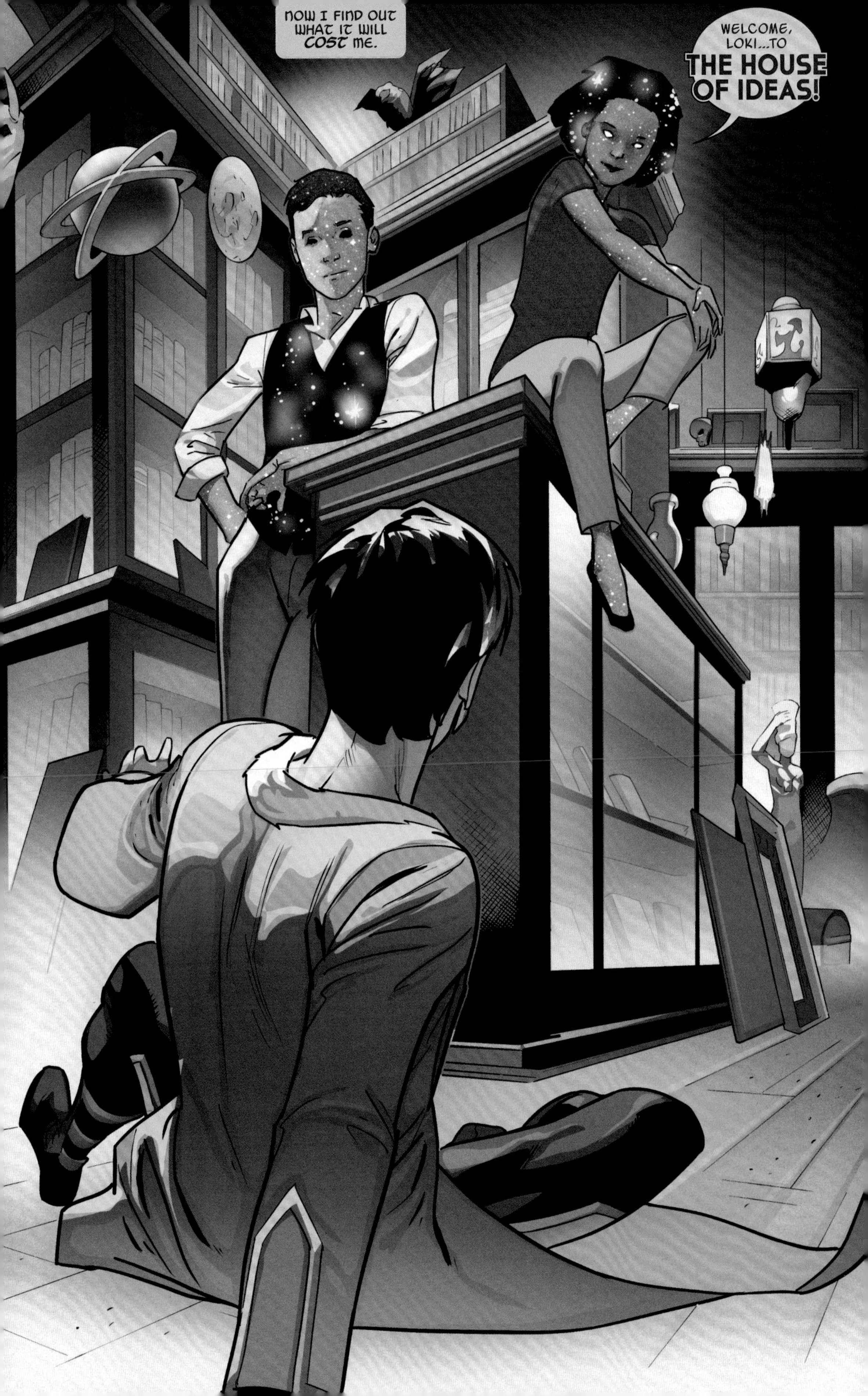
NOW I FIND OUT WHAT IT WILL COST ME.
WELCOME, LOKI...TO THE HOUSE OF IDEAS!

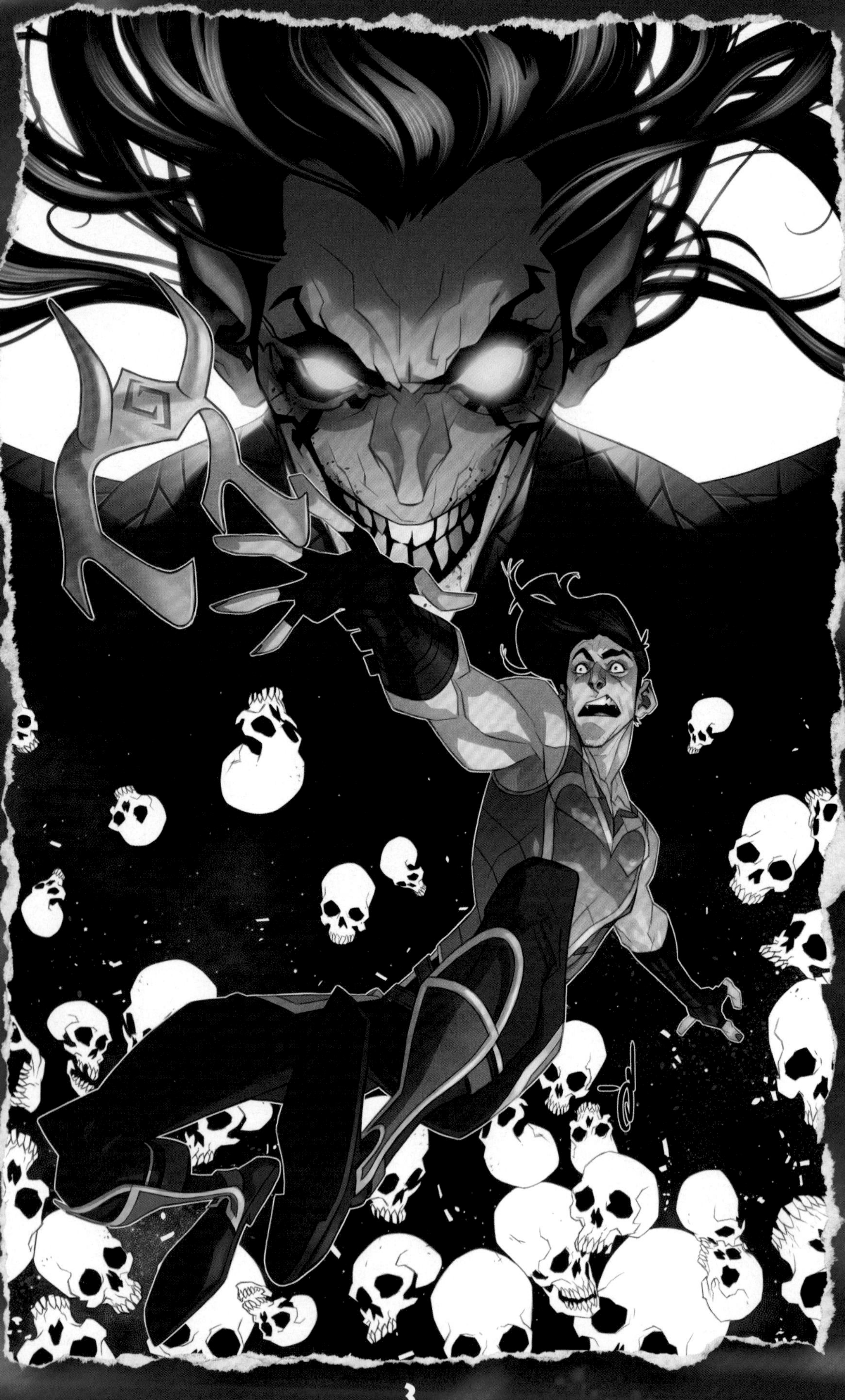

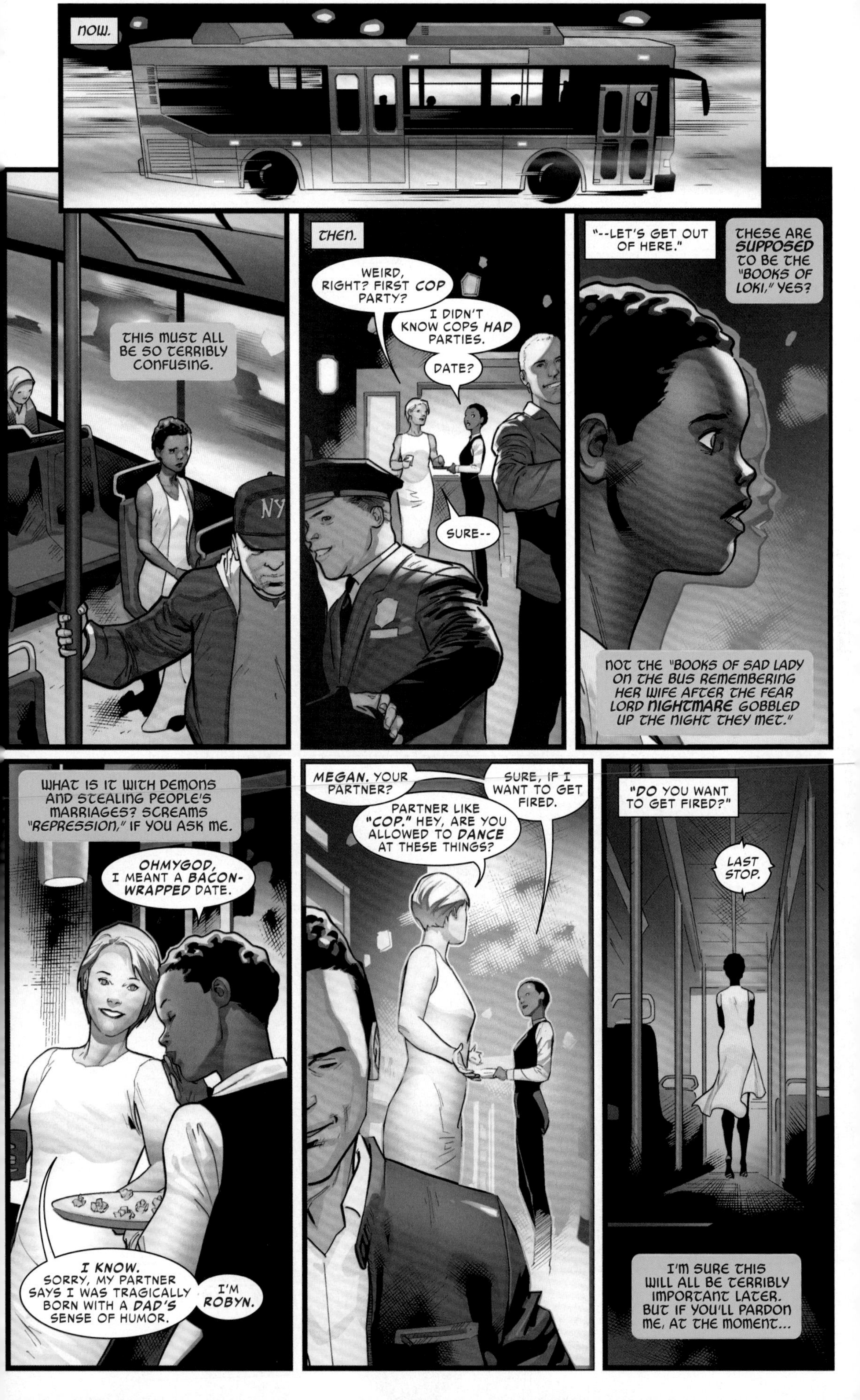
NOW.
THIS MUST ALL BE SO TERRIBLY CONFUSING.
NY
THEN.
WEIRD, RIGHT? FIRST COP PARTY?
I DIDN'T KNOW COPS HAD PARTIES.
DATE?
SURE--
"--LET'S GET OUT OF HERE."
THESE ARE SUPPOSED TO BE THE "BOOKS OF LOKI," YES?
NOT THE "BOOKS OF SAD LADY ON THE BUS REMEMBERING HER WIFE AFTER THE FEAR LORD NIGHTMARE GOBBLED UP THE NIGHT THEY MET."
WHAT IS IT WITH DEMONS AND STEALING PEOPLE'S MARRIAGES? SCREAMS "REPRESSION," IF YOU ASK ME.
OHMYGOD, I MEANT A BACON-WRAPPED DATE.
I KNOW. SORRY, MY PARTNER SAYS I WAS TRAGICALLY BORN WITH A DAD'S SENSE OF HUMOR.
I'M ROBYN.
MEGAN. YOUR PARTNER?
SURE, IF I WANT TO GET FIRED.
PARTNER LIKE "COP." HEY, ARE YOU ALLOWED TO DANCE AT THESE THINGS?
"DO YOU WANT TO GET FIRED?"
LAST STOP.
I'M SURE THIS WILL ALL BE TERRIBLY IMPORTANT LATER. BUT IF YOU'LL PARDON ME, AT THE MOMENT...

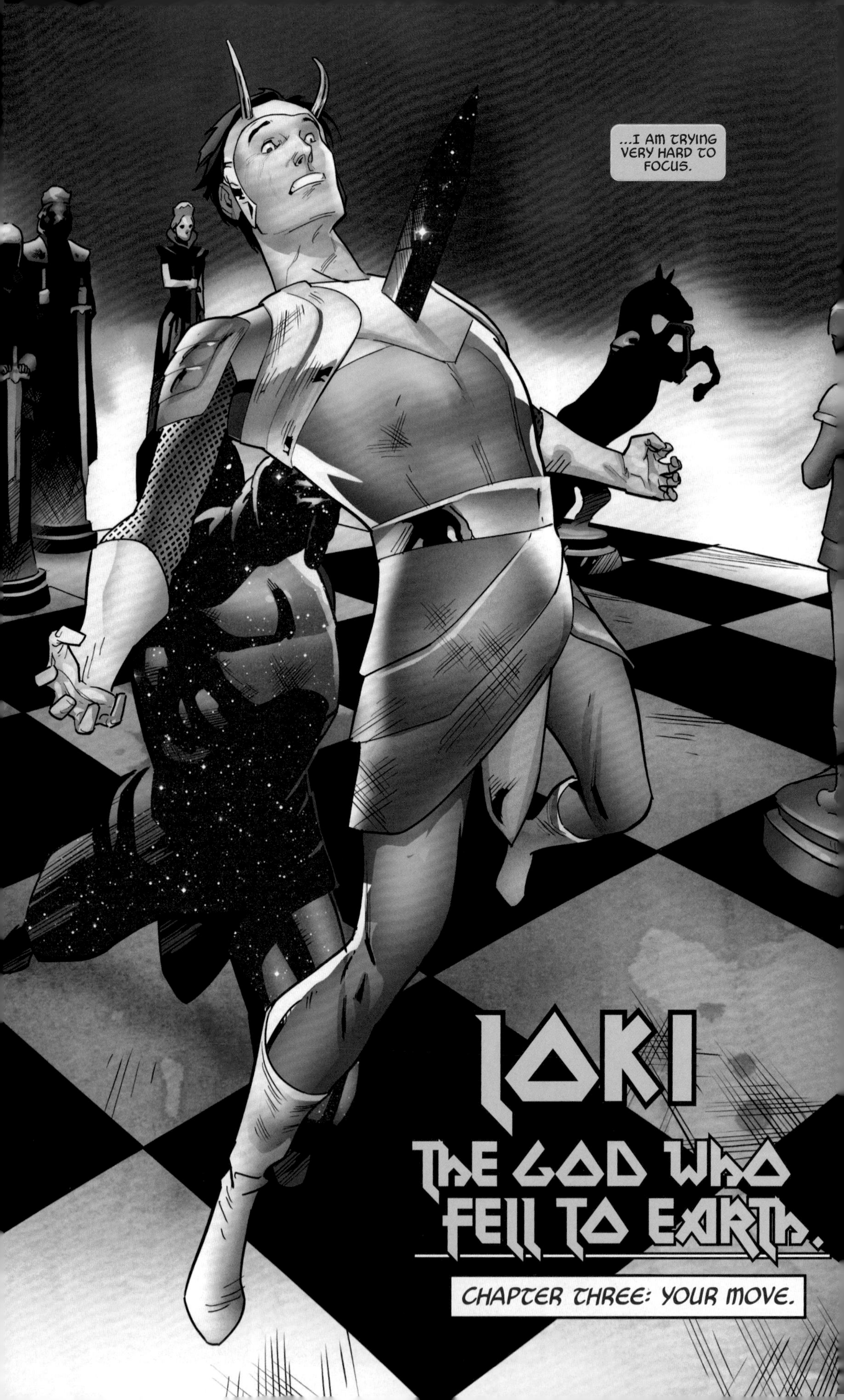
...I AM TRYING VERY HARD TO FOCUS.
LOKI
THE GOD WHO FELL TO EARTH.
CHAPTER THREE: YOUR MOVE.

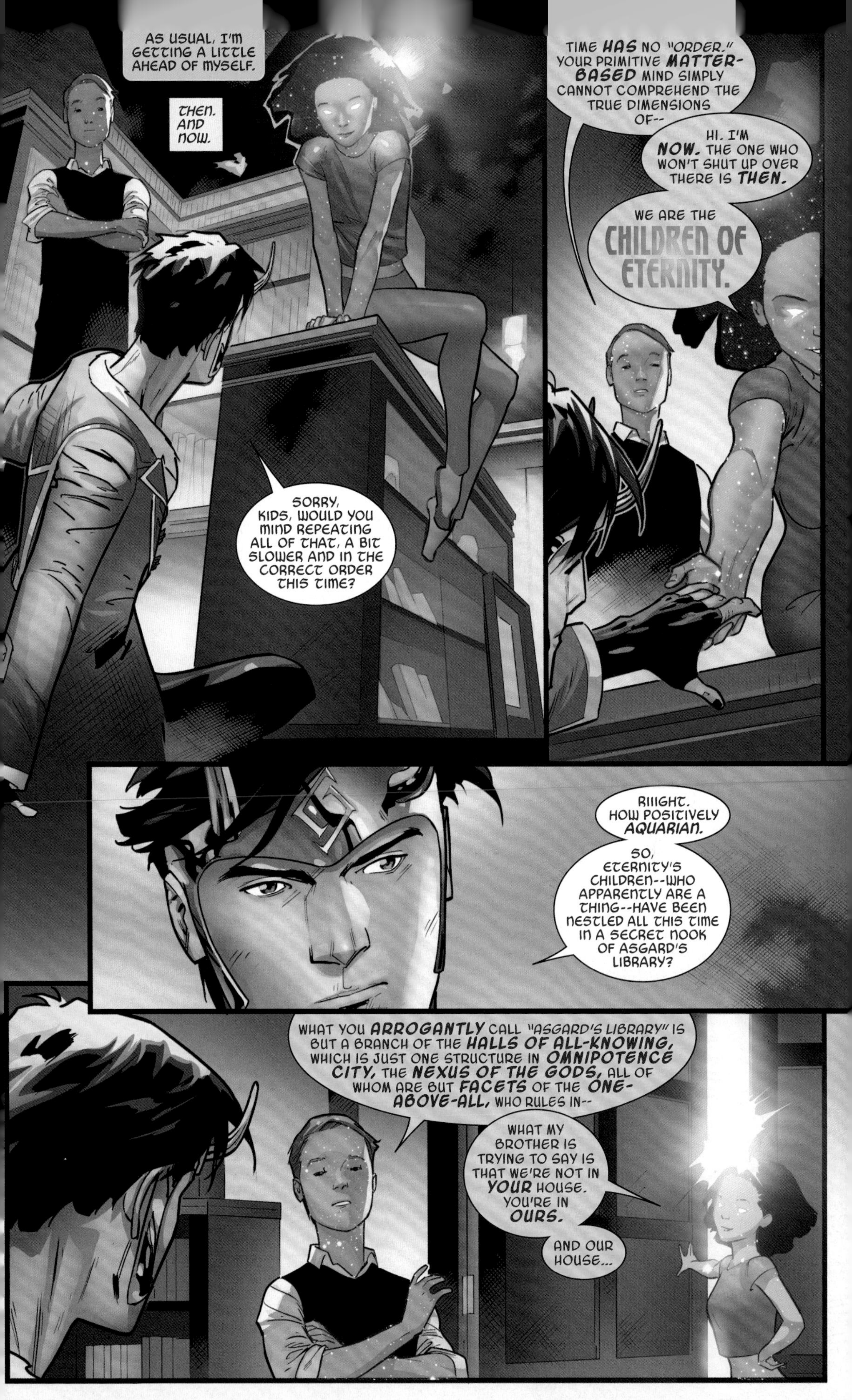

AS USUAL, I'M GETTING A LITTLE AHEAD OF MYSELF.
THEN. AND NOW.
SORRY, KIDS, WOULD YOU MIND REPEATING ALL OF THAT, A BIT SLOWER AND IN THE CORRECT ORDER THIS TIME?
TIME HAS NO "ORDER." YOUR PRIMITIVE MATTER-BASED MIND SIMPLY CANNOT COMPREHEND THE TRUE DIMENSIONS OF--
HI. I'M NOW. THE ONE WHO WON'T SHUT UP OVER THERE IS THEN.
WE ARE THE CHILDREN OF ETERNITY.
RIIIGHT. HOW POSITIVELY AQUARIAN.
SO, ETERNITY'S CHILDREN--WHO APPARENTLY ARE A THING--HAVE BEEN NESTLED ALL THIS TIME IN A SECRET NOOK OF ASGARD'S LIBRARY?
WHAT YOU ARROGANTLY CALL "ASGARD'S LIBRARY" IS BUT A BRANCH OF THE HALLS OF ALL-KNOWING, WHICH IS JUST ONE STRUCTURE IN OMNIPOTENCE CITY, THE NEXUS OF THE GODS, ALL OF WHOM ARE BUT FACETS OF THE ONE-ABOVE-ALL, WHO RULES IN--
WHAT MY BROTHER IS TRYING TO SAY IS THAT WE'RE NOT IN YOUR HOUSE. YOU'RE IN OURS.
AND OUR HOUSE...

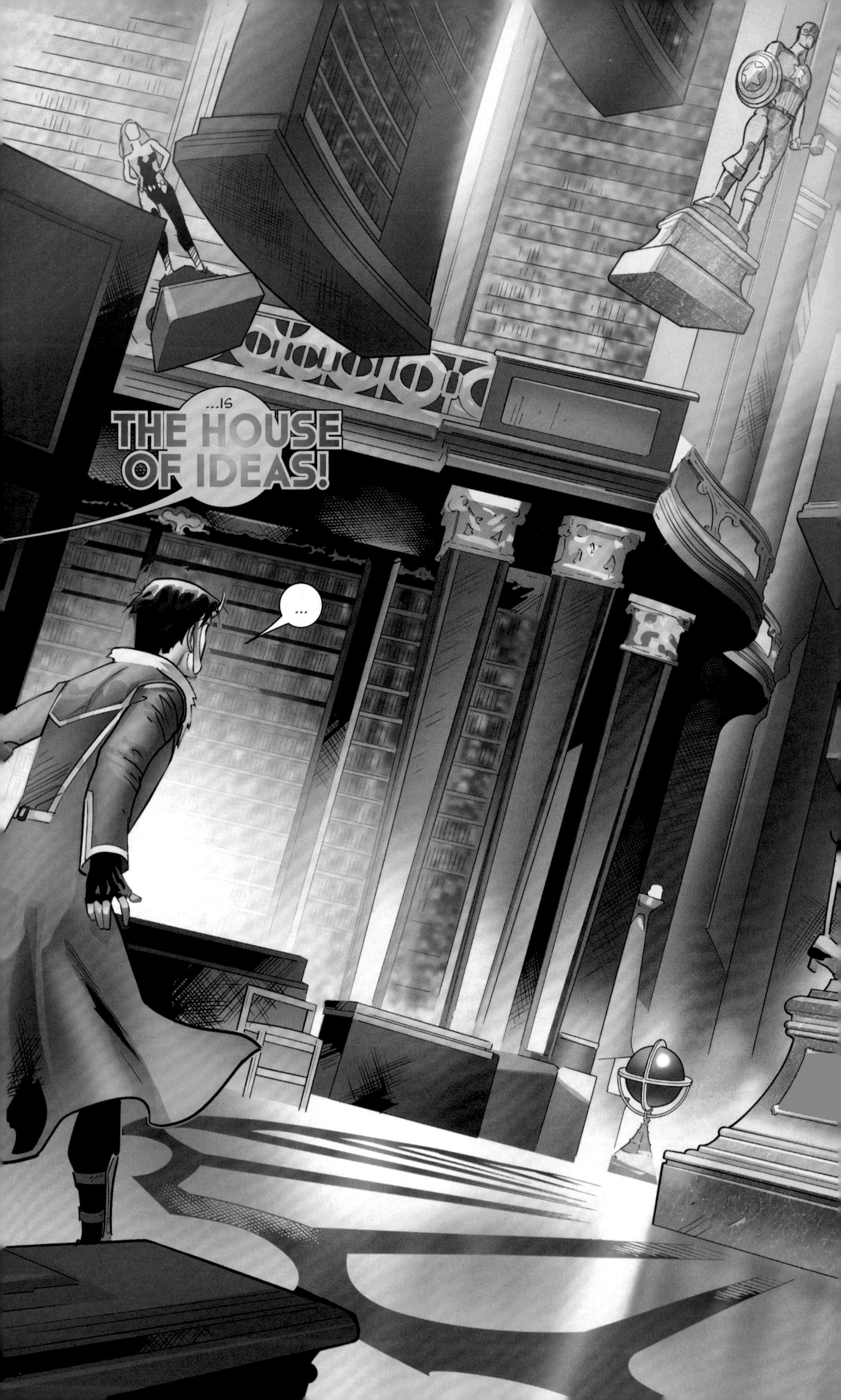

...IS THE HOUSE OF IDEAS!
...

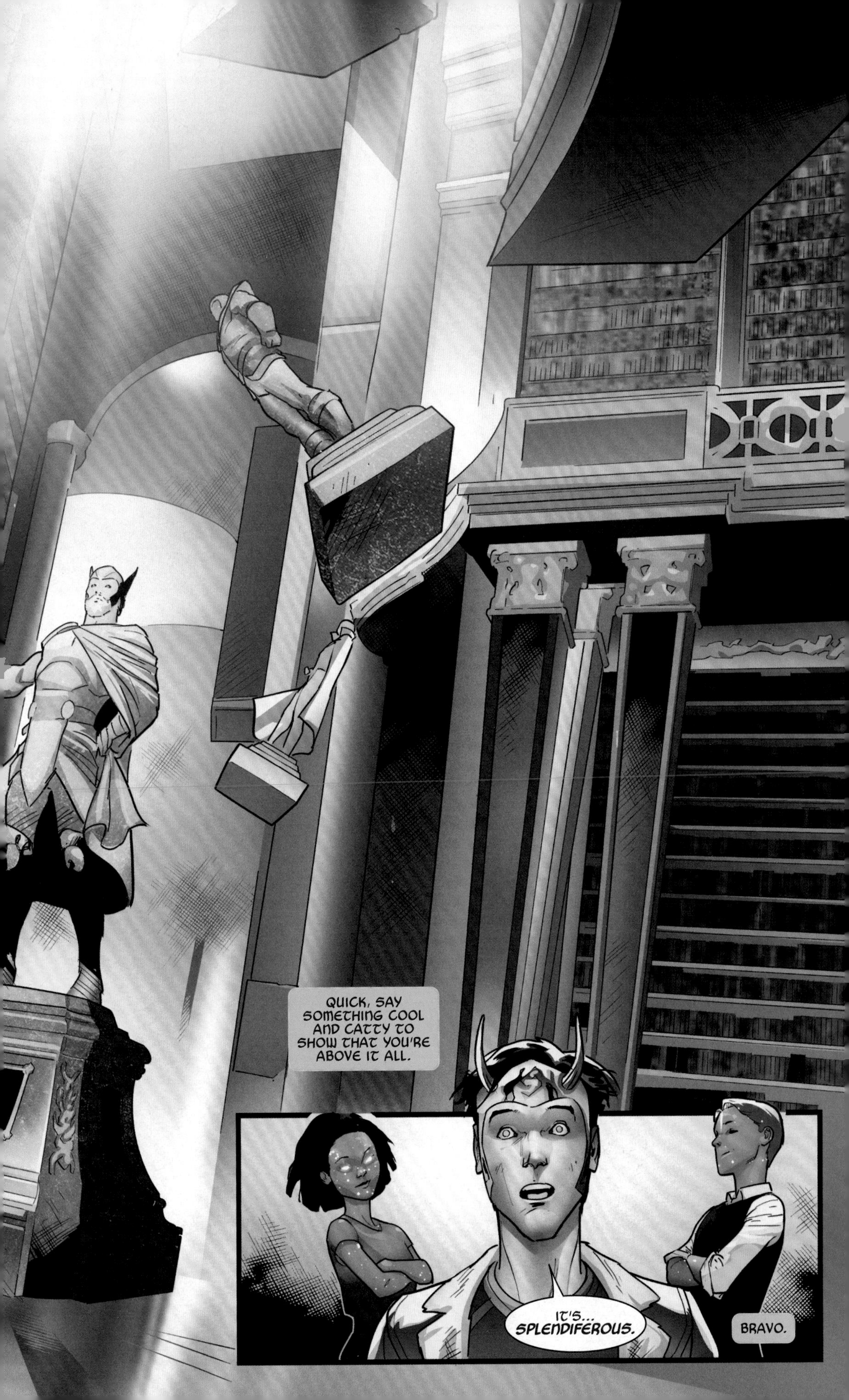
QUICK, SAY SOMETHING COOL AND CATTY TO SHOW THAT YOU'RE ABOVE IT ALL.
IT'S... SPLENDIFEROUS.
BRAVO.

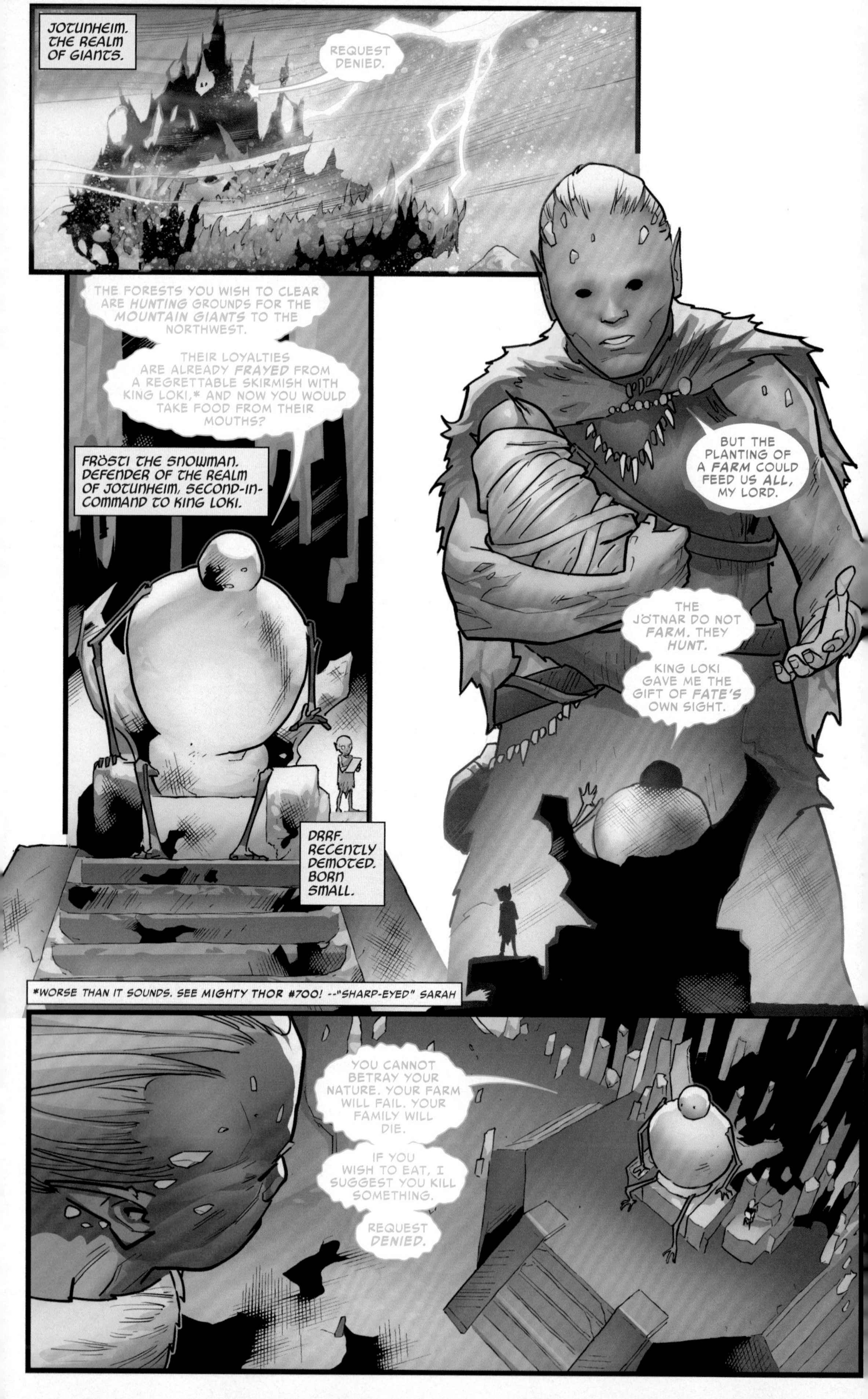
JOTUNHEIM. THE REALM OF GIANTS.
REQUEST DENIED.
THE FORESTS YOU WISH TO CLEAR ARE HUNTING GROUNDS FOR THE MOUNTAIN GIANTS TO THE NORTHWEST.
THEIR LOYALTIES ARE ALREADY FRAYED FROM A REGRETTABLE SKIRMISH WITH KING LOKI,* AND NOW YOU WOULD TAKE FOOD FROM THEIR MOUTHS?
FRÖSTI THE SNOWMAN. DEFENDER OF THE REALM OF JOTUNHEIM, SECOND-IN-COMMAND TO KING LOKI.
BUT THE PLANTING OF A FARM COULD FEED US ALL, MY LORD.
THE JÖTNAR DO NOT FARM. THEY HUNT.
KING LOKI GAVE ME THE GIFT OF FATE'S OWN SIGHT.
DRRF. RECENTLY DEMOTED. BORN SMALL.
*WORSE THAN IT SOUNDS. SEE MIGHTY THOR #700! --"SHARP-EYED" SARAH
YOU CANNOT BETRAY YOUR NATURE. YOUR FARM WILL FAIL. YOUR FAMILY WILL DIE.
IF YOU WISH TO EAT, I SUGGEST YOU KILL SOMETHING.
REQUEST DENIED.

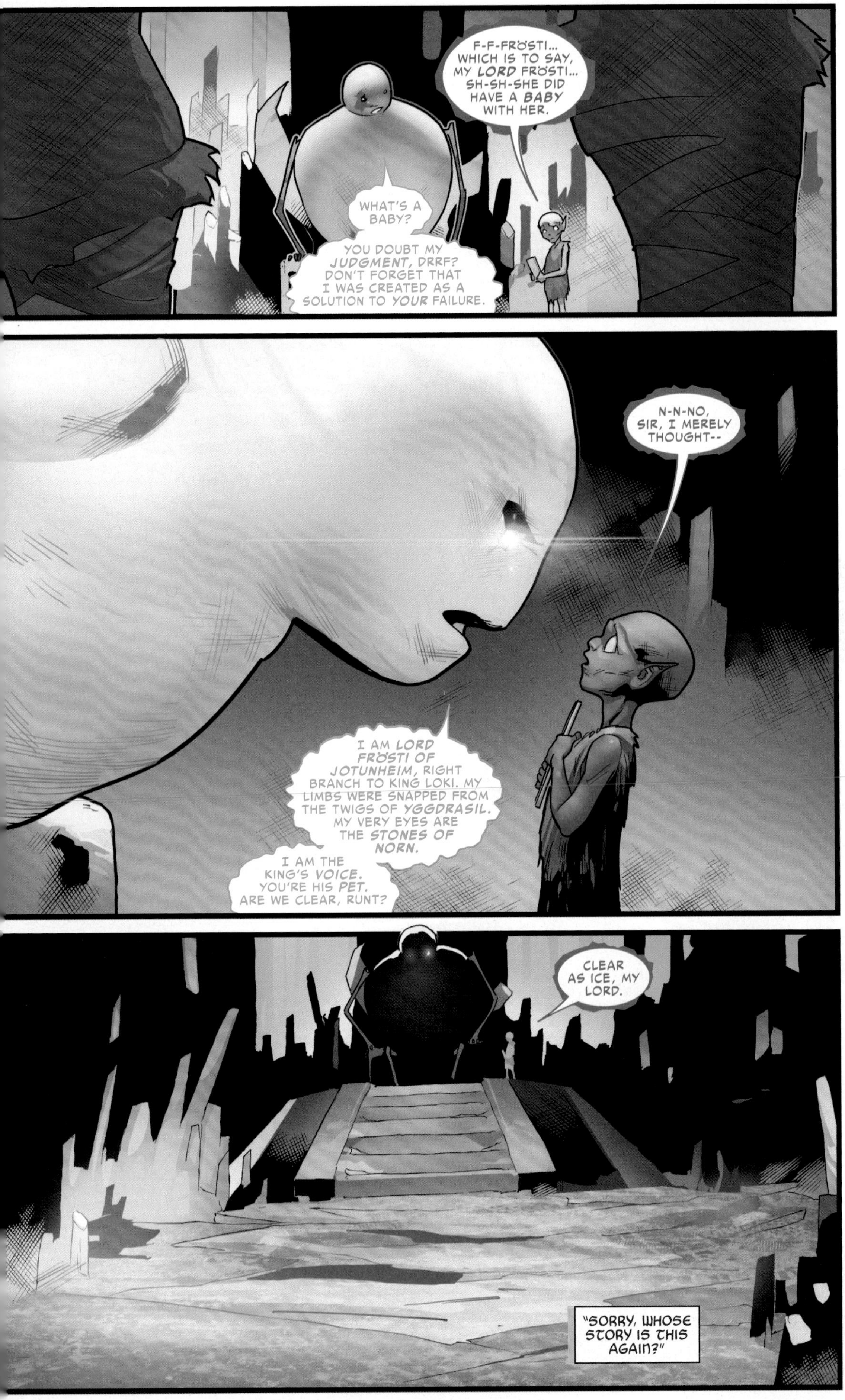
F-F-FRÖSTI... WHICH IS TO SAY, MY LORD FRÖSTI... SH-SH-SHE DID HAVE A BABY WITH HER.
WHAT'S A BABY?
YOU DOUBT MY JUDGMENT, DRRF? DON'T FORGET THAT I WAS CREATED AS A SOLUTION TO YOUR FAILURE.
N-N-NO, SIR, I MERELY THOUGHT--
I AM LORD FRÖSTI OF JOTUNHEIM, RIGHT BRANCH TO KING LOKI. MY LIMBS WERE SNAPPED FROM THE TWIGS OF YGGDRASIL. MY VERY EYES ARE THE STONES OF NORN.
I AM THE KING'S VOICE. YOU'RE HIS PET. ARE WE CLEAR, RUNT?
CLEAR AS ICE, MY LORD.
"SORRY, WHOSE STORY IS THIS AGAIN?"

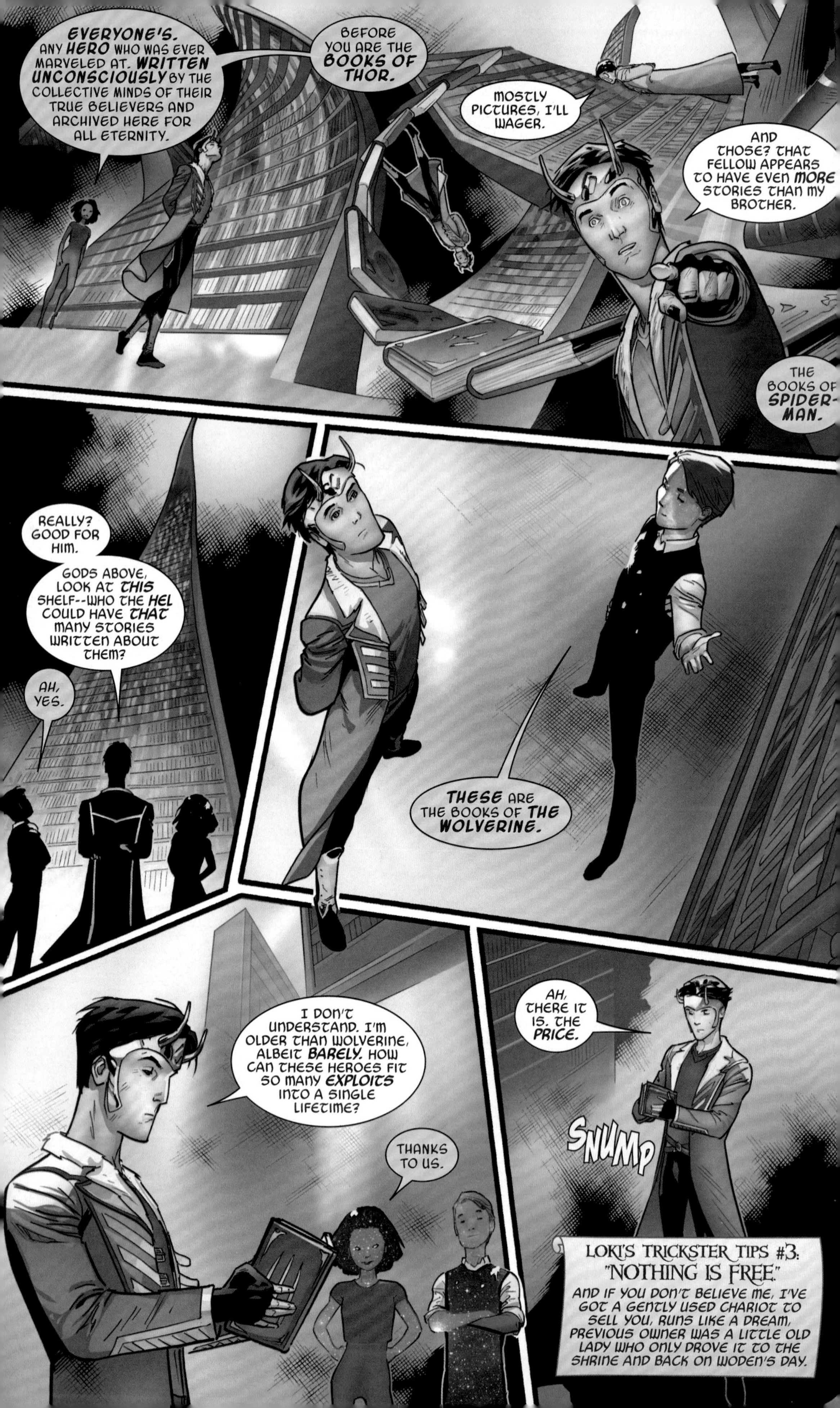
EVERYONE'S. ANY HERO WHO WAS EVER MARVELED AT. WRITTEN UNCONSCIOUSLY BY THE COLLECTIVE MINDS OF THEIR TRUE BELIEVERS AND ARCHIVED HERE FOR ALL ETERNITY.
BEFORE YOU ARE THE BOOKS OF THOR.
MOSTLY PICTURES, I'LL WAGER.
AND THOSE? THAT FELLOW APPEARS TO HAVE EVEN MORE STORIES THAN MY BROTHER.
THE BOOKS OF SPIDER-MAN.
REALLY? GOOD FOR HIM.
GODS ABOVE, LOOK AT THIS SHELF--WHO THE HEL COULD HAVE THAT MANY STORIES WRITTEN ABOUT THEM?
AH, YES.
THESE ARE THE BOOKS OF THE WOLVERINE.
I DON'T UNDERSTAND. I'M OLDER THAN WOLVERINE, ALBEIT BARELY. HOW CAN THESE HEROES FIT SO MANY EXPLOITS INTO A SINGLE LIFETIME?
THANKS TO US.
AH, THERE IT IS. THE PRICE.
SNUMP
LOKI'S TRICKSTER TIPS #3: "NOTHING IS FREE."
AND IF YOU DON'T BELIEVE ME, I'VE GOT A GENTLY USED CHARIOT TO SELL YOU, RUNS LIKE A DREAM, PREVIOUS OWNER WAS A LITTLE OLD LADY WHO ONLY DROVE IT TO THE SHRINE AND BACK ON WODEN'S DAY.

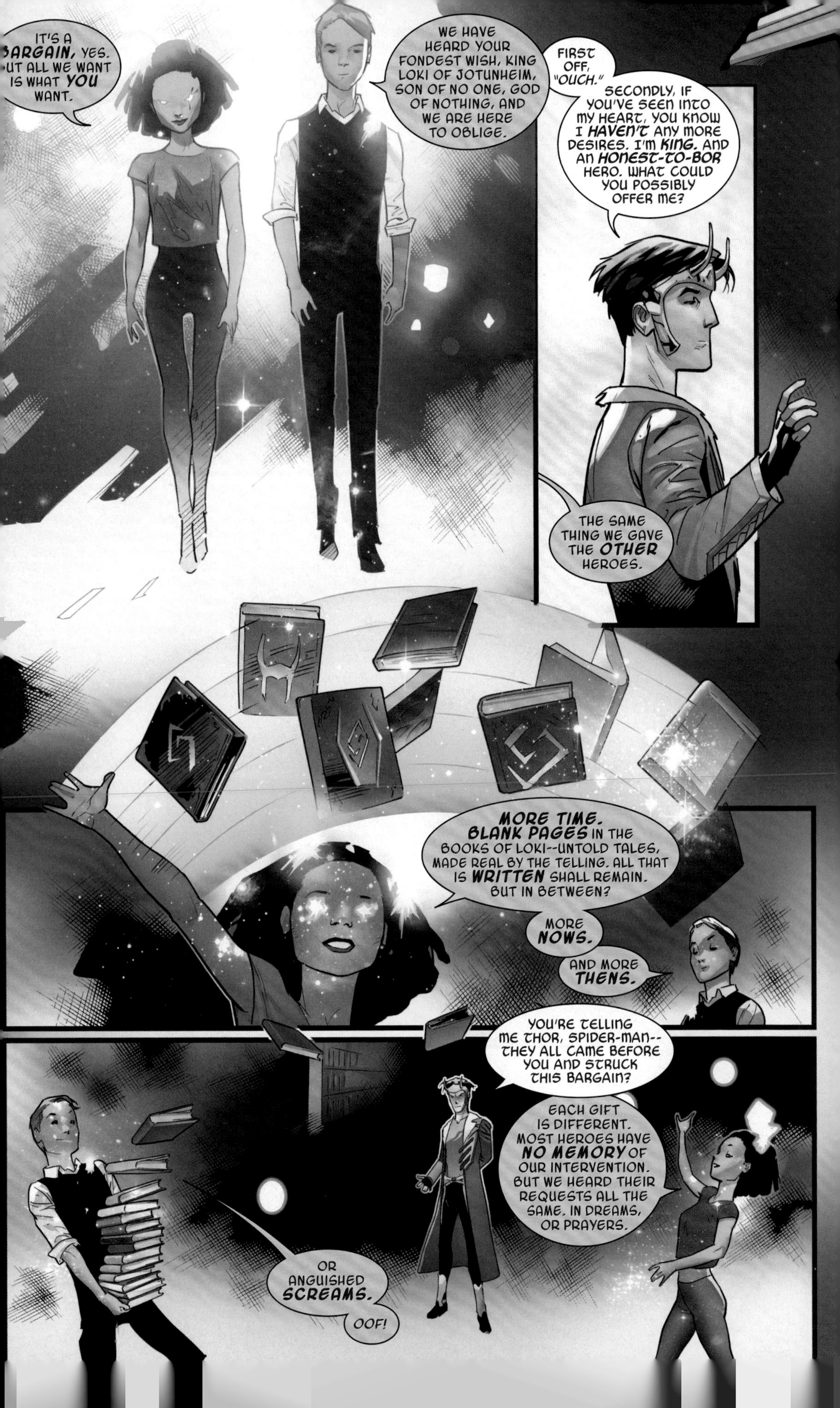
IT'S A BARGAIN, YES. BUT ALL WE WANT IS WHAT YOU WANT.
WE HAVE HEARD YOUR FONDEST WISH, KING LOKI OF JOTUNHEIM, SON OF NO ONE, GOD OF NOTHING, AND WE ARE HERE TO OBLIGE.
FIRST OFF, "OUCH."
SECONDLY, IF YOU'VE SEEN INTO MY HEART, YOU KNOW I HAVEN'T ANY MORE DESIRES. I'M KING. AND AN HONEST-TO-BOR HERO. WHAT COULD YOU POSSIBLY OFFER ME?
THE SAME THING WE GAVE THE OTHER HEROES.
MORE TIME. BLANK PAGES IN THE BOOKS OF LOKI--UNTOLD TALES, MADE REAL BY THE TELLING. ALL THAT IS WRITTEN SHALL REMAIN. BUT IN BETWEEN?
MORE NOWS.
AND MORE THENS.
YOU'RE TELLING ME THOR, SPIDER-MAN-- THEY ALL CAME BEFORE YOU AND STRUCK THIS BARGAIN?
EACH GIFT IS DIFFERENT. MOST HEROES HAVE NO MEMORY OF OUR INTERVENTION. BUT WE HEARD THEIR REQUESTS ALL THE SAME. IN DREAMS, OR PRAYERS.
OR ANGUISHED SCREAMS.
OOF!

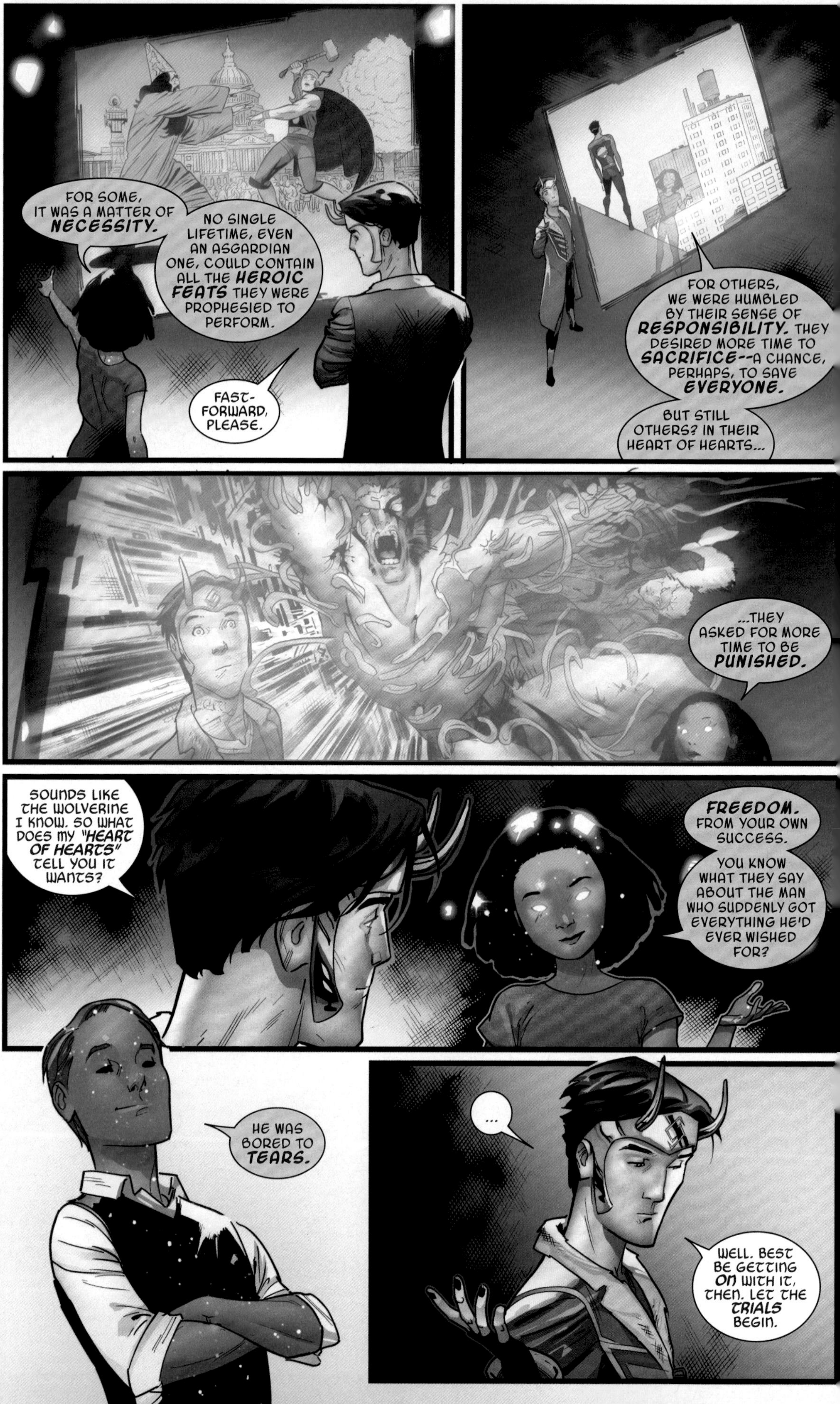
FOR SOME, IT WAS A MATTER OF NECESSITY.
NO SINGLE LIFETIME, EVEN AN ASGARDIAN ONE, COULD CONTAIN ALL THE HEROIC FEATS THEY WERE PROPHESIED TO PERFORM.
FAST-FORWARD, PLEASE.
FOR OTHERS, WE WERE HUMBLED BY THEIR SENSE OF RESPONSIBILITY. THEY DESIRED MORE TIME TO SACRIFICE--A CHANCE, PERHAPS, TO SAVE EVERYONE.
BUT STILL OTHERS? IN THEIR HEART OF HEARTS...
...THEY ASKED FOR MORE TIME TO BE PUNISHED.
SOUNDS LIKE THE WOLVERINE I KNOW. SO WHAT DOES MY "HEART OF HEARTS" TELL YOU IT WANTS?
FREEDOM. FROM YOUR OWN SUCCESS.
YOU KNOW WHAT THEY SAY ABOUT THE MAN WHO SUDDENLY GOT EVERYTHING HE'D EVER WISHED FOR?
HE WAS BORED TO TEARS.
...
WELL. BEST BE GETTING ON WITH IT, THEN. LET THE TRIALS BEGIN.

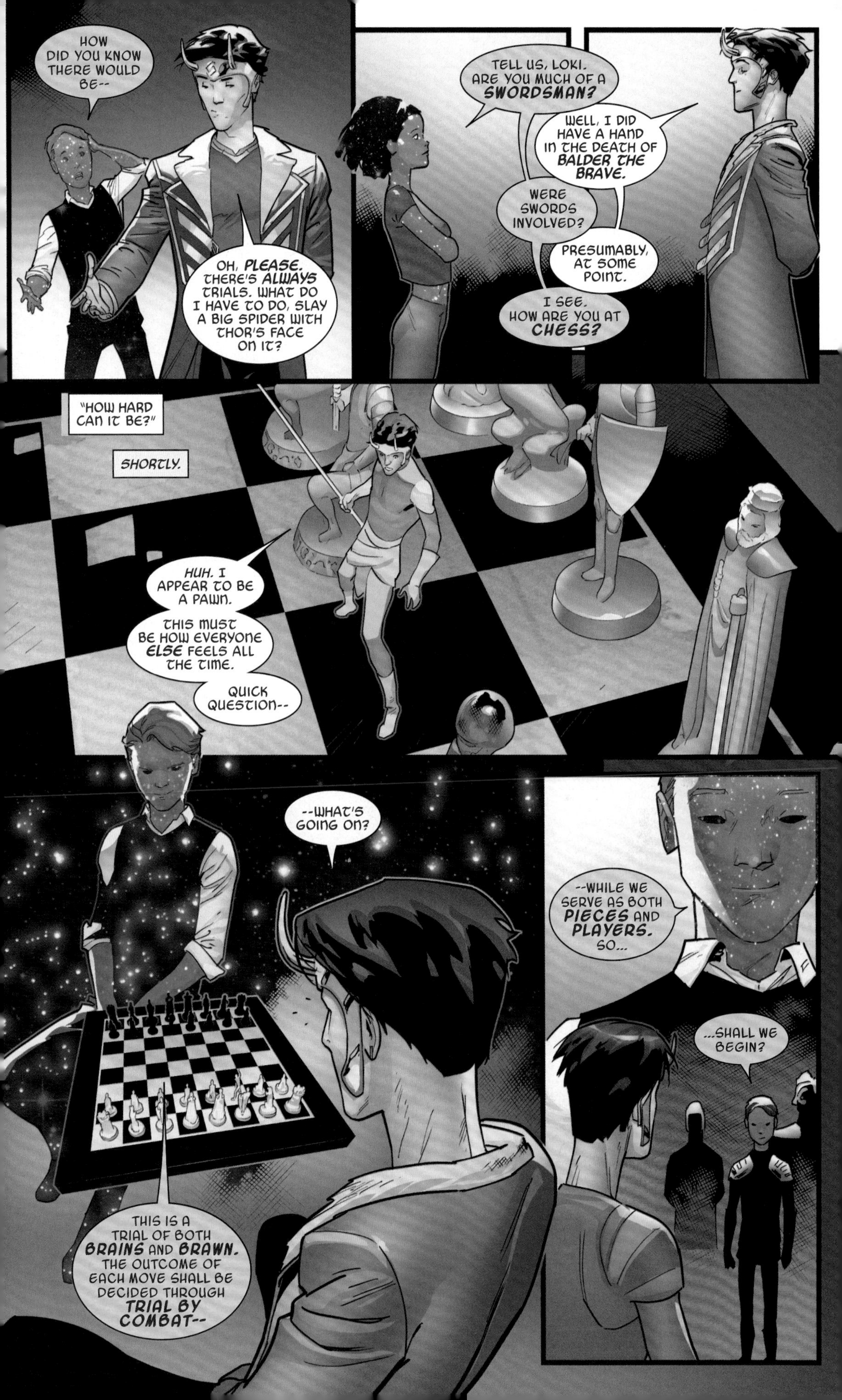
HOW DID YOU KNOW THERE WOULD BE--
OH, PLEASE. THERE'S ALWAYS TRIALS. WHAT DO I HAVE TO DO, SLAY A BIG SPIDER WITH THOR'S FACE ON IT?
TELL US, LOKI. ARE YOU MUCH OF A SWORDSMAN?
WELL, I DID HAVE A HAND IN THE DEATH OF BALDER THE BRAVE.
WERE SWORDS INVOLVED?
PRESUMABLY, AT SOME POINT.
I SEE. HOW ARE YOU AT CHESS?
"HOW HARD CAN IT BE?"
SHORTLY.
HUH. I APPEAR TO BE A PAWN.
THIS MUST BE HOW EVERYONE ELSE FEELS ALL THE TIME.
QUICK QUESTION--
--WHAT'S GOING ON?
THIS IS A TRIAL OF BOTH BRAINS AND BRAWN. THE OUTCOME OF EACH MOVE SHALL BE DECIDED THROUGH TRIAL BY COMBAT--
--WHILE WE SERVE AS BOTH PIECES AND PLAYERS. SO...
...SHALL WE BEGIN?

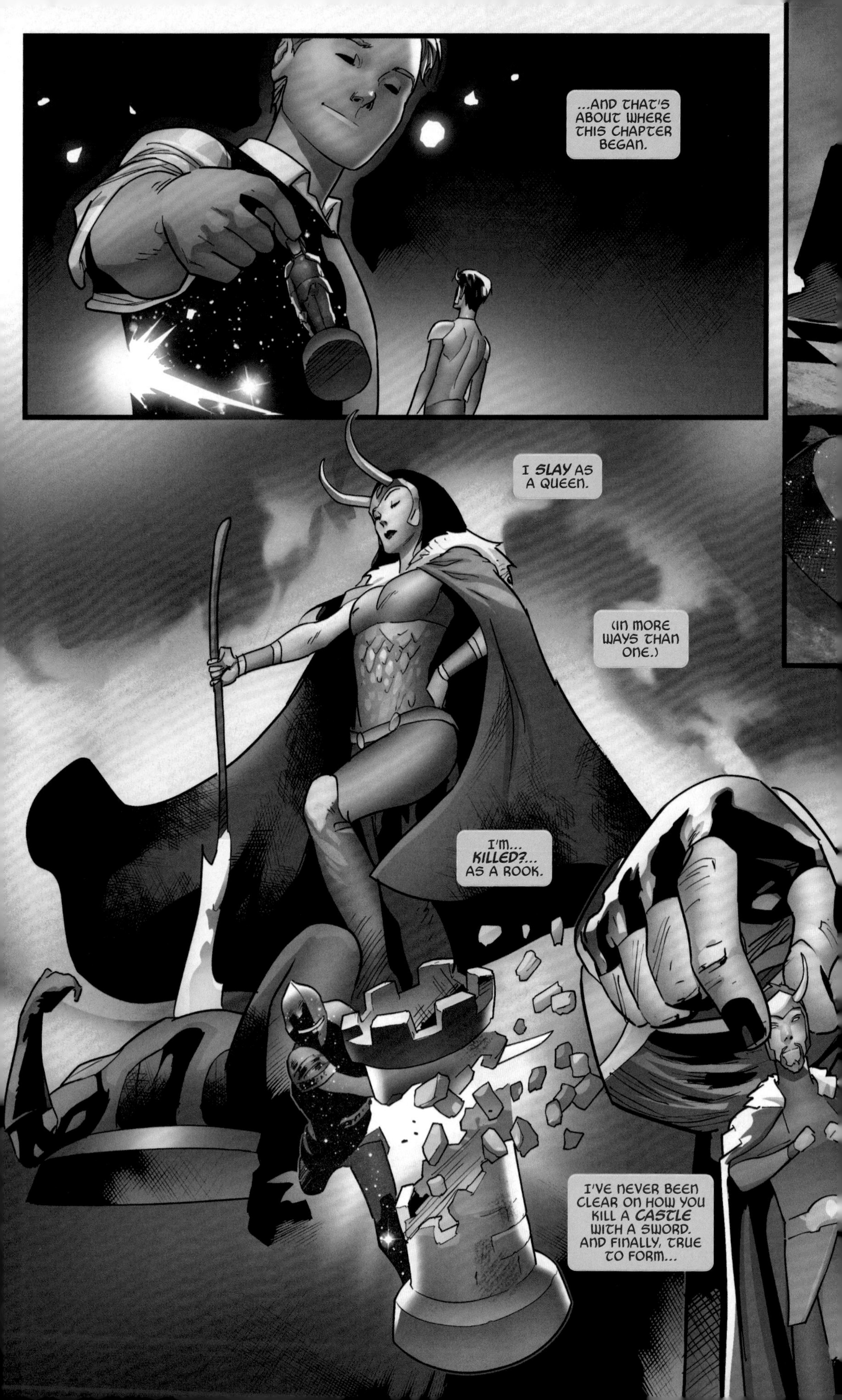
...AND THAT'S ABOUT WHERE THIS CHAPTER BEGAN.
I SLAY AS A QUEEN.
(IN MORE WAYS THAN ONE.)
I'M... KILLED?... AS A ROOK.
I'VE NEVER BEEN CLEAR ON HOW YOU KILL A CASTLE WITH A SWORD. AND FINALLY, TRUE TO FORM...

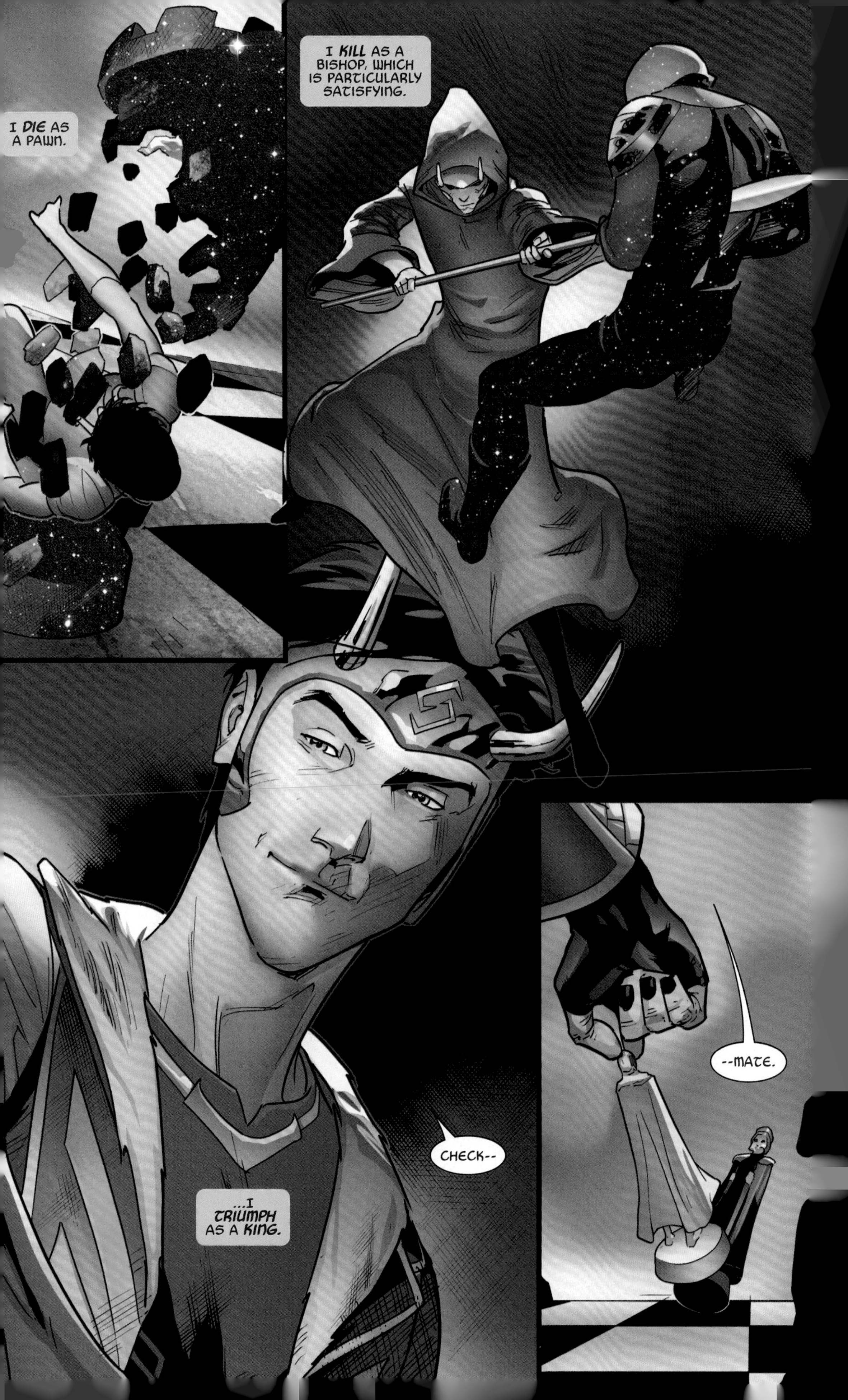
I DIE AS A PAWN.
I KILL AS A BISHOP, WHICH IS PARTICULARLY SATISFYING.
...I TRIUMPH AS A KING.
CHECK--
--MATE.

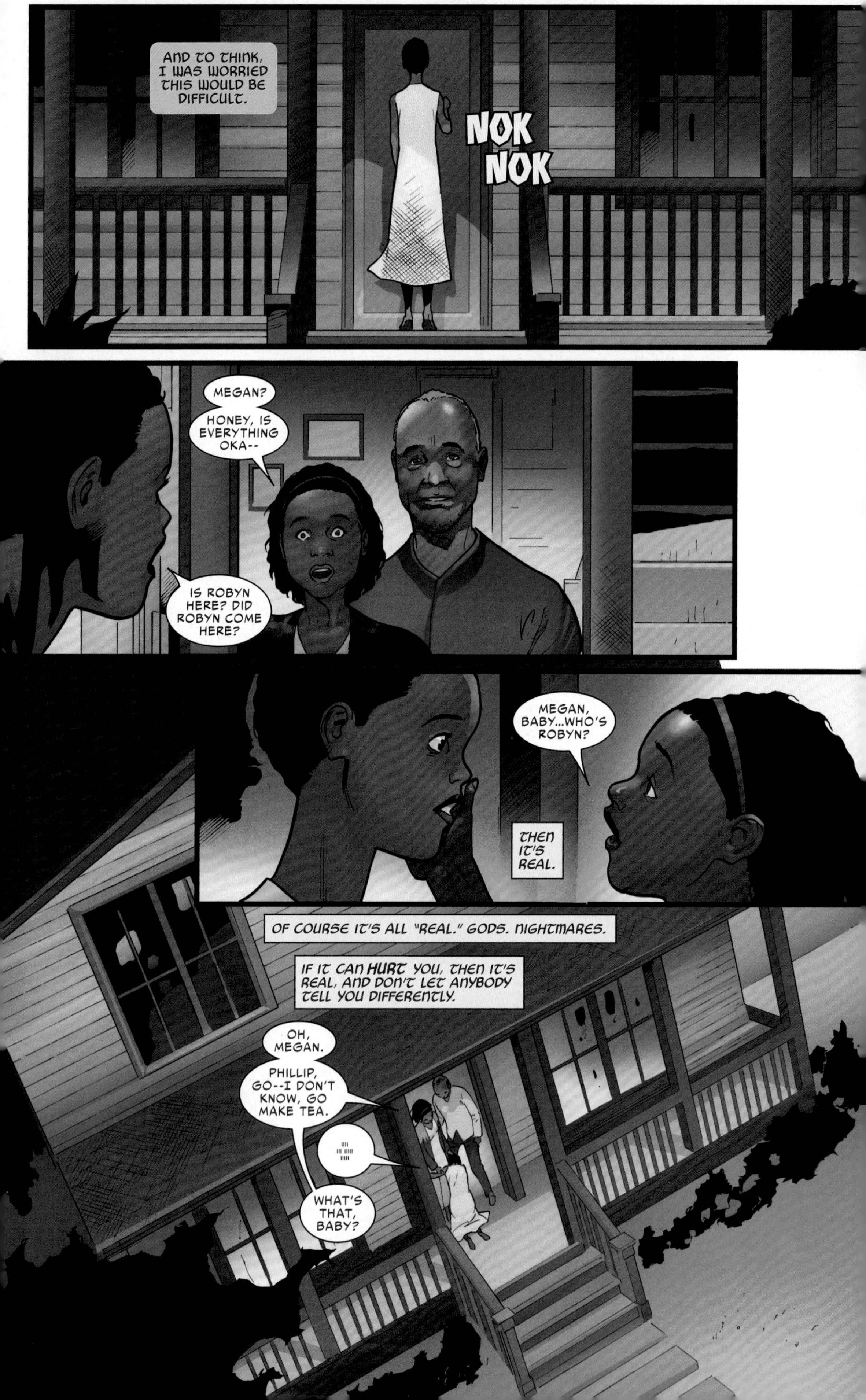
AND TO THINK, I WAS WORRIED THIS WOULD BE DIFFICULT.
NOK NOK
MEGAN?
HONEY, IS EVERYTHING OKA--
IS ROBYN HERE? DID ROBYN COME HERE?
MEGAN, BABY...WHO'S ROBYN?
THEN IT'S REAL.
OF COURSE IT'S ALL "REAL." GODS. NIGHTMARES.
IF IT CAN HURT YOU, THEN IT'S REAL, AND DON'T LET ANYBODY TELL YOU DIFFERENTLY.
OH, MEGAN.
PHILLIP, GO--I DON'T KNOW, GO MAKE TEA.
WHAT'S THAT, BABY?

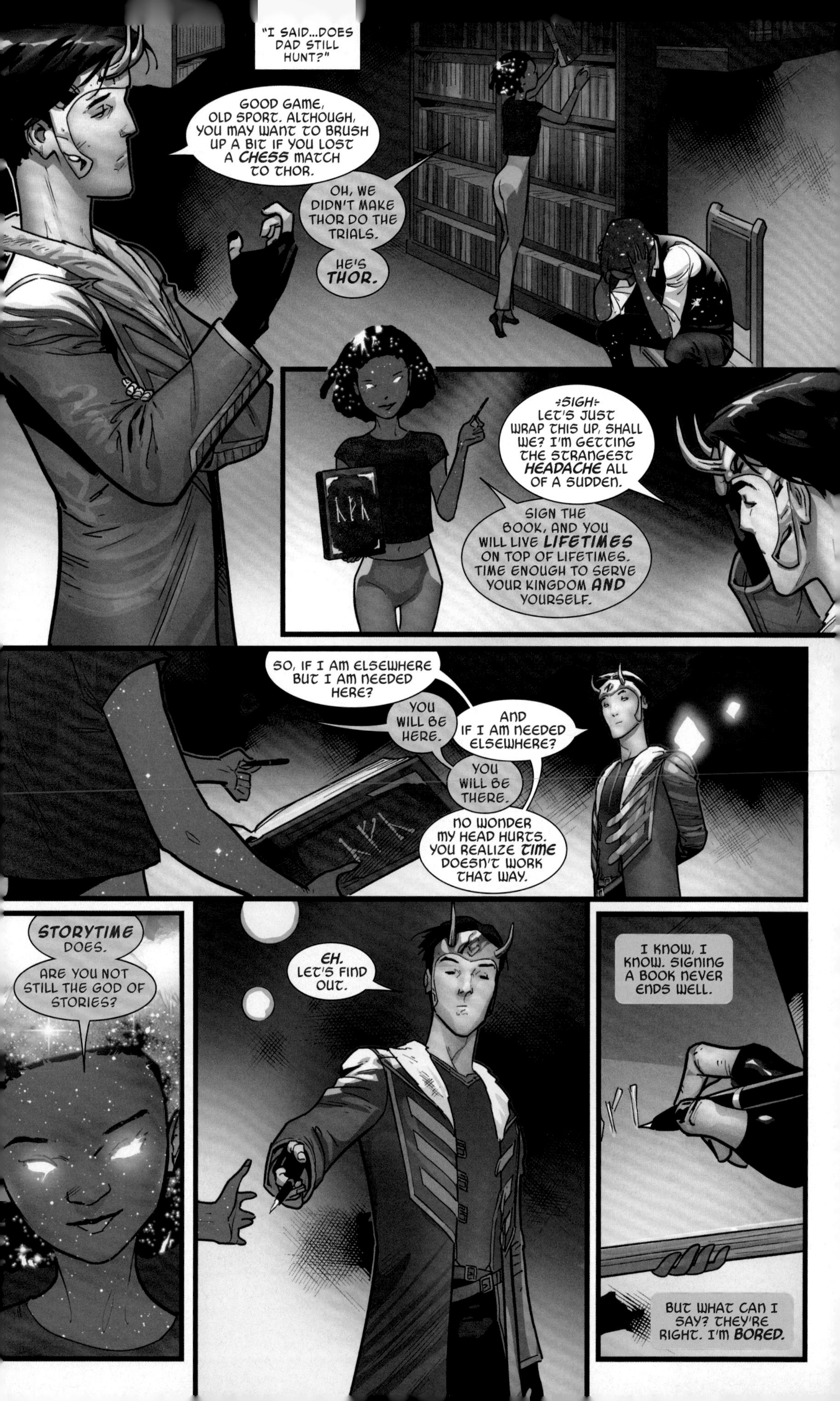
"I SAID...DOES DAD STILL HUNT?"
GOOD GAME, OLD SPORT. ALTHOUGH, YOU MAY WANT TO BRUSH UP A BIT IF YOU LOST A CHESS MATCH TO THOR.
OH, WE DIDN'T MAKE THOR DO THE TRIALS.
HE'S THOR.
SIGH LET'S JUST WRAP THIS UP, SHALL WE? I'M GETTING THE STRANGEST HEADACHE ALL OF A SUDDEN.
SIGN THE BOOK, AND YOU WILL LIVE LIFETIMES ON TOP OF LIFETIMES. TIME ENOUGH TO SERVE YOUR KINGDOM AND YOURSELF.
SO, IF I AM ELSEWHERE BUT I AM NEEDED HERE?
YOU WILL BE HERE.
AND IF I AM NEEDED ELSEWHERE?
YOU WILL BE THERE.
NO WONDER MY HEAD HURTS. YOU REALIZE TIME DOESN'T WORK THAT WAY.
STORYTIME DOES.
ARE YOU NOT STILL THE GOD OF STORIES?
EH. LET'S FIND OUT.
I KNOW, I KNOW. SIGNING A BOOK NEVER ENDS WELL.
BUT WHAT CAN I SAY? THEY'RE RIGHT. I'M BORED.

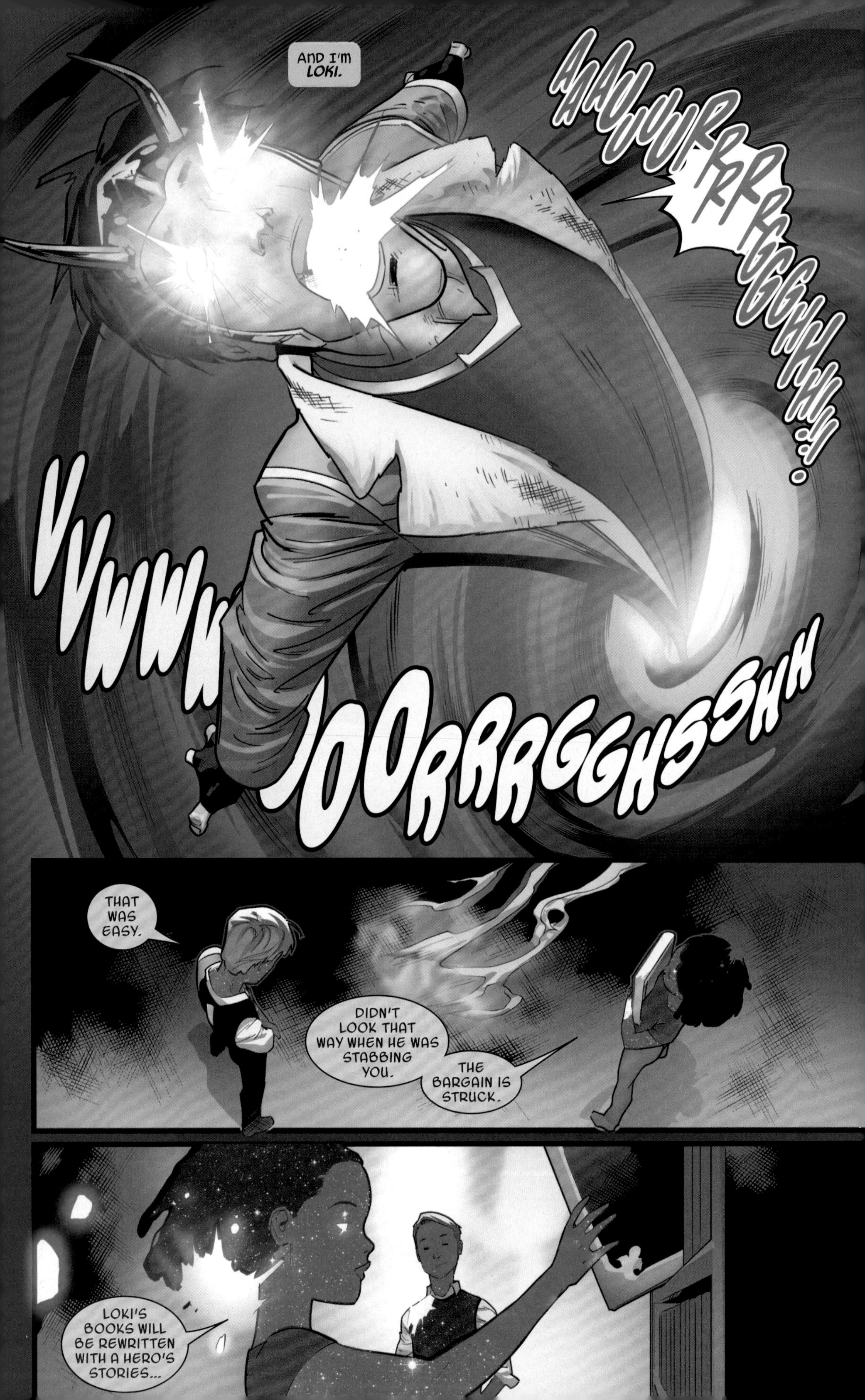
AND I'M LOKI.
AAAUUURRRRRGGHHH!!..
VVWWW
OORRRGGHSSHH
THAT WAS EASY.
DIDN'T LOOK THAT WAY WHEN HE WAS STABBING YOU.
THE BARGAIN IS STRUCK.
LOKI'S BOOKS WILL BE REWRITTEN WITH A HERO'S STORIES...

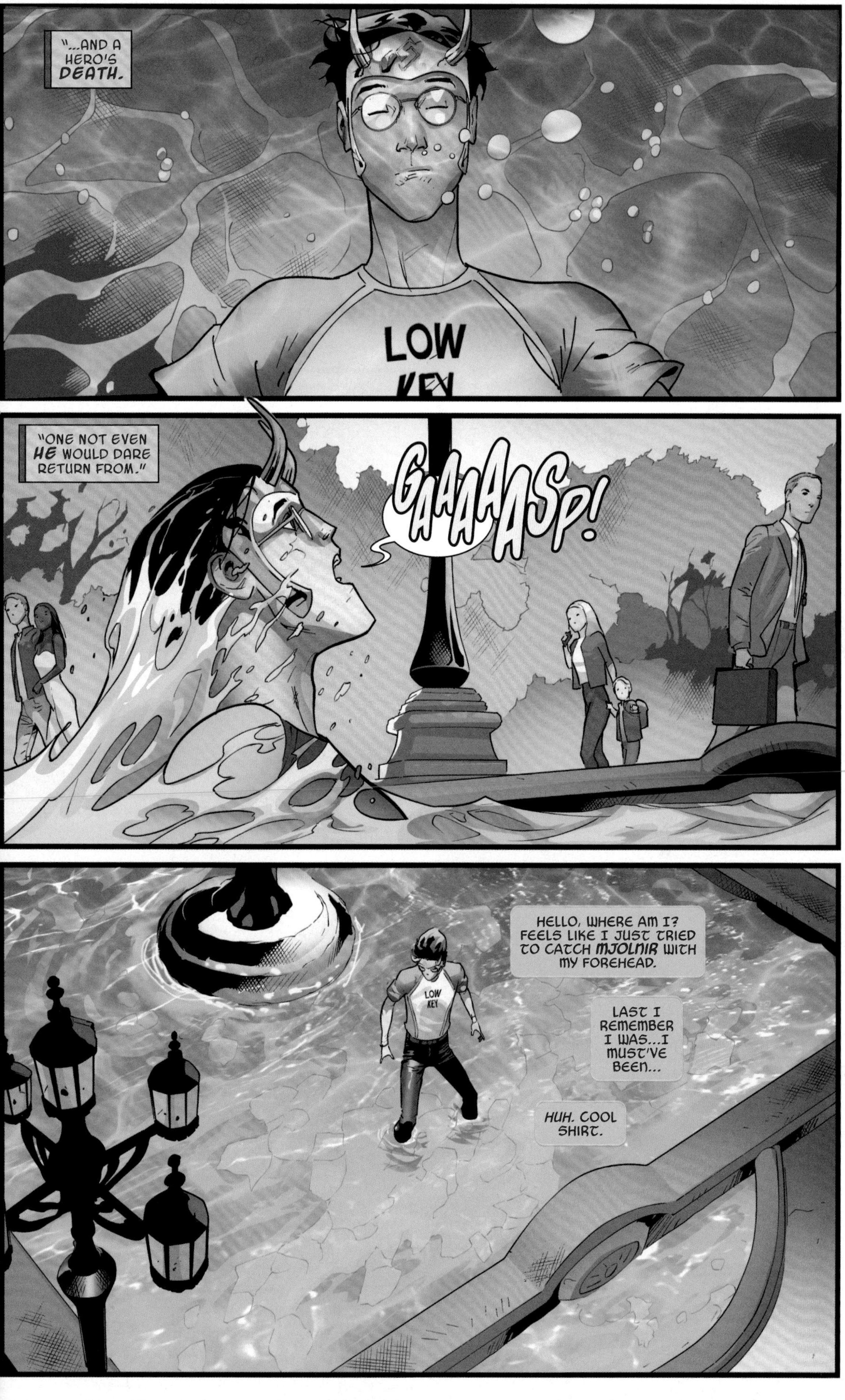
"...AND A HERO'S DEATH.
"ONE NOT EVEN HE WOULD DARE RETURN FROM."
GAAAAASP!
HELLO, WHERE AM I? FEELS LIKE I JUST TRIED TO CATCH MJOLNIR WITH MY FOREHEAD.
LAST I REMEMBER I WAS...I MUST'VE BEEN...
HUH. COOL SHIRT.
LOW KEY

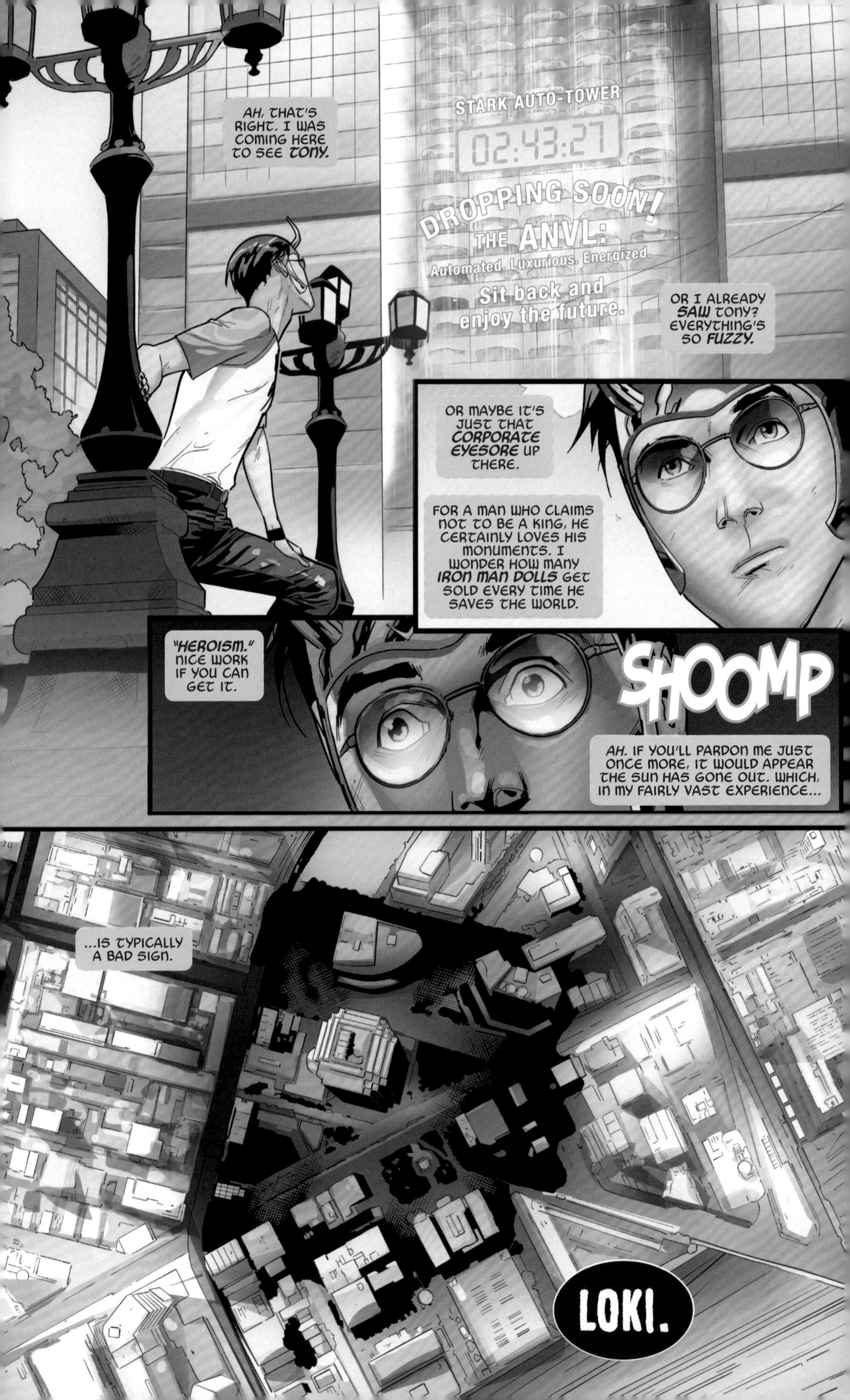
AH, THAT'S RIGHT. I WAS COMING HERE TO SEE TONY.
STARK AUTO-TOWER
02:43:27
DROPPING SOON!
THE ANVL:
Automated. Luxurious. Energized.
Sit back and enjoy the future.
OR I ALREADY SAW TONY? EVERYTHING'S SO FUZZY.
OR MAYBE IT'S JUST THAT CORPORATE EYESORE UP THERE.
FOR A MAN WHO CLAIMS NOT TO BE A KING, HE CERTAINLY LOVES HIS MONUMENTS. I WONDER HOW MANY IRON MAN DOLLS GET SOLD EVERY TIME HE SAVES THE WORLD.
"HEROISM." NICE WORK IF YOU CAN GET IT.
SHOOMP
AH. IF YOU'LL PARDON ME JUST ONCE MORE, IT WOULD APPEAR THE SUN HAS GONE OUT. WHICH, IN MY FAIRLY VAST EXPERIENCE...
...IS TYPICALLY A BAD SIGN.
LOKI.

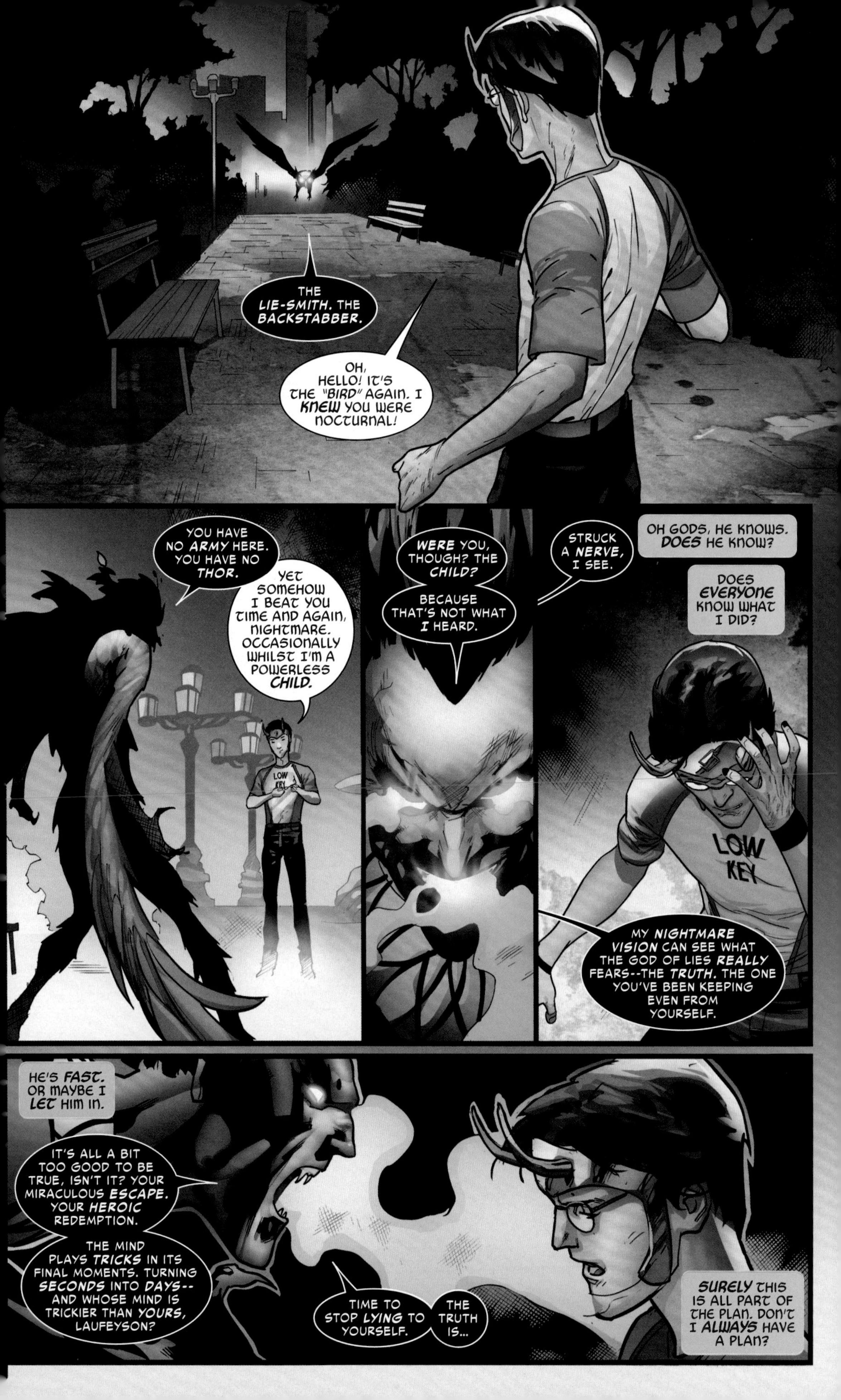
THE LIE-SMITH. THE BACKSTABBER.
OH, HELLO! IT'S THE "BIRD" AGAIN. I KNEW YOU WERE NOCTURNAL!
YOU HAVE NO ARMY HERE. YOU HAVE NO THOR.
YET SOMEHOW I BEAT YOU TIME AND AGAIN, NIGHTMARE. OCCASIONALLY WHILST I'M A POWERLESS CHILD.
LOW KEY
WERE YOU, THOUGH? THE CHILD?
BECAUSE THAT'S NOT WHAT I HEARD.
STRUCK A NERVE, I SEE.
OH GODS, HE KNOWS. DOES HE KNOW?
DOES EVERYONE KNOW WHAT I DID?
LOW KEY
MY NIGHTMARE VISION CAN SEE WHAT THE GOD OF LIES REALLY FEARS--THE TRUTH. THE ONE YOU'VE BEEN KEEPING EVEN FROM YOURSELF.
HE'S FAST. OR MAYBE I LET HIM IN.
IT'S ALL A BIT TOO GOOD TO BE TRUE, ISN'T IT? YOUR MIRACULOUS ESCAPE. YOUR HEROIC REDEMPTION.
THE MIND PLAYS TRICKS IN ITS FINAL MOMENTS. TURNING SECONDS INTO DAYS-- AND WHOSE MIND IS TRICKIER THAN YOURS, LAUFEYSON?
TIME TO STOP LYING TO YOURSELF.
THE TRUTH IS...
SURELY THIS IS ALL PART OF THE PLAN. DON'T I ALWAYS HAVE A PLAN?

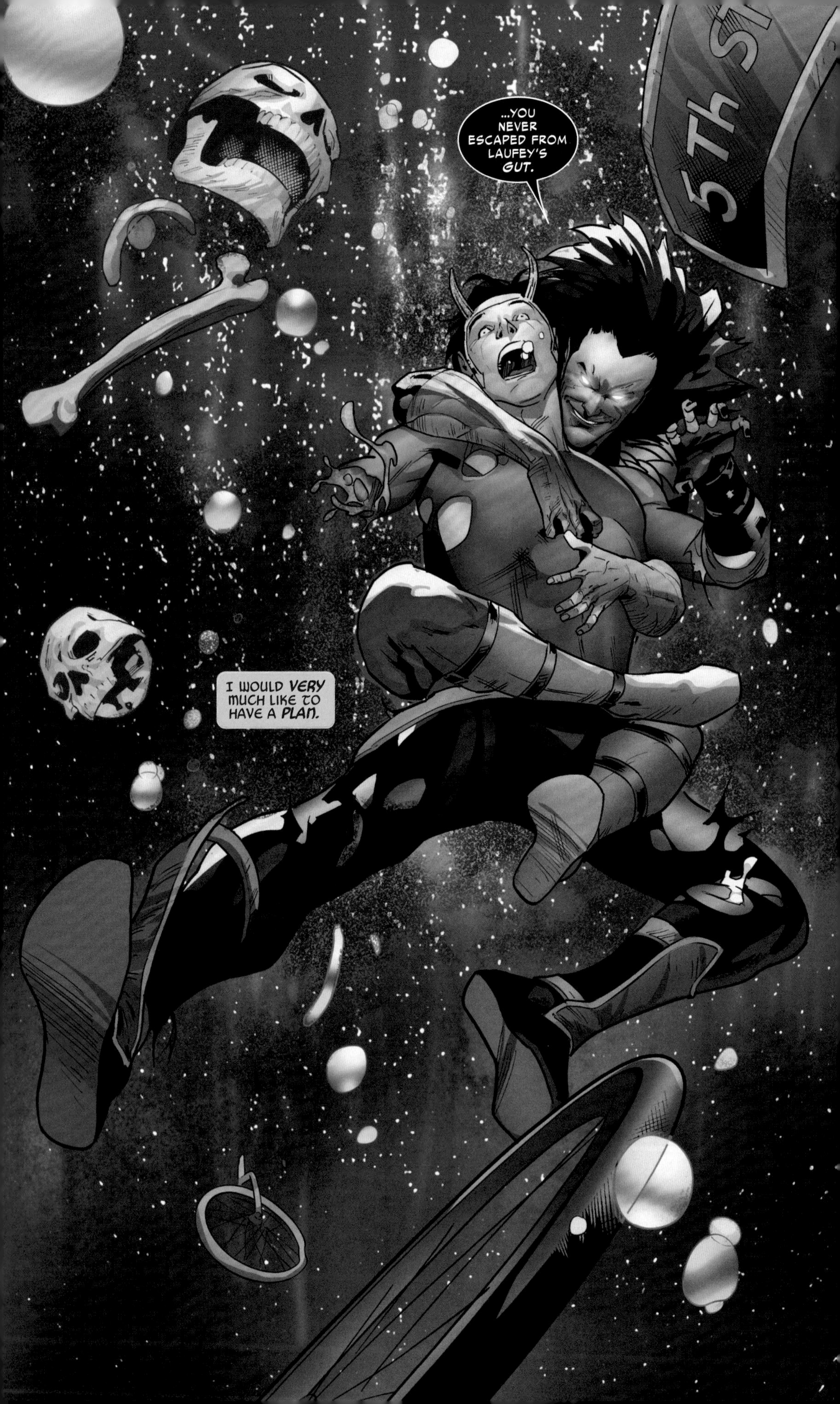
...YOU NEVER ESCAPED FROM LAUFEY'S GUT.
I WOULD VERY MUCH LIKE TO HAVE A PLAN.
5Th St

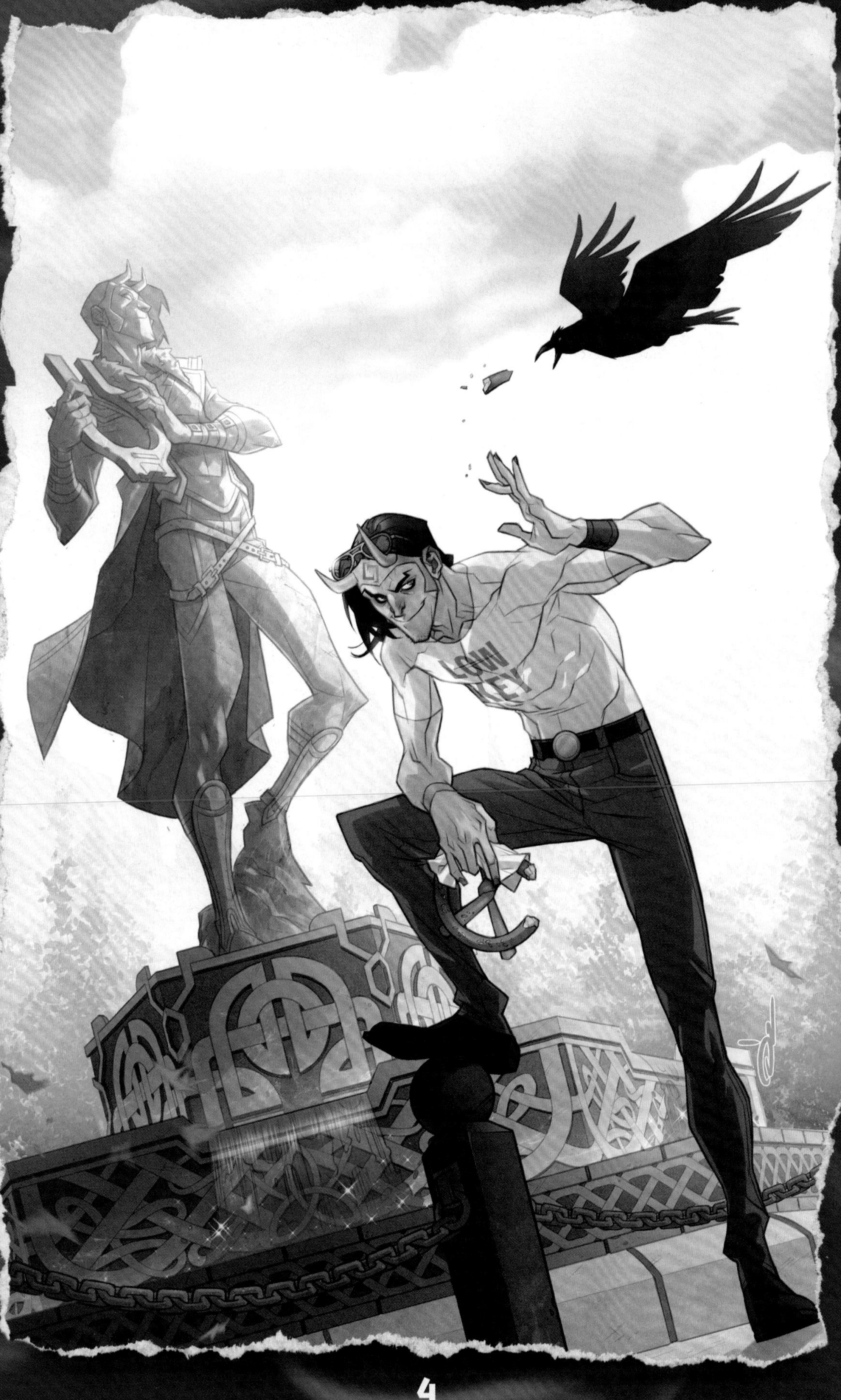

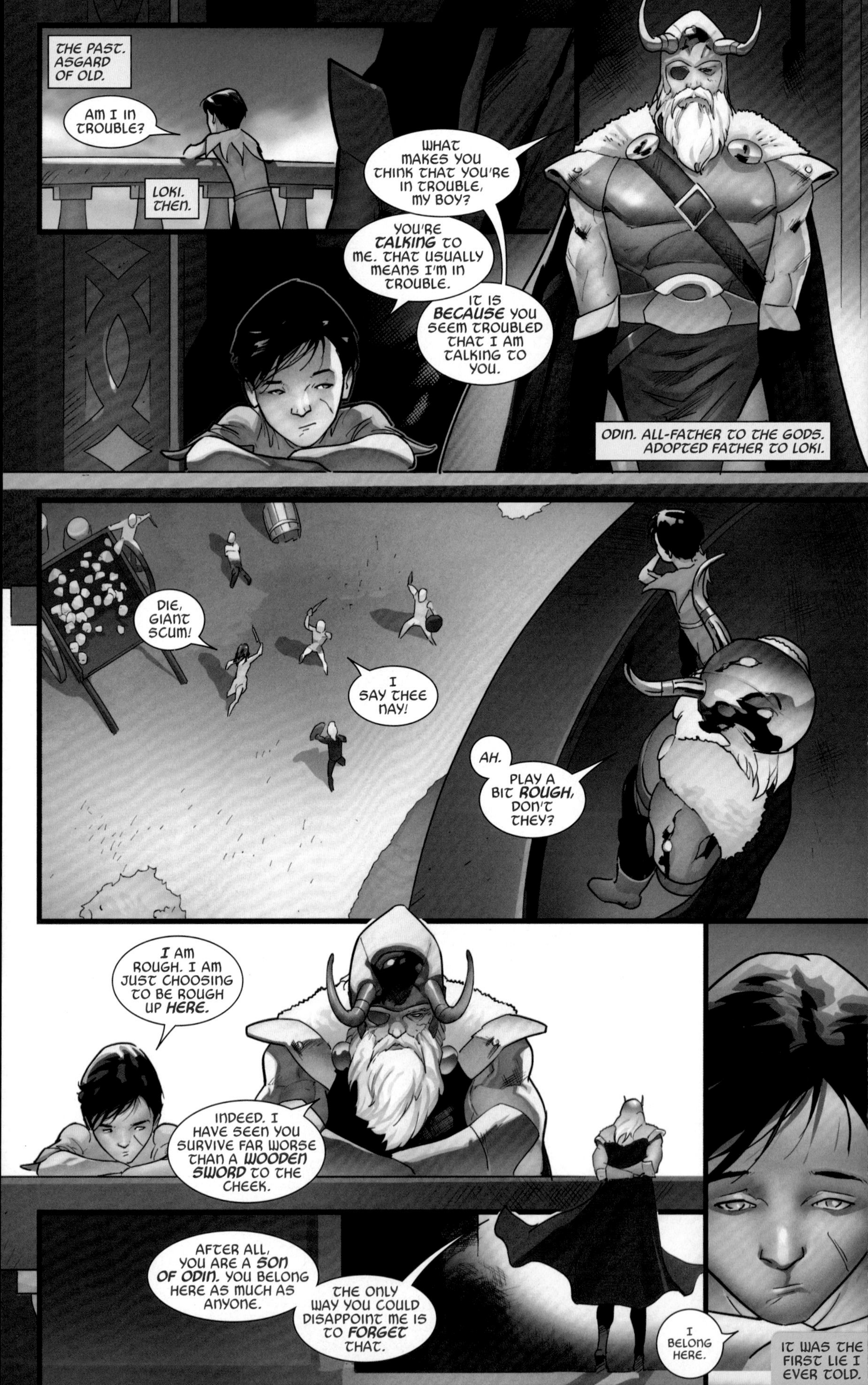
THE PAST. ASGARD OF OLD.
AM I IN TROUBLE?
LOKI. THEN.
WHAT MAKES YOU THINK THAT YOU'RE IN TROUBLE, MY BOY?
YOU'RE TALKING TO ME. THAT USUALLY MEANS I'M IN TROUBLE.
IT IS BECAUSE YOU SEEM TROUBLED THAT I AM TALKING TO YOU.
ODIN. ALL-FATHER TO THE GODS. ADOPTED FATHER TO LOKI.
DIE, GIANT SCUM!
I SAY THEE NAY!
AH.
PLAY A BIT ROUGH, DON'T THEY?
I AM ROUGH. I AM JUST CHOOSING TO BE ROUGH UP HERE.
INDEED. I HAVE SEEN YOU SURVIVE FAR WORSE THAN A WOODEN SWORD TO THE CHEEK.
AFTER ALL, YOU ARE A SON OF ODIN. YOU BELONG HERE AS MUCH AS ANYONE.
THE ONLY WAY YOU COULD DISAPPOINT ME IS TO FORGET THAT.
I BELONG HERE.
IT WAS THE FIRST LIE I EVER TOLD.

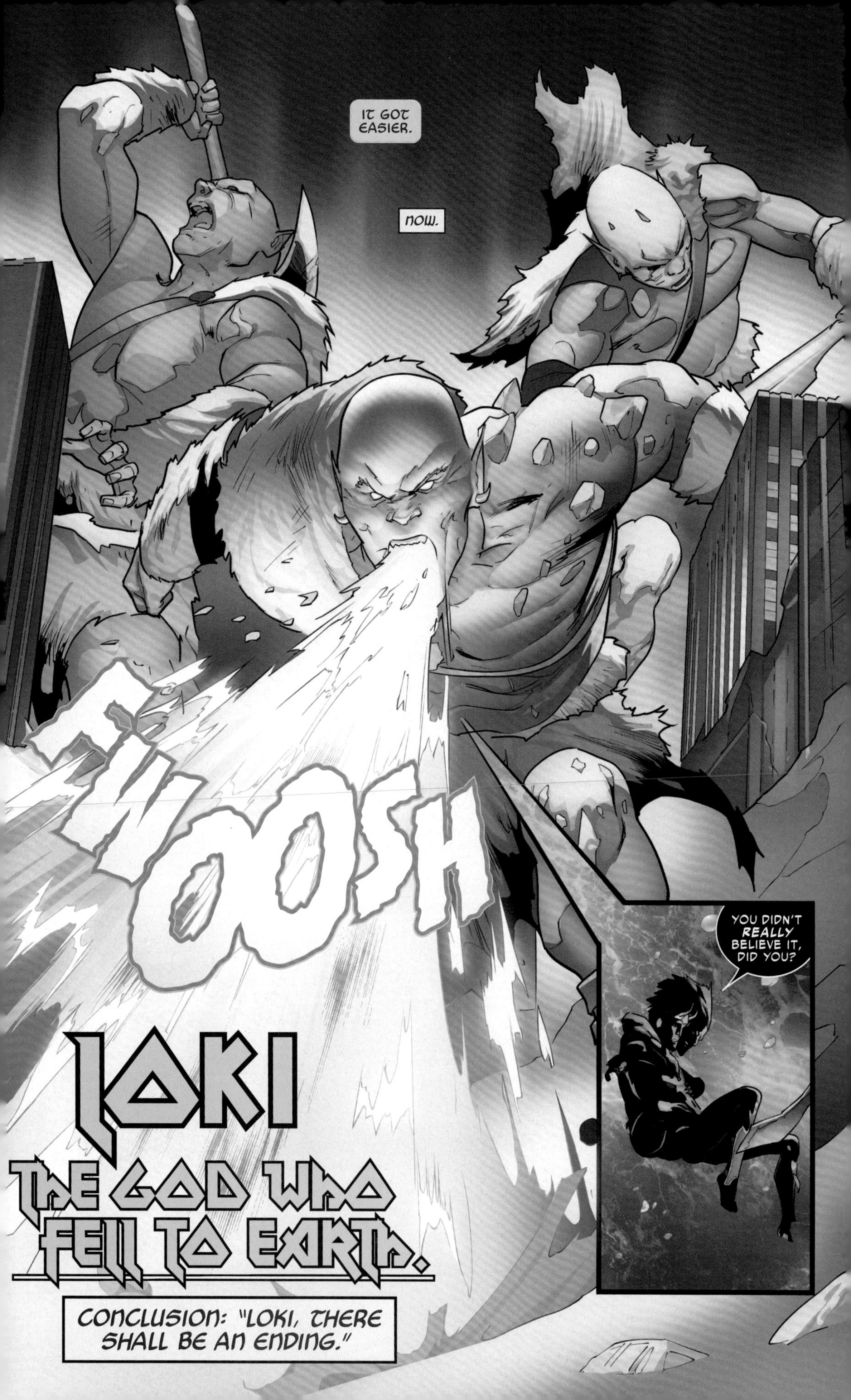
IT GOT EASIER.
NOW.
FWOOSH
YOU DIDN'T REALLY BELIEVE IT, DID YOU?
LOKI
THE GOD WHO FELL TO EARTH.
CONCLUSION: "LOKI, THERE SHALL BE AN ENDING."

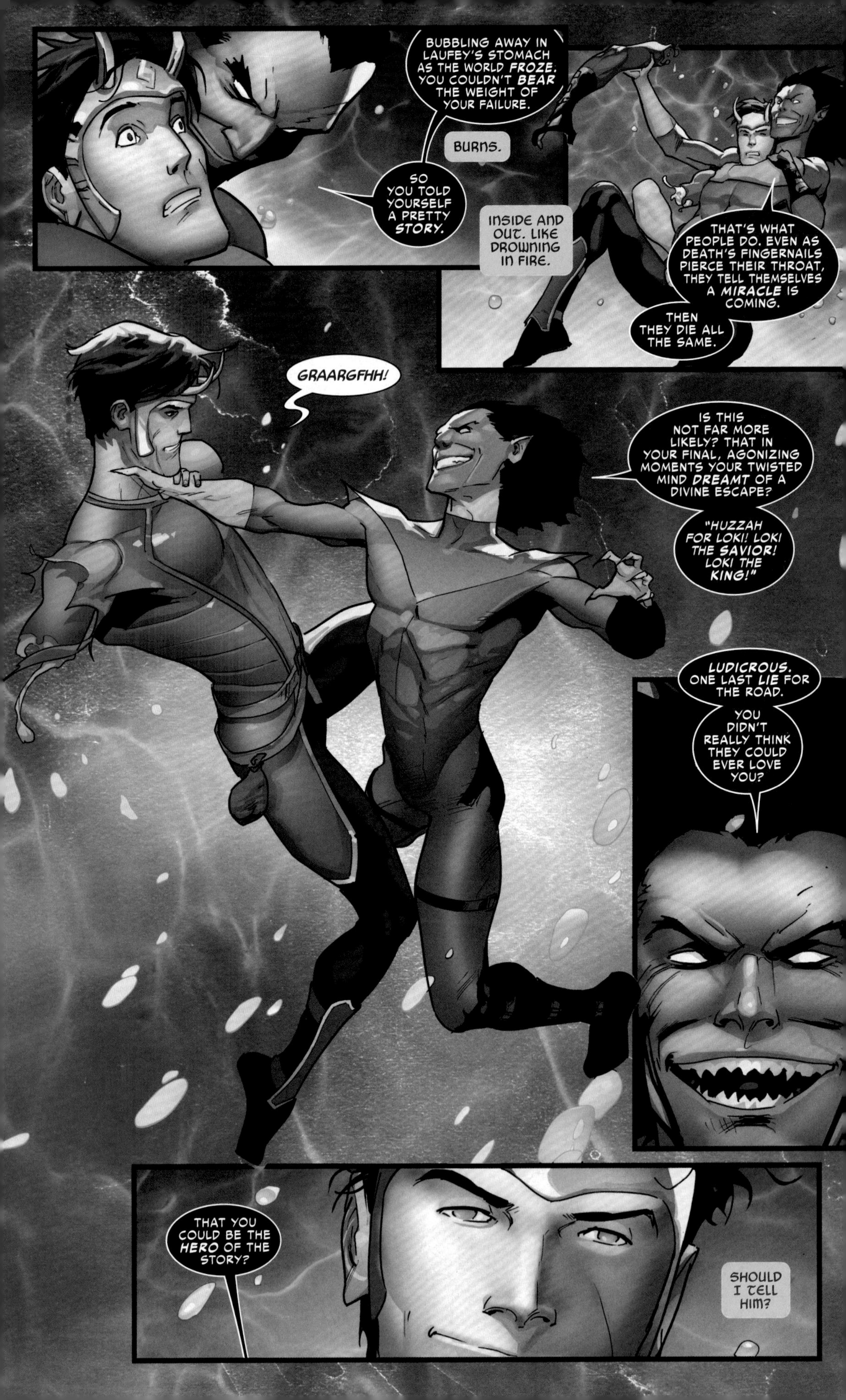

BUBBLING AWAY IN LAUFEY'S STOMACH AS THE WORLD FROZE. YOU COULDN'T BEAR THE WEIGHT OF YOUR FAILURE.
BURNS.
SO YOU TOLD YOURSELF A PRETTY STORY.
INSIDE AND OUT. LIKE DROWNING IN FIRE.
THAT'S WHAT PEOPLE DO. EVEN AS DEATH'S FINGERNAILS PIERCE THEIR THROAT, THEY TELL THEMSELVES A MIRACLE IS COMING.
THEN THEY DIE ALL THE SAME.
GRAARGFHH!
IS THIS NOT FAR MORE LIKELY? THAT IN YOUR FINAL, AGONIZING MOMENTS YOUR TWISTED MIND DREAMT OF A DIVINE ESCAPE?
"HUZZAH FOR LOKI! LOKI THE SAVIOR! LOKI THE KING!"
LUDICROUS. ONE LAST LIE FOR THE ROAD.
YOU DIDN'T REALLY THINK THEY COULD EVER LOVE YOU?
THAT YOU COULD BE THE HERO OF THE STORY?
SHOULD I TELL HIM?

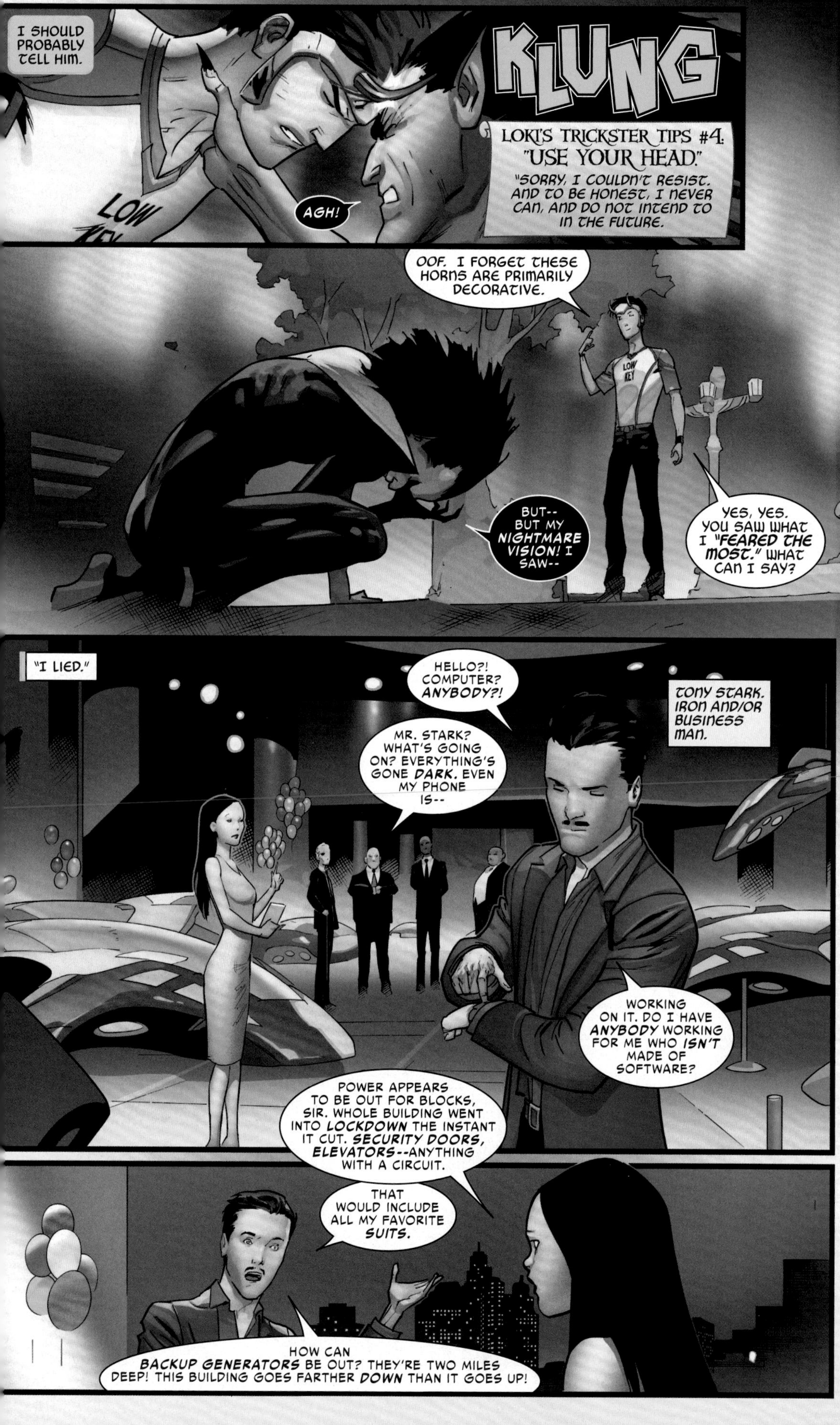

I SHOULD PROBABLY TELL HIM.
KLUNG
LOKI'S TRICKSTER TIPS #4:
"USE YOUR HEAD."
"SORRY, I COULDN'T RESIST. AND TO BE HONEST, I NEVER CAN, AND DO NOT INTEND TO IN THE FUTURE.
AGH!
LOW
OOF. I FORGET THESE HORNS ARE PRIMARILY DECORATIVE.
LOW KEY
BUT-- BUT MY NIGHTMARE VISION! I SAW--
YES, YES. YOU SAW WHAT I "FEARED THE MOST." WHAT CAN I SAY?
"I LIED."
HELLO?! COMPUTER? ANYBODY?!
TONY STARK. IRON AND/OR BUSINESS MAN.
MR. STARK? WHAT'S GOING ON? EVERYTHING'S GONE DARK. EVEN MY PHONE IS--
WORKING ON IT. DO I HAVE ANYBODY WORKING FOR ME WHO ISN'T MADE OF SOFTWARE?
POWER APPEARS TO BE OUT FOR BLOCKS, SIR. WHOLE BUILDING WENT INTO LOCKDOWN THE INSTANT IT CUT. SECURITY DOORS, ELEVATORS--ANYTHING WITH A CIRCUIT.
THAT WOULD INCLUDE ALL MY FAVORITE SUITS.
HOW CAN BACKUP GENERATORS BE OUT? THEY'RE TWO MILES DEEP! THIS BUILDING GOES FARTHER DOWN THAN IT GOES UP!

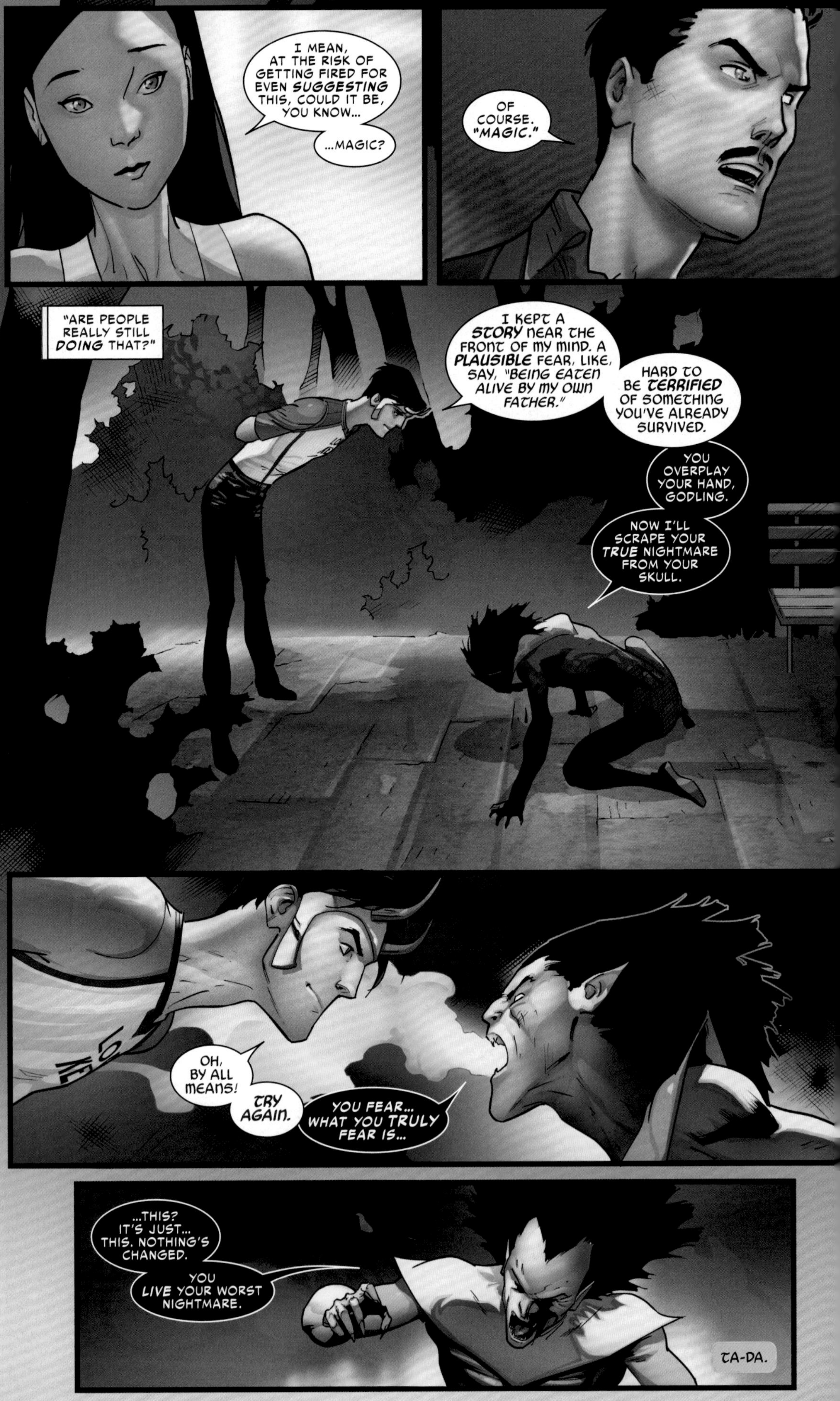

I MEAN, AT THE RISK OF GETTING FIRED FOR EVEN SUGGESTING THIS, COULD IT BE, YOU KNOW...
...MAGIC?
OF COURSE. "MAGIC."
"ARE PEOPLE REALLY STILL DOING THAT?"
I KEPT A STORY NEAR THE FRONT OF MY MIND. A PLAUSIBLE FEAR, LIKE, SAY, "BEING EATEN ALIVE BY MY OWN FATHER."
HARD TO BE TERRIFIED OF SOMETHING YOU'VE ALREADY SURVIVED.
YOU OVERPLAY YOUR HAND, GODLING.
NOW I'LL SCRAPE YOUR TRUE NIGHTMARE FROM YOUR SKULL.
OH, BY ALL MEANS!
TRY AGAIN.
YOU FEAR... WHAT YOU TRULY FEAR IS...
...THIS? IT'S JUST... THIS. NOTHING'S CHANGED.
YOU LIVE YOUR WORST NIGHTMARE.
TA-DA.

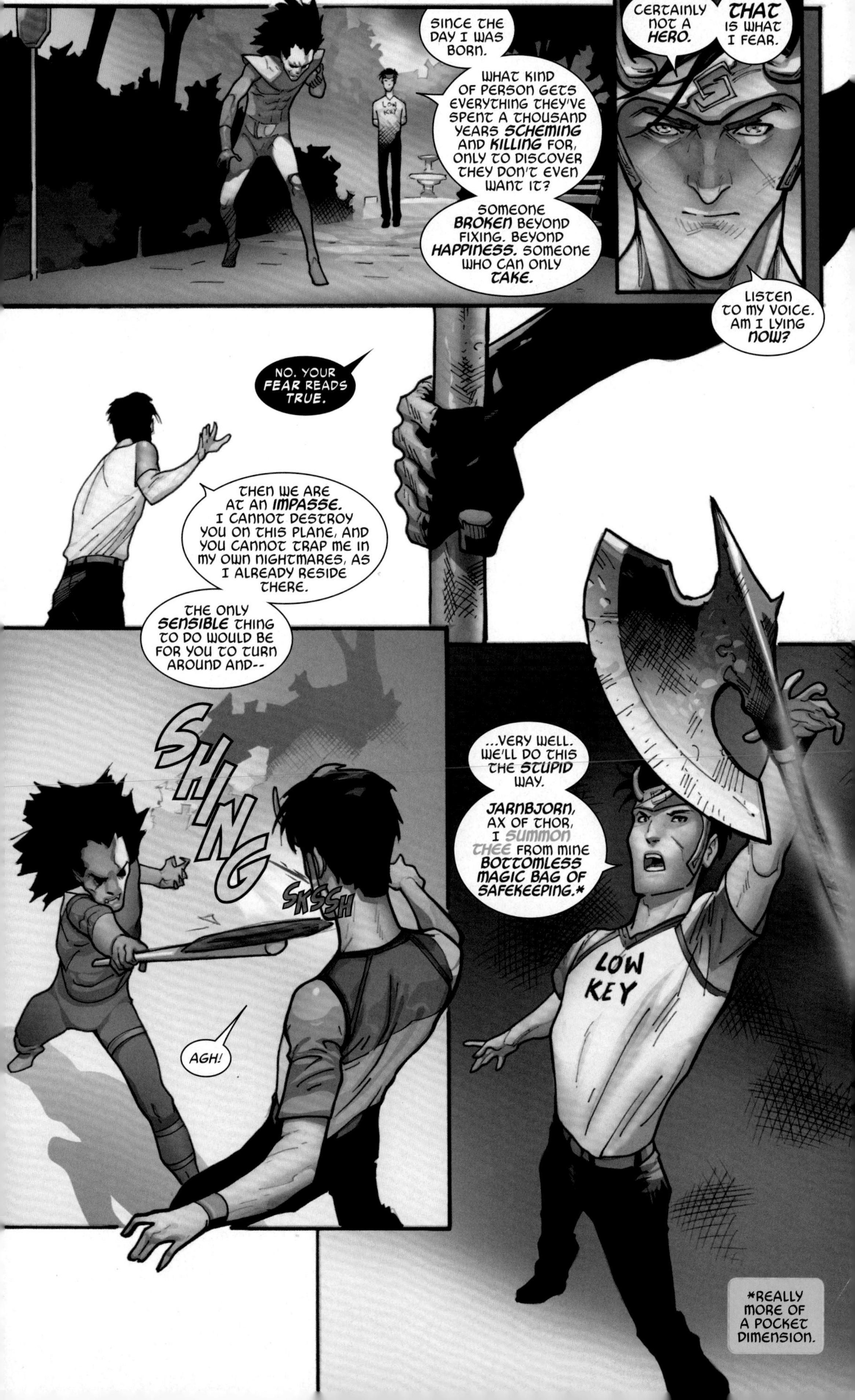
SINCE THE DAY I WAS BORN.
WHAT KIND OF PERSON GETS EVERYTHING THEY'VE SPENT A THOUSAND YEARS SCHEMING AND KILLING FOR, ONLY TO DISCOVER THEY DON'T EVEN WANT IT?
SOMEONE BROKEN BEYOND FIXING. BEYOND HAPPINESS. SOMEONE WHO CAN ONLY TAKE.
CERTAINLY NOT A HERO.
THAT IS WHAT I FEAR.
LISTEN TO MY VOICE. AM I LYING NOW?
NO. YOUR FEAR READS TRUE.
THEN WE ARE AT AN IMPASSE. I CANNOT DESTROY YOU ON THIS PLANE, AND YOU CANNOT TRAP ME IN MY OWN NIGHTMARES, AS I ALREADY RESIDE THERE.
THE ONLY SENSIBLE THING TO DO WOULD BE FOR YOU TO TURN AROUND AND--
SHING
SKSSH
AGH!
...VERY WELL. WE'LL DO THIS THE STUPID WAY.
JARNBJORN, AX OF THOR, I SUMMON THEE FROM MINE BOTTOMLESS MAGIC BAG OF SAFEKEEPING.*
LOW KEY
*REALLY MORE OF A POCKET DIMENSION.

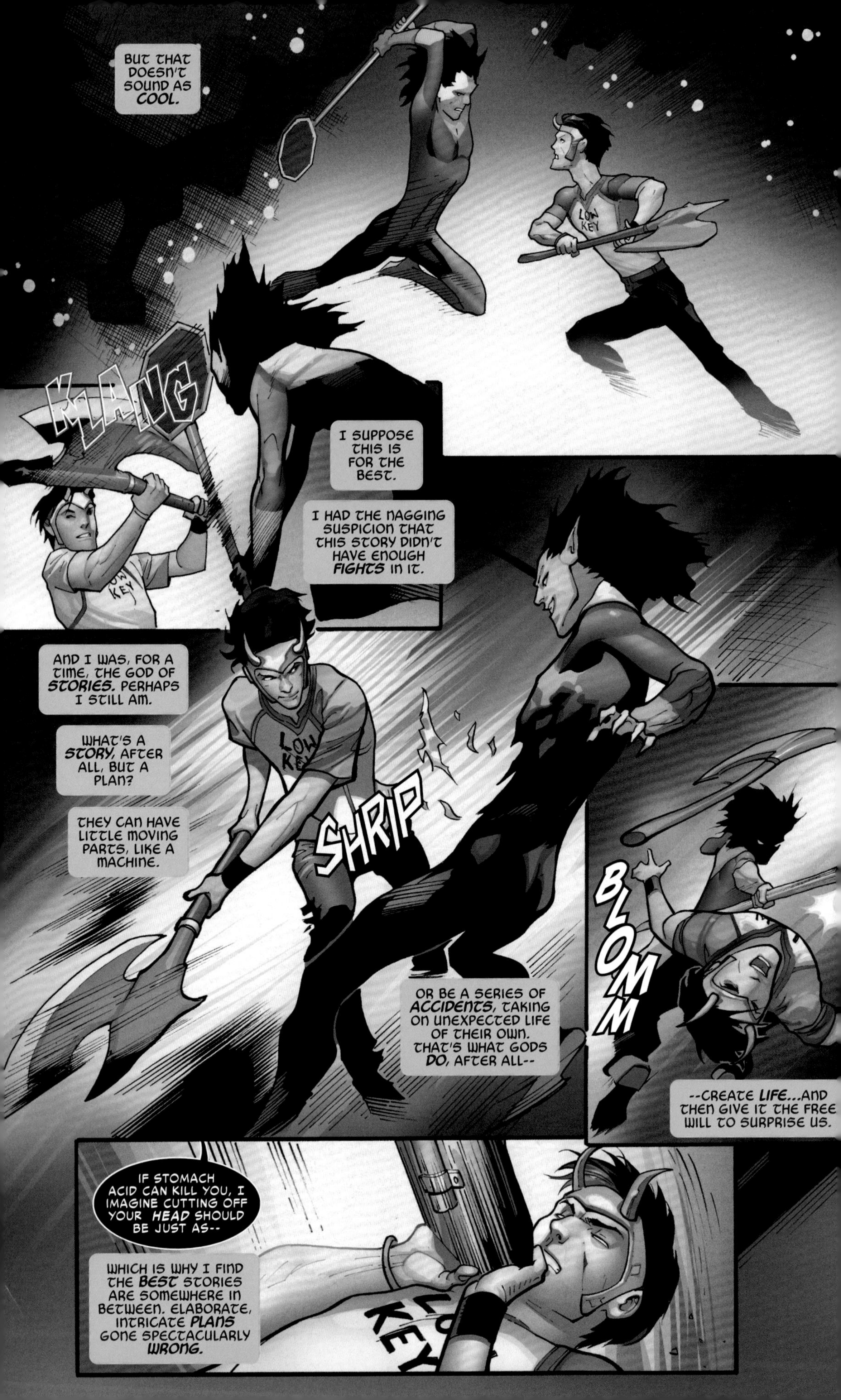

BUT THAT DOESN'T SOUND AS COOL.
KLANG
I SUPPOSE THIS IS FOR THE BEST.
I HAD THE NAGGING SUSPICION THAT THIS STORY DIDN'T HAVE ENOUGH FIGHTS IN IT.
LOW KEY
AND I WAS, FOR A TIME, THE GOD OF STORIES. PERHAPS I STILL AM.
WHAT'S A STORY, AFTER ALL, BUT A PLAN?
THEY CAN HAVE LITTLE MOVING PARTS, LIKE A MACHINE.
SHRIP
OR BE A SERIES OF ACCIDENTS, TAKING ON UNEXPECTED LIFE OF THEIR OWN. THAT'S WHAT GODS DO, AFTER ALL--
BLOMM
--CREATE LIFE...AND THEN GIVE IT THE FREE WILL TO SURPRISE US.
IF STOMACH ACID CAN KILL YOU, I IMAGINE CUTTING OFF YOUR HEAD SHOULD BE JUST AS--
WHICH IS WHY I FIND THE BEST STORIES ARE SOMEWHERE IN BETWEEN. ELABORATE, INTRICATE PLANS GONE SPECTACULARLY WRONG.

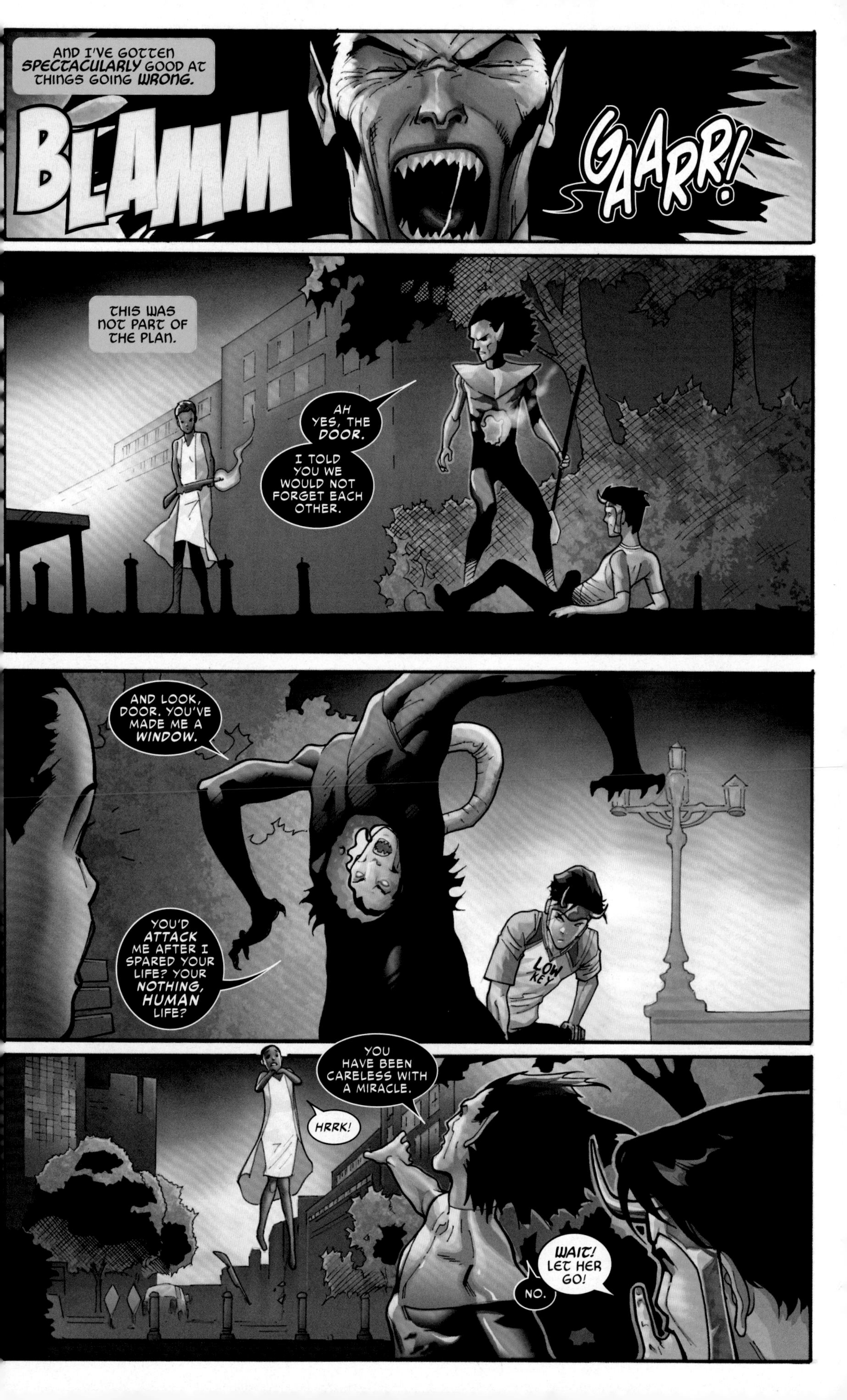
AND I'VE GOTTEN SPECTACULARLY GOOD AT THINGS GOING WRONG.
BLAMM
GAARR!
THIS WAS NOT PART OF THE PLAN.
AH YES, THE DOOR.
I TOLD YOU WE WOULD NOT FORGET EACH OTHER.
AND LOOK, DOOR. YOU'VE MADE ME A WINDOW.
YOU'D ATTACK ME AFTER I SPARED YOUR LIFE? YOUR NOTHING, HUMAN LIFE?
LOW KEY
YOU HAVE BEEN CARELESS WITH A MIRACLE.
HRRK!
WAIT! LET HER GO!
NO.

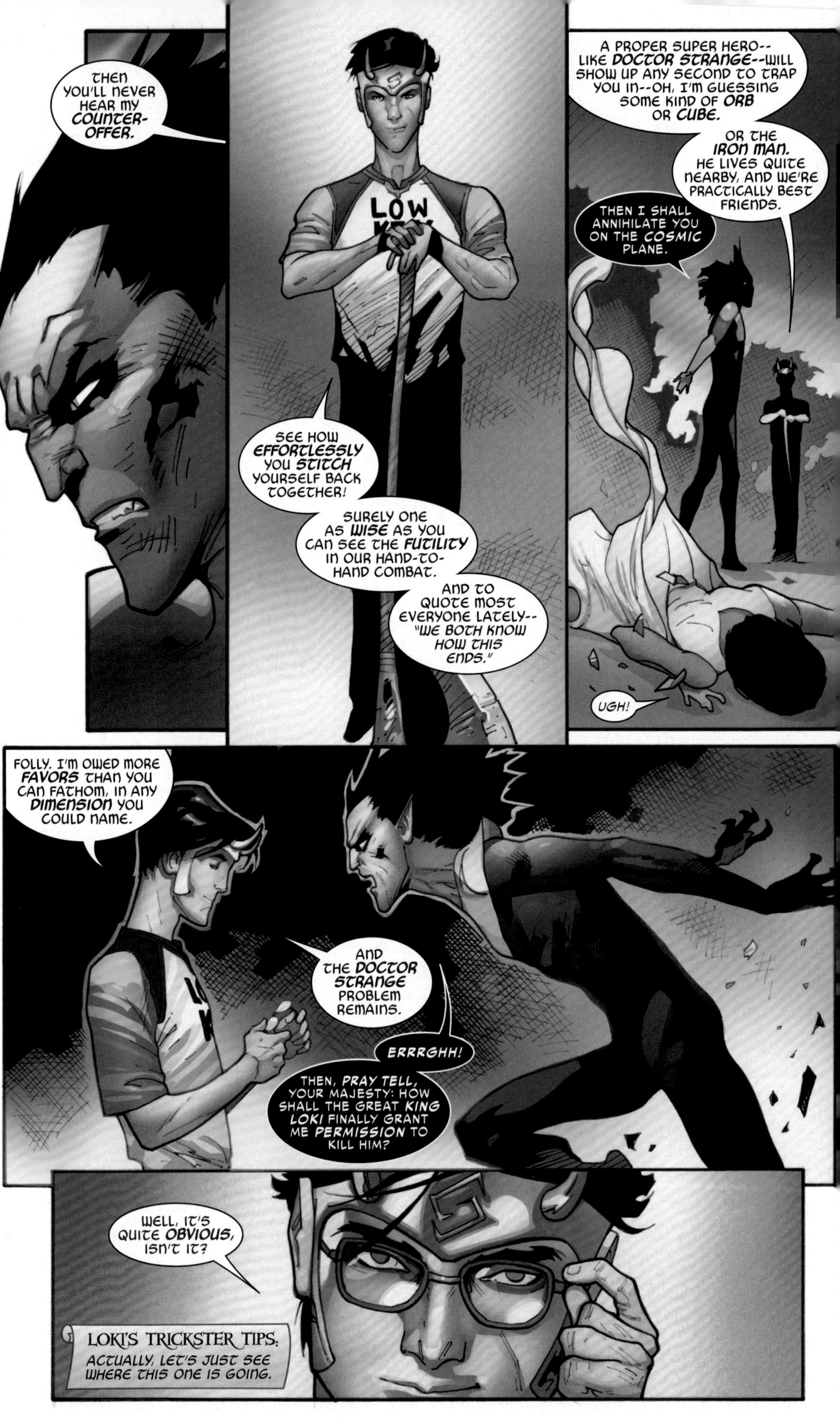
THEN YOU'LL NEVER HEAR MY COUNTER-OFFER.
SEE HOW EFFORTLESSLY YOU STITCH YOURSELF BACK TOGETHER!
SURELY ONE AS WISE AS YOU CAN SEE THE FUTILITY IN OUR HAND-TO-HAND COMBAT.
AND TO QUOTE MOST EVERYONE LATELY-- "WE BOTH KNOW HOW THIS ENDS."
A PROPER SUPER HERO-- LIKE DOCTOR STRANGE--WILL SHOW UP ANY SECOND TO TRAP YOU IN--OH, I'M GUESSING SOME KIND OF ORB OR CUBE.
OR THE IRON MAN. HE LIVES QUITE NEARBY, AND WE'RE PRACTICALLY BEST FRIENDS.
THEN I SHALL ANNIHILATE YOU ON THE COSMIC PLANE.
UGH!
FOLLY. I'M OWED MORE FAVORS THAN YOU CAN FATHOM, IN ANY DIMENSION YOU COULD NAME.
AND THE DOCTOR STRANGE PROBLEM REMAINS.
ERRRGHH!
THEN, PRAY TELL, YOUR MAJESTY: HOW SHALL THE GREAT KING LOKI FINALLY GRANT ME PERMISSION TO KILL HIM?
WELL, IT'S QUITE OBVIOUS, ISN'T IT?
LOKI'S TRICKSTER TIPS:
ACTUALLY, LET'S JUST SEE WHERE THIS ONE IS GOING.

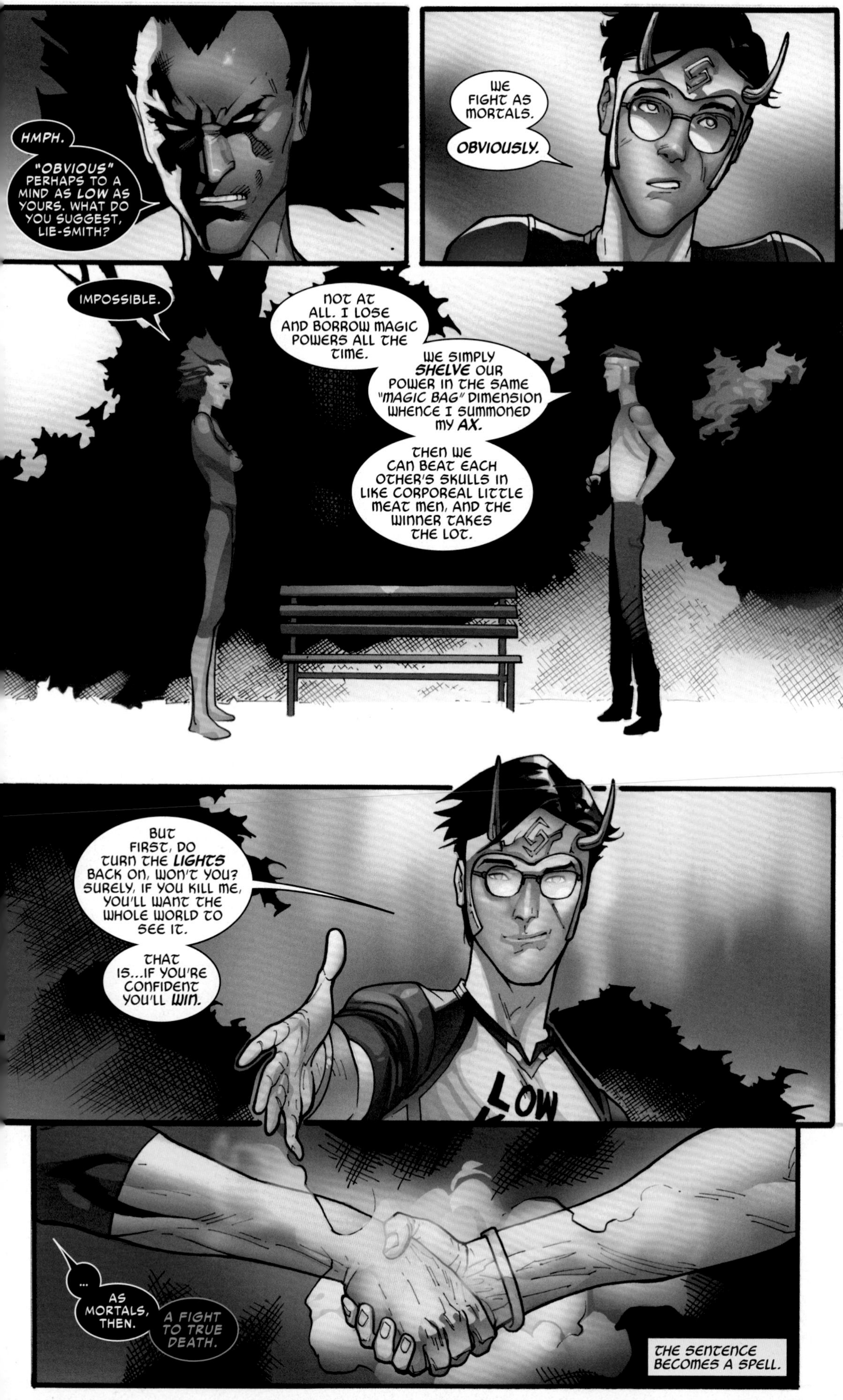
HMPH.
"OBVIOUS" PERHAPS TO A MIND AS LOW AS YOURS. WHAT DO YOU SUGGEST, LIE-SMITH?
WE FIGHT AS MORTALS.
OBVIOUSLY.
IMPOSSIBLE.
NOT AT ALL. I LOSE AND BORROW MAGIC POWERS ALL THE TIME.
WE SIMPLY SHELVE OUR POWER IN THE SAME "MAGIC BAG" DIMENSION WHENCE I SUMMONED MY AX.
THEN WE CAN BEAT EACH OTHER'S SKULLS IN LIKE CORPOREAL LITTLE MEAT MEN, AND THE WINNER TAKES THE LOT.
BUT FIRST, DO TURN THE LIGHTS BACK ON, WON'T YOU? SURELY, IF YOU KILL ME, YOU'LL WANT THE WHOLE WORLD TO SEE IT.
THAT IS...IF YOU'RE CONFIDENT YOU'LL WIN.
LOW
...AS MORTALS, THEN.
A FIGHT TO TRUE DEATH.
THE SENTENCE BECOMES A SPELL.

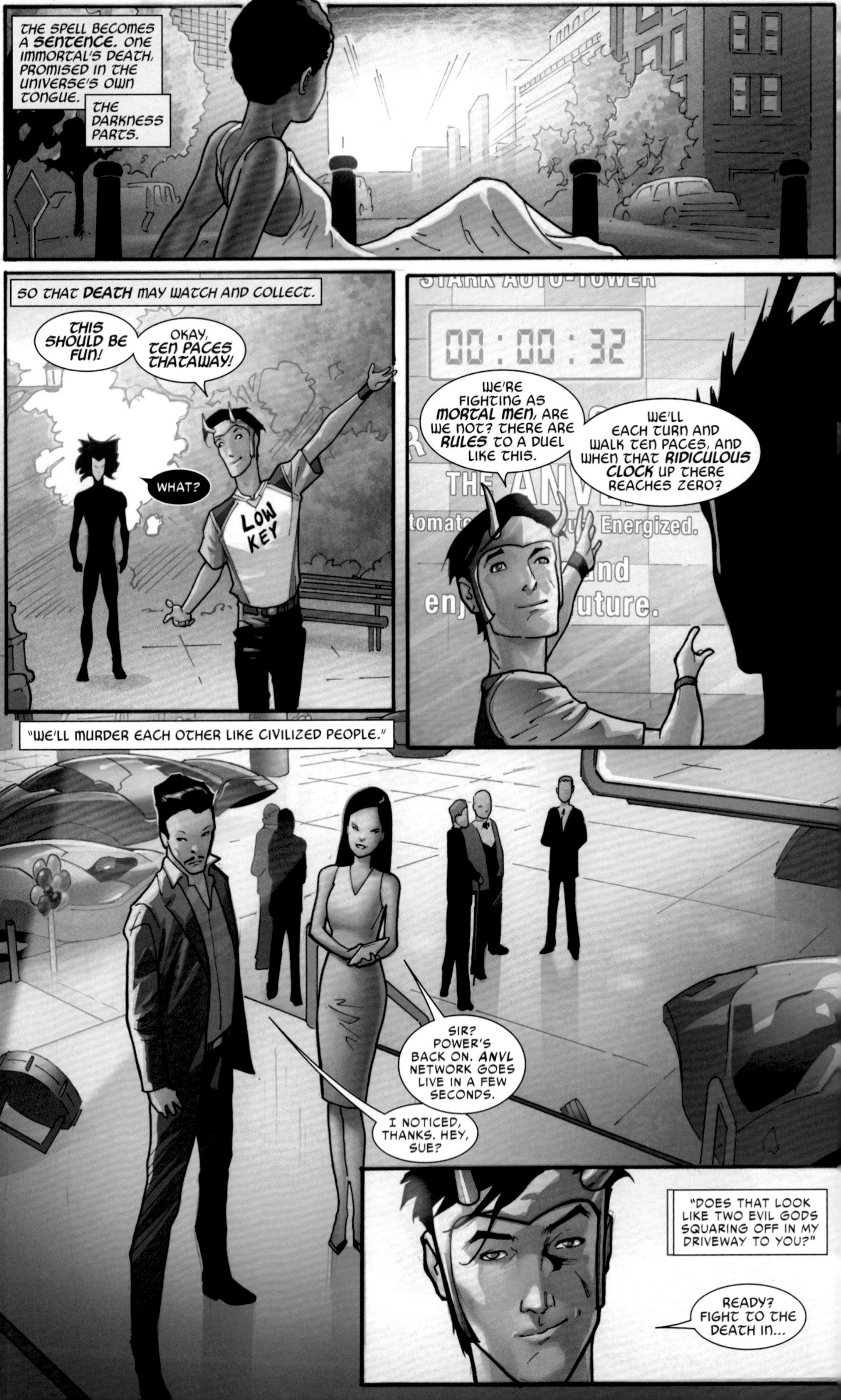
THE SPELL BECOMES A SENTENCE. ONE IMMORTAL'S DEATH, PROMISED IN THE UNIVERSE'S OWN TONGUE.
THE DARKNESS PARTS.
SO THAT DEATH MAY WATCH AND COLLECT.
THIS SHOULD BE FUN!
OKAY, TEN PACES THATAWAY!
WHAT?
LOW KEY
"WE'LL MURDER EACH OTHER LIKE CIVILIZED PEOPLE."
STARK AUTO-TOWER
00 : 00 : 32
WE'RE FIGHTING AS MORTAL MEN, ARE WE NOT? THERE ARE RULES TO A DUEL LIKE THIS.
WE'LL EACH TURN AND WALK TEN PACES, AND WHEN THAT RIDICULOUS CLOCK UP THERE REACHES ZERO?
SIR? POWER'S BACK ON. ANVL NETWORK GOES LIVE IN A FEW SECONDS.
I NOTICED, THANKS. HEY, SUE?
"DOES THAT LOOK LIKE TWO EVIL GODS SQUARING OFF IN MY DRIVEWAY TO YOU?"
READY? FIGHT TO THE DEATH IN...

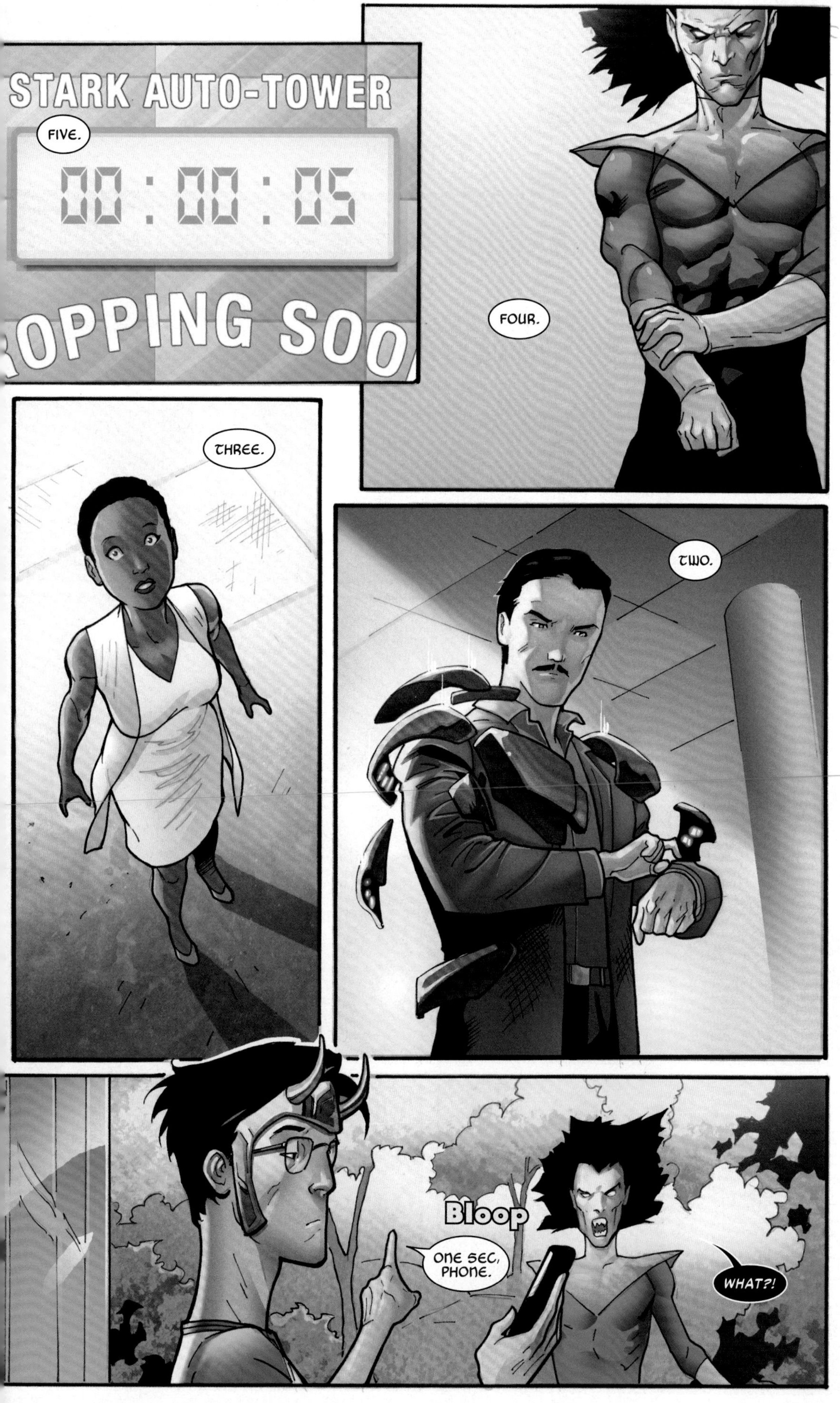
STARK AUTO-TOWER
FIVE.
00 : 00 : 05
OPPING SOO
FOUR.
THREE.
TWO.
Bloop
ONE SEC, PHONE.
WHAT?!

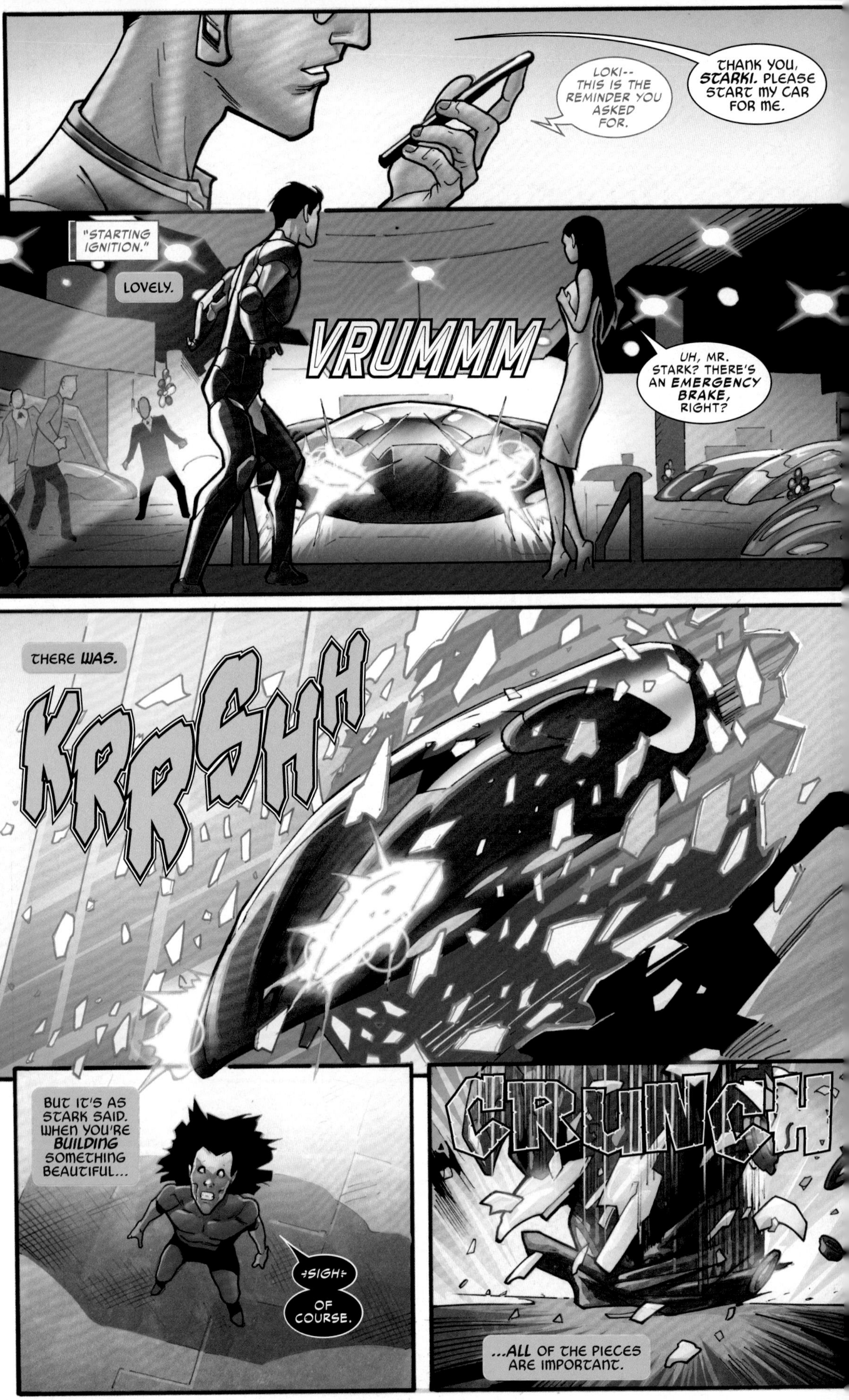
LOKI-- THIS IS THE REMINDER YOU ASKED FOR.
THANK YOU, STARKI. PLEASE START MY CAR FOR ME.
"STARTING IGNITION."
LOVELY.
VRUMMM
UH, MR. STARK? THERE'S AN EMERGENCY BRAKE, RIGHT?
THERE WAS.
KRRSHH
BUT IT'S AS STARK SAID. WHEN YOU'RE BUILDING SOMETHING BEAUTIFUL...
+SIGH+
OF COURSE.
CRUNCH
...ALL OF THE PIECES ARE IMPORTANT.

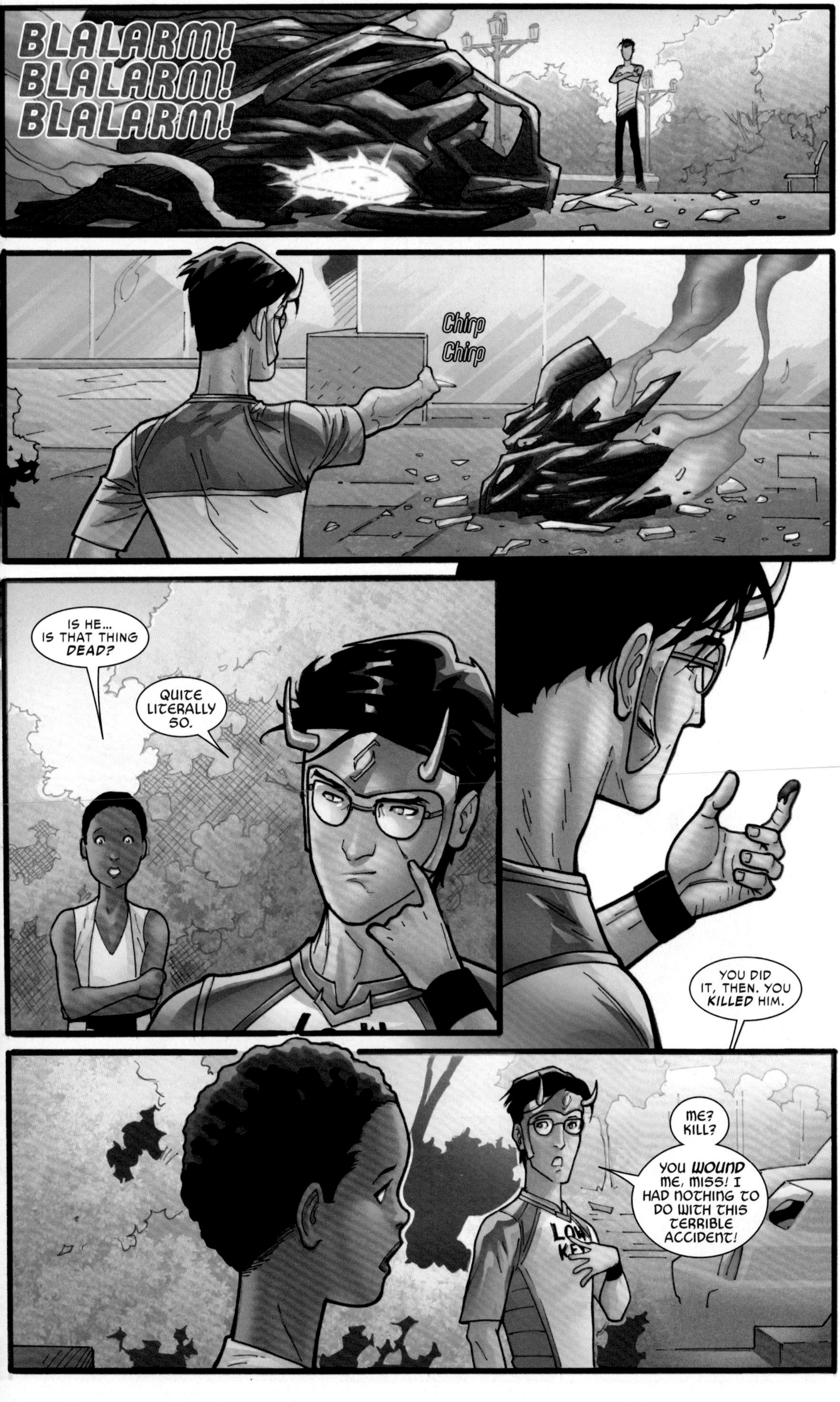
BLALARM! BLALARM! BLALARM!
Chirp Chirp
IS HE... IS THAT THING DEAD?
QUITE LITERALLY SO.
YOU DID IT, THEN. YOU KILLED HIM.
ME? KILL?
YOU WOUND ME, MISS! I HAD NOTHING TO DO WITH THIS TERRIBLE ACCIDENT!

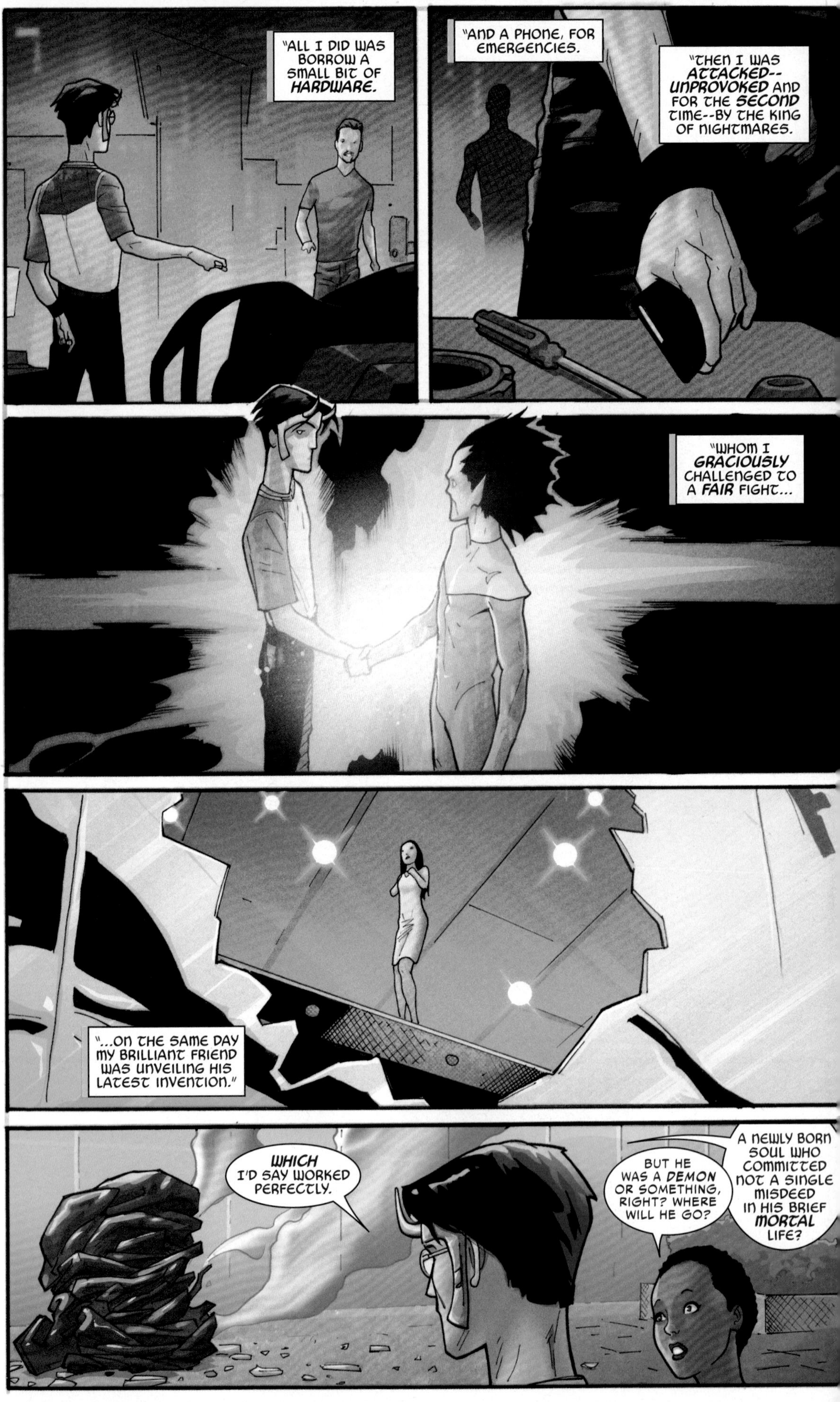
"ALL I DID WAS BORROW A SMALL BIT OF HARDWARE.
"AND A PHONE, FOR EMERGENCIES.
"THEN I WAS ATTACKED--UNPROVOKED AND FOR THE SECOND TIME--BY THE KING OF NIGHTMARES.
"WHOM I GRACIOUSLY CHALLENGED TO A FAIR FIGHT...
"...ON THE SAME DAY MY BRILLIANT FRIEND WAS UNVEILING HIS LATEST INVENTION."
WHICH I'D SAY WORKED PERFECTLY.
BUT HE WAS A DEMON OR SOMETHING, RIGHT? WHERE WILL HE GO?
A NEWLY BORN SOUL WHO COMMITTED NOT A SINGLE MISDEED IN HIS BRIEF MORTAL LIFE?

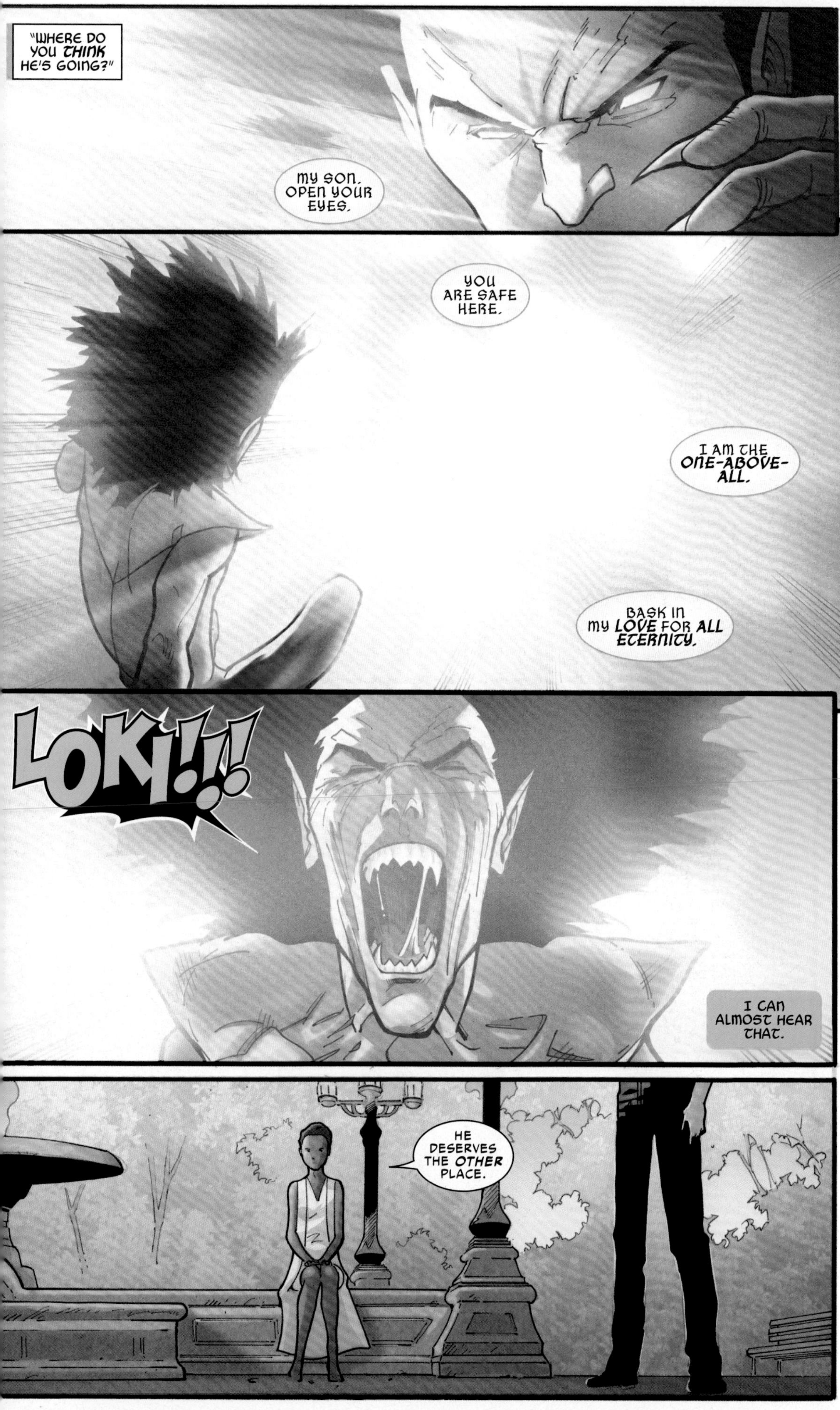
"WHERE DO YOU THINK HE'S GOING?"
MY SON. OPEN YOUR EYES.
YOU ARE SAFE HERE.
I AM THE ONE-ABOVE-ALL.
BASK IN MY LOVE FOR ALL ETERNITY.
LOKI!!!
I CAN ALMOST HEAR THAT.
HE DESERVES THE OTHER PLACE.

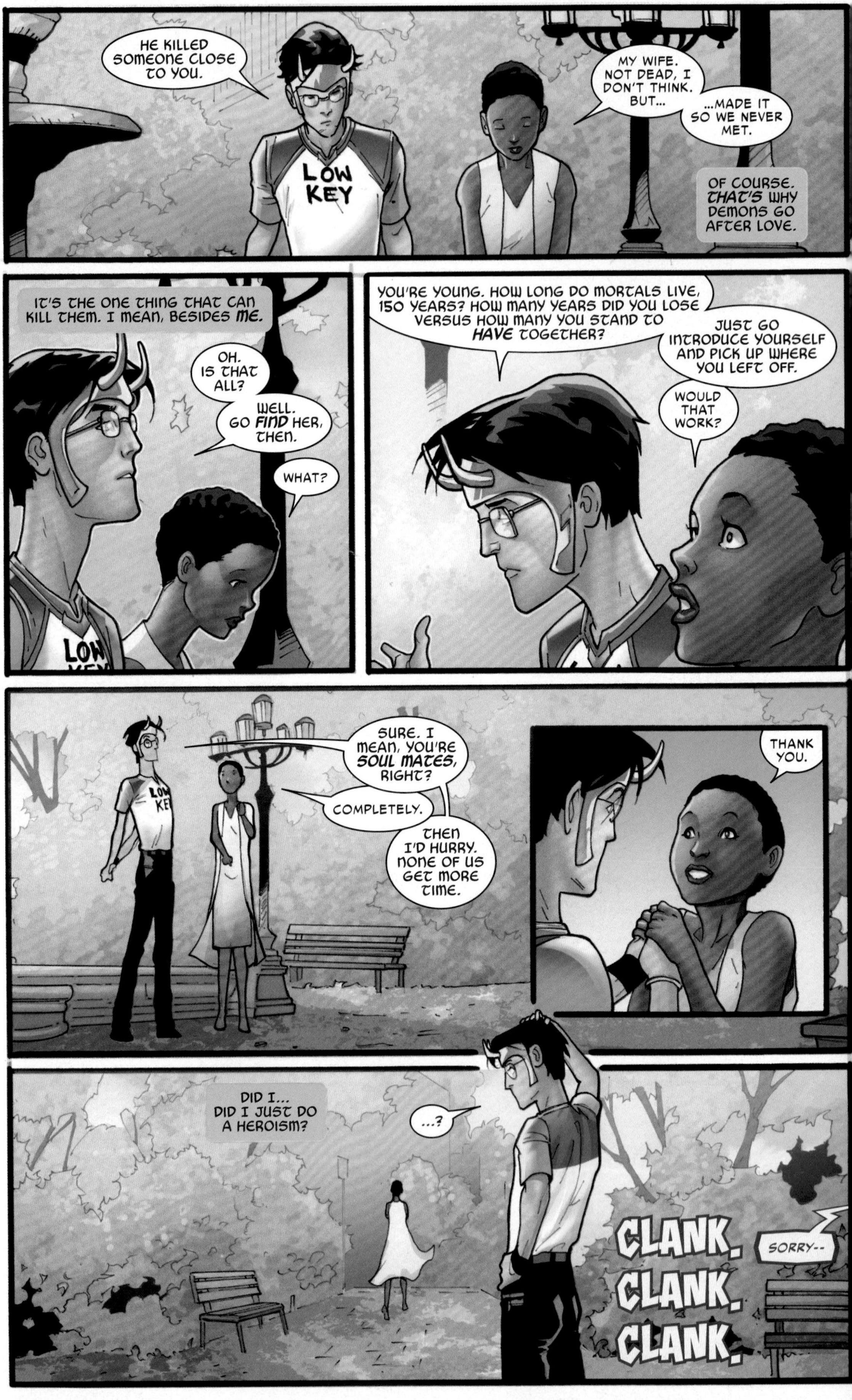
HE KILLED SOMEONE CLOSE TO YOU.
MY WIFE. NOT DEAD, I DON'T THINK. BUT...
...MADE IT SO WE NEVER MET.
OF COURSE. THAT'S WHY DEMONS GO AFTER LOVE.
IT'S THE ONE THING THAT CAN KILL THEM. I MEAN, BESIDES ME.
OH. IS THAT ALL?
WELL. GO FIND HER, THEN.
WHAT?
YOU'RE YOUNG. HOW LONG DO MORTALS LIVE, 150 YEARS? HOW MANY YEARS DID YOU LOSE VERSUS HOW MANY YOU STAND TO HAVE TOGETHER?
JUST GO INTRODUCE YOURSELF AND PICK UP WHERE YOU LEFT OFF.
WOULD THAT WORK?
SURE. I MEAN, YOU'RE SOUL MATES, RIGHT?
COMPLETELY.
THEN I'D HURRY. NONE OF US GET MORE TIME.
THANK YOU.
DID I... DID I JUST DO A HEROISM?
...?
CLANK. CLANK. CLANK.
SORRY--

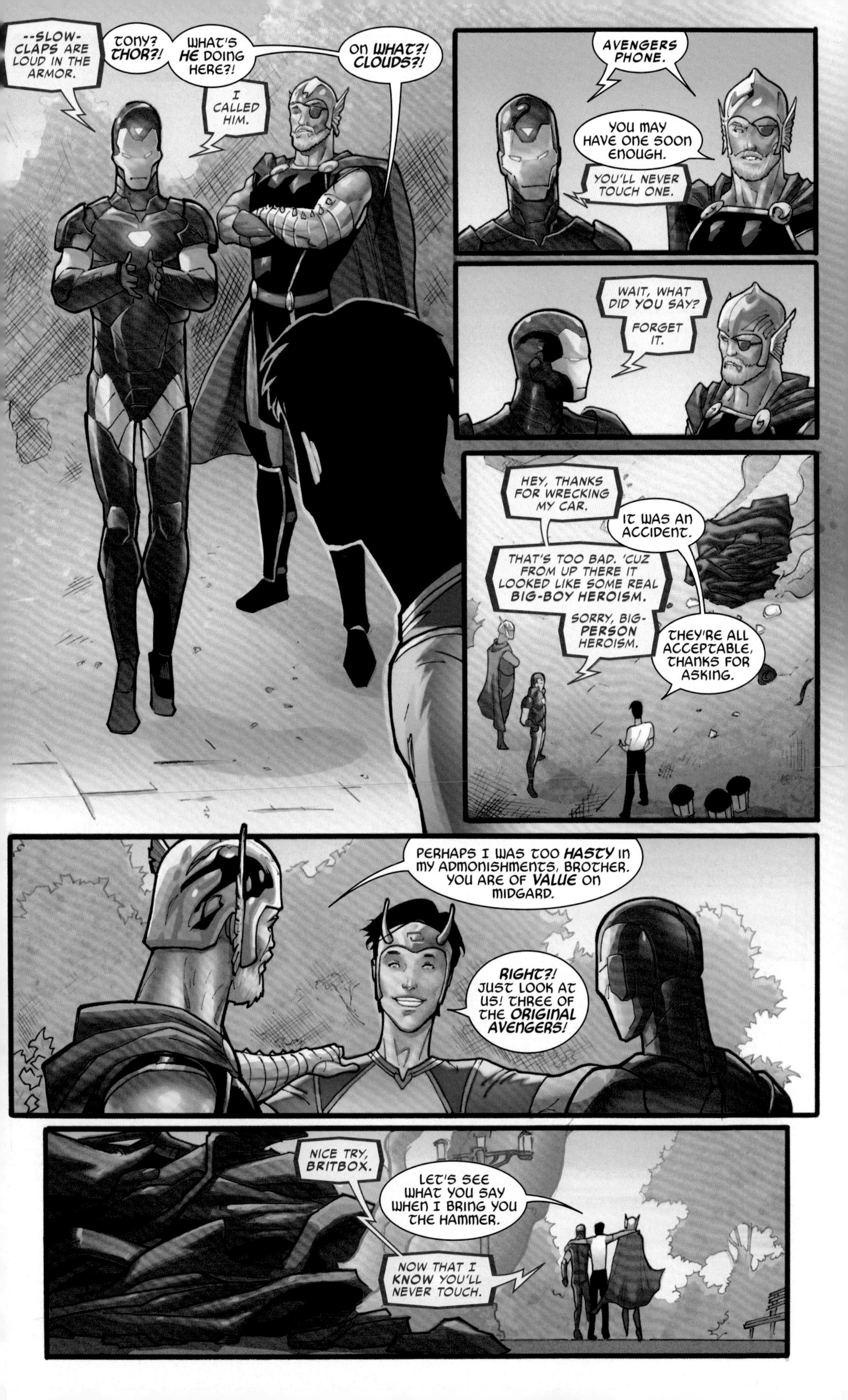
--SLOW-CLAPS ARE LOUD IN THE ARMOR.
TONY? THOR?!
WHAT'S HE DOING HERE?!
I CALLED HIM.
ON WHAT?! CLOUDS?!
AVENGERS PHONE.
YOU MAY HAVE ONE SOON ENOUGH.
YOU'LL NEVER TOUCH ONE.
WAIT, WHAT DID YOU SAY?
FORGET IT.
HEY, THANKS FOR WRECKING MY CAR.
IT WAS AN ACCIDENT.
THAT'S TOO BAD. 'CUZ FROM UP THERE IT LOOKED LIKE SOME REAL BIG-BOY HEROISM.
SORRY, BIG-PERSON HEROISM.
THEY'RE ALL ACCEPTABLE, THANKS FOR ASKING.
PERHAPS I WAS TOO HASTY IN MY ADMONISHMENTS, BROTHER. YOU ARE OF VALUE ON MIDGARD.
RIGHT?! JUST LOOK AT US! THREE OF THE ORIGINAL AVENGERS!
NICE TRY, BRITBOX.
LET'S SEE WHAT YOU SAY WHEN I BRING YOU THE HAMMER.
NOW THAT I KNOW YOU'LL NEVER TOUCH.

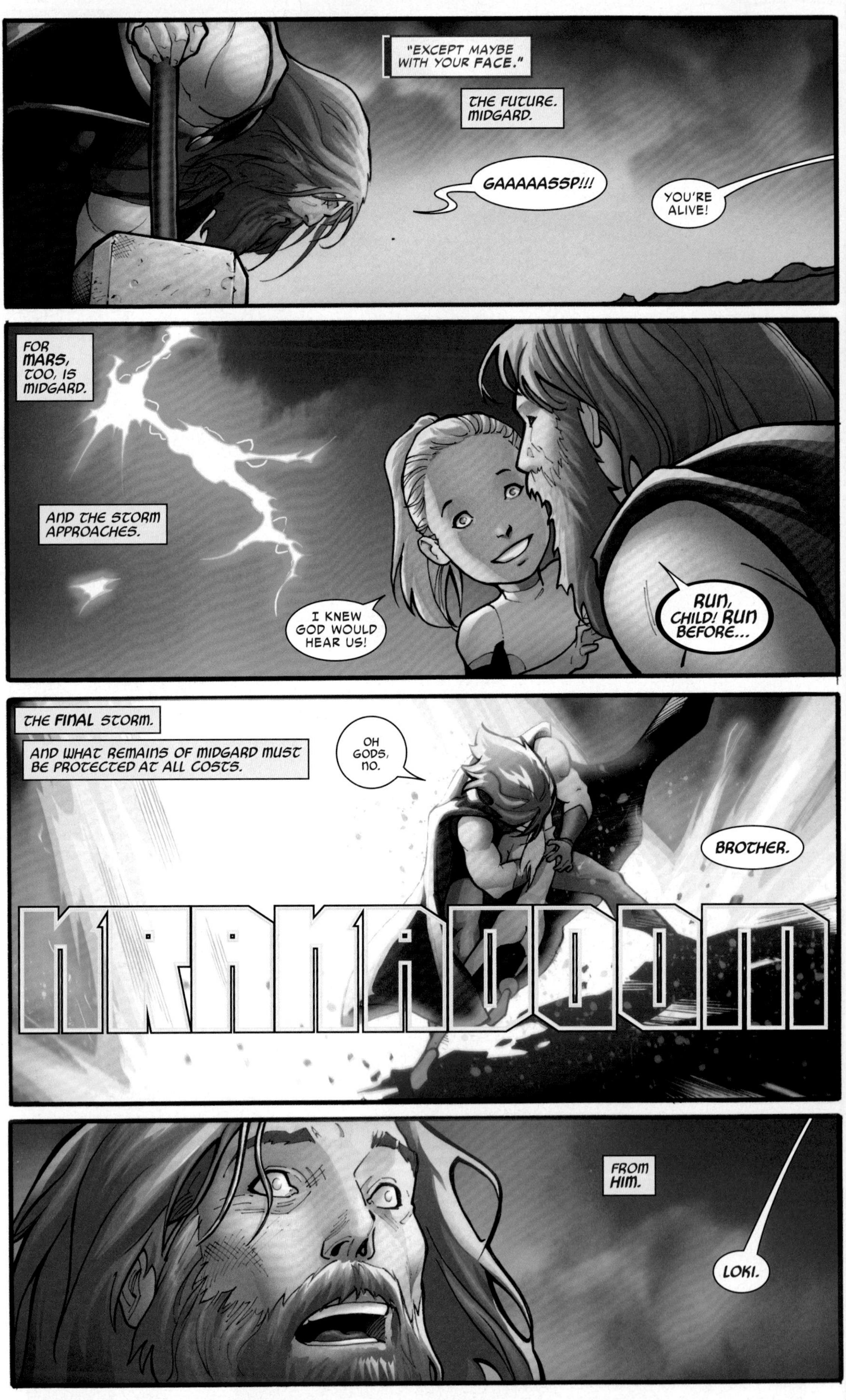
"EXCEPT MAYBE WITH YOUR FACE."
THE FUTURE. MIDGARD.
GAAAAASSP!!!
YOU'RE ALIVE!
FOR MARS, TOO, IS MIDGARD.
AND THE STORM APPROACHES.
I KNEW GOD WOULD HEAR US!
RUN, CHILD! RUN BEFORE...
THE FINAL STORM.
AND WHAT REMAINS OF MIDGARD MUST BE PROTECTED AT ALL COSTS.
OH GODS, NO.
BROTHER.
KRAKADOOM
FROM HIM.
LOKI.

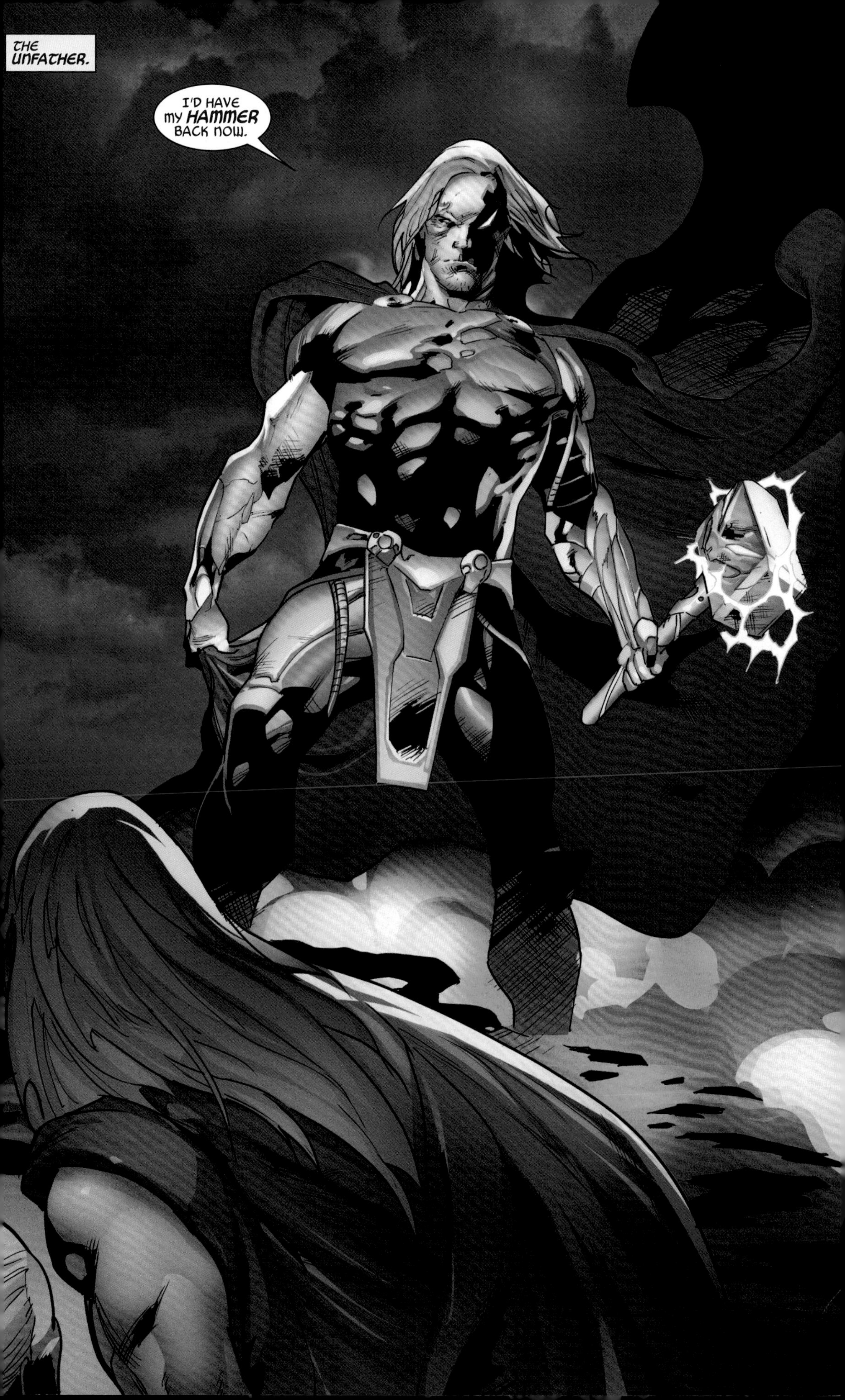
THE UNFATHER.
I'D HAVE my HAMMER BACK NOW.

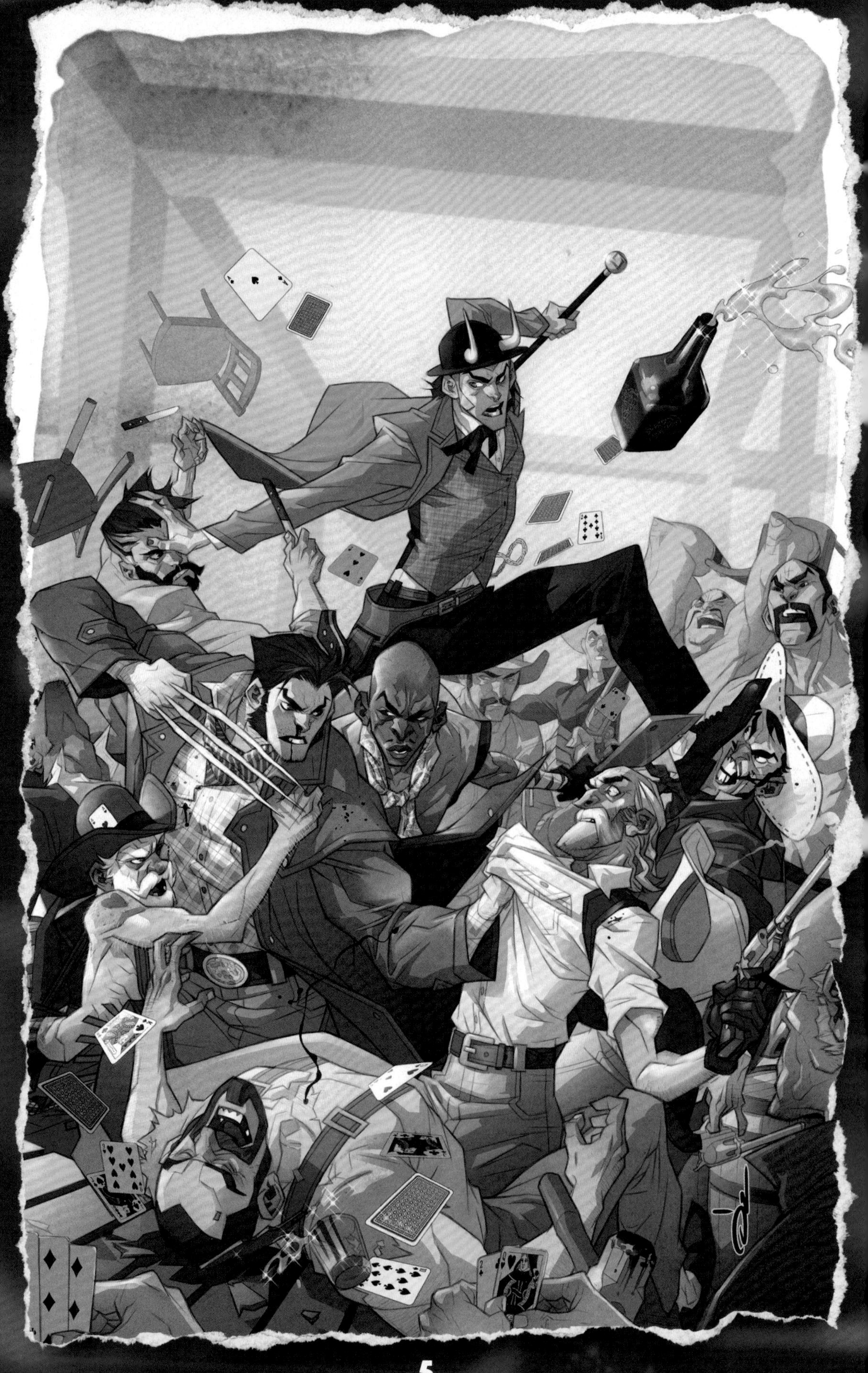

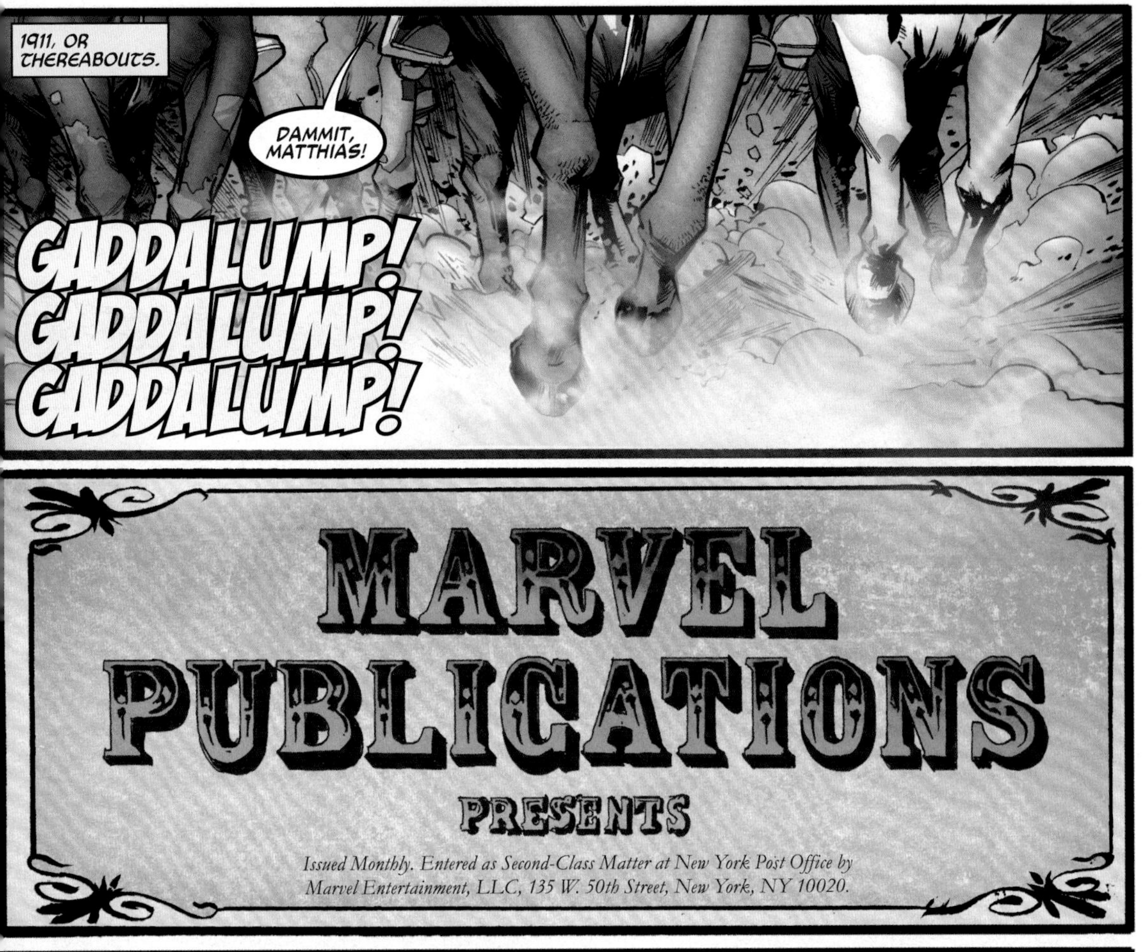
1911, OR THEREABOUTS.
DAMMIT, MATTHIAS!
GADDALUMP! GADDALUMP! GADDALUMP!

MARVEL PUBLICATIONS

PRESENTS

Issued Monthly. Entered as Second-Class Matter at New York Post Office by Marvel Entertainment, LLC, 135 W. 50th Street, New York, NY 10020.

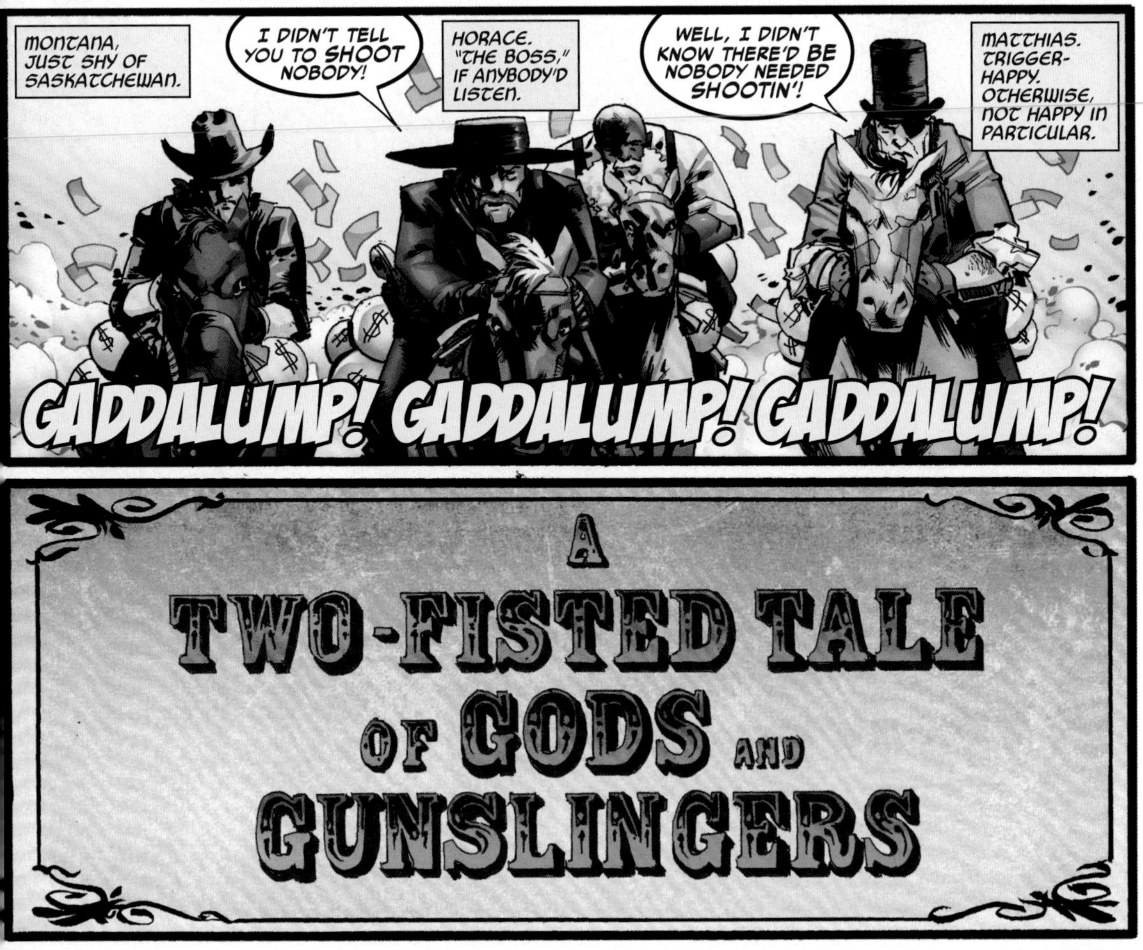
MONTANA, JUST SHY OF SASKATCHEWAN.
I DIDN'T TELL YOU TO SHOOT NOBODY!
HORACE. "THE BOSS," IF ANYBODY'D LISTEN.
WELL, I DIDN'T KNOW THERE'D BE NOBODY NEEDED SHOOTIN'!
MATTHIAS. TRIGGER-HAPPY. OTHERWISE, NOT HAPPY IN PARTICULAR.
GADDALUMP! GADDALUMP! GADDALUMP!

A TWO-FISTED TALE OF GODS AND GUNSLINGERS

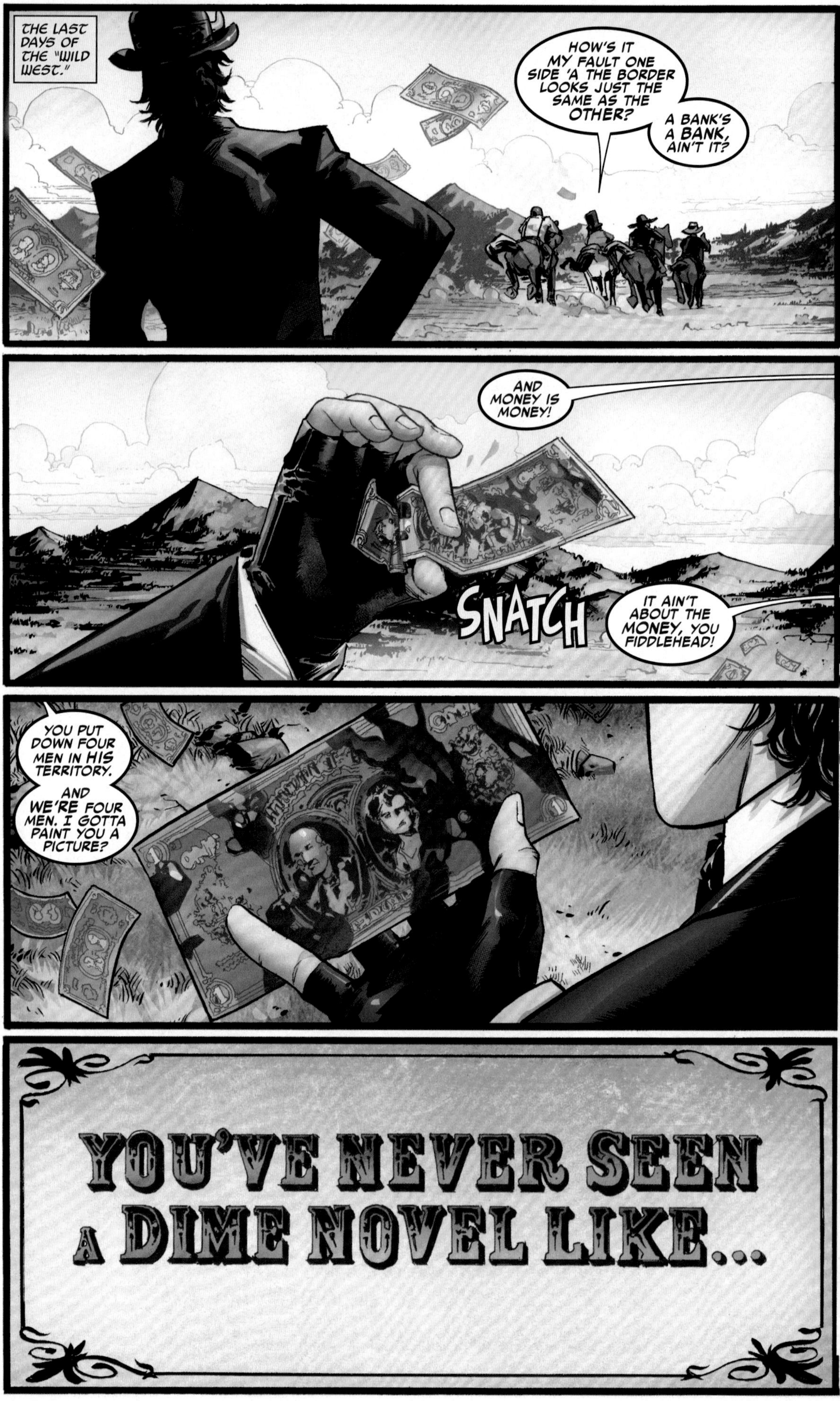
THE LAST DAYS OF THE "WILD WEST."
HOW'S IT MY FAULT ONE SIDE 'A THE BORDER LOOKS JUST THE SAME AS THE OTHER?
A BANK'S A BANK, AIN'T IT?
AND MONEY IS MONEY!
SNATCH
IT AIN'T ABOUT THE MONEY, YOU FIDDLEHEAD!
YOU PUT DOWN FOUR MEN IN HIS TERRITORY.
AND WE'RE FOUR MEN. I GOTTA PAINT YOU A PICTURE?
YOU'VE NEVER SEEN A DIME NOVEL LIKE...

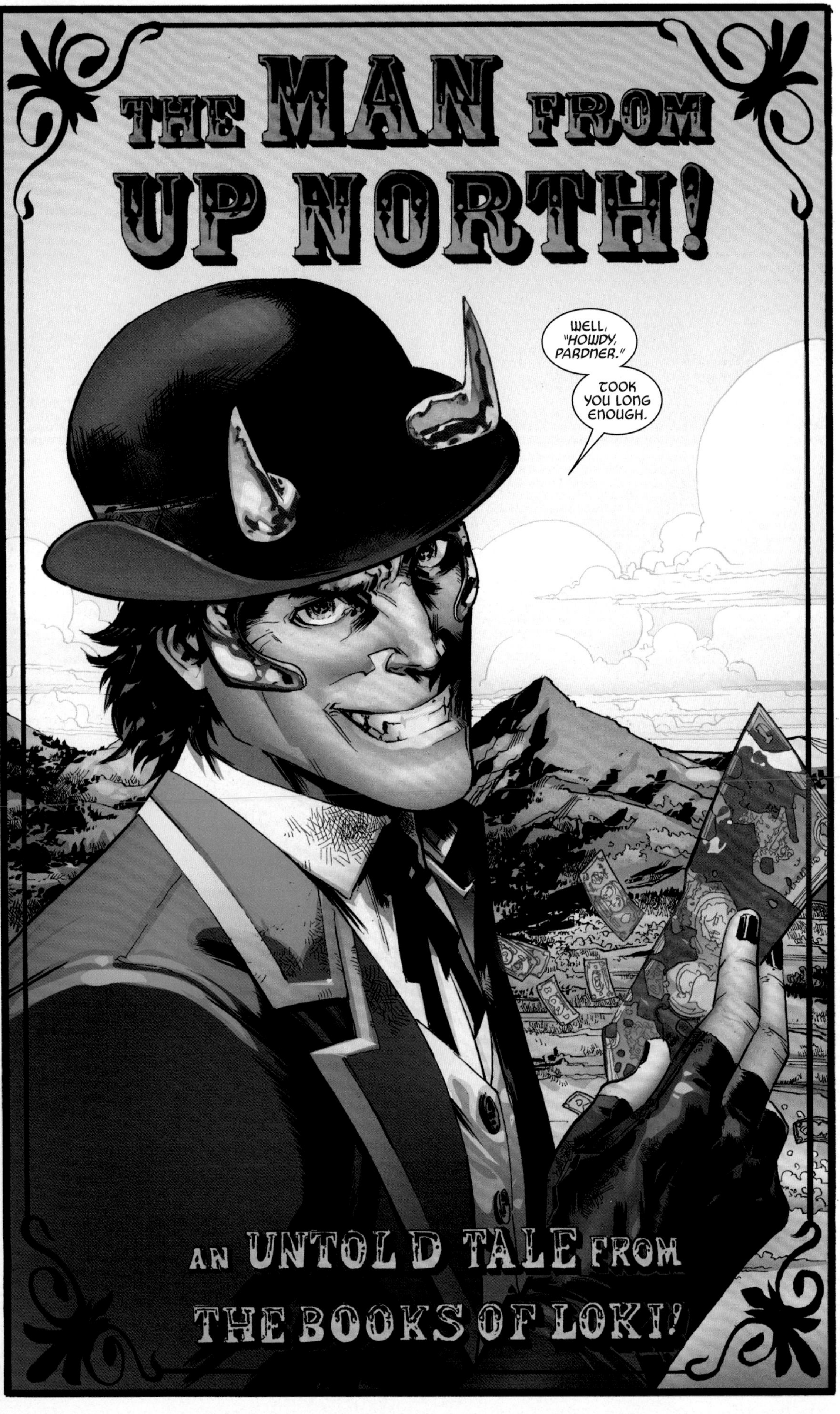
THE MAN FROM UP NORTH!
WELL, "HOWDY, PARDNER."
TOOK YOU LONG ENOUGH.
AN UNTOLD TALE FROM THE BOOKS OF LOKI!

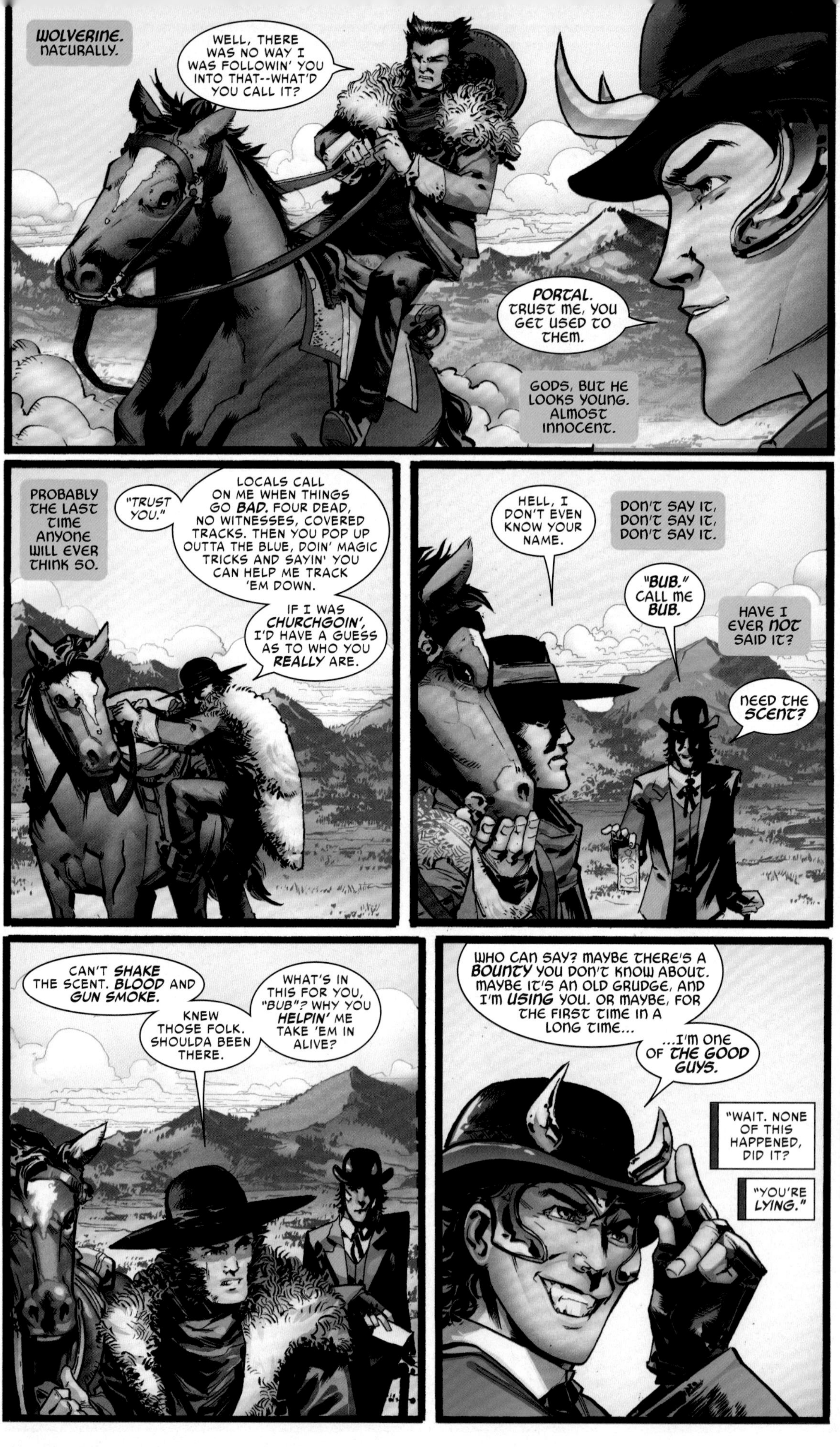
WOLVERINE. NATURALLY.
WELL, THERE WAS NO WAY I WAS FOLLOWIN' YOU INTO THAT--WHAT'D YOU CALL IT?
PORTAL. TRUST ME, YOU GET USED TO THEM.
GODS, BUT HE LOOKS YOUNG. ALMOST INNOCENT.
PROBABLY THE LAST TIME ANYONE WILL EVER THINK SO.
"TRUST YOU."
LOCALS CALL ON ME WHEN THINGS GO BAD. FOUR DEAD, NO WITNESSES, COVERED TRACKS. THEN YOU POP UP OUTTA THE BLUE, DOIN' MAGIC TRICKS AND SAYIN' YOU CAN HELP ME TRACK 'EM DOWN.
IF I WAS CHURCHGOIN', I'D HAVE A GUESS AS TO WHO YOU REALLY ARE.
HELL, I DON'T EVEN KNOW YOUR NAME.
DON'T SAY IT, DON'T SAY IT, DON'T SAY IT.
"BUB." CALL ME BUB.
HAVE I EVER NOT SAID IT?
NEED THE SCENT?
CAN'T SHAKE THE SCENT. BLOOD AND GUN SMOKE.
KNEW THOSE FOLK. SHOULDA BEEN THERE.
WHAT'S IN THIS FOR YOU, "BUB"? WHY YOU HELPIN' ME TAKE 'EM IN ALIVE?
WHO CAN SAY? MAYBE THERE'S A BOUNTY YOU DON'T KNOW ABOUT. MAYBE IT'S AN OLD GRUDGE, AND I'M USING YOU. OR MAYBE, FOR THE FIRST TIME IN A LONG TIME...
...I'M ONE OF THE GOOD GUYS.
"WAIT. NONE OF THIS HAPPENED, DID IT?
"YOU'RE LYING."

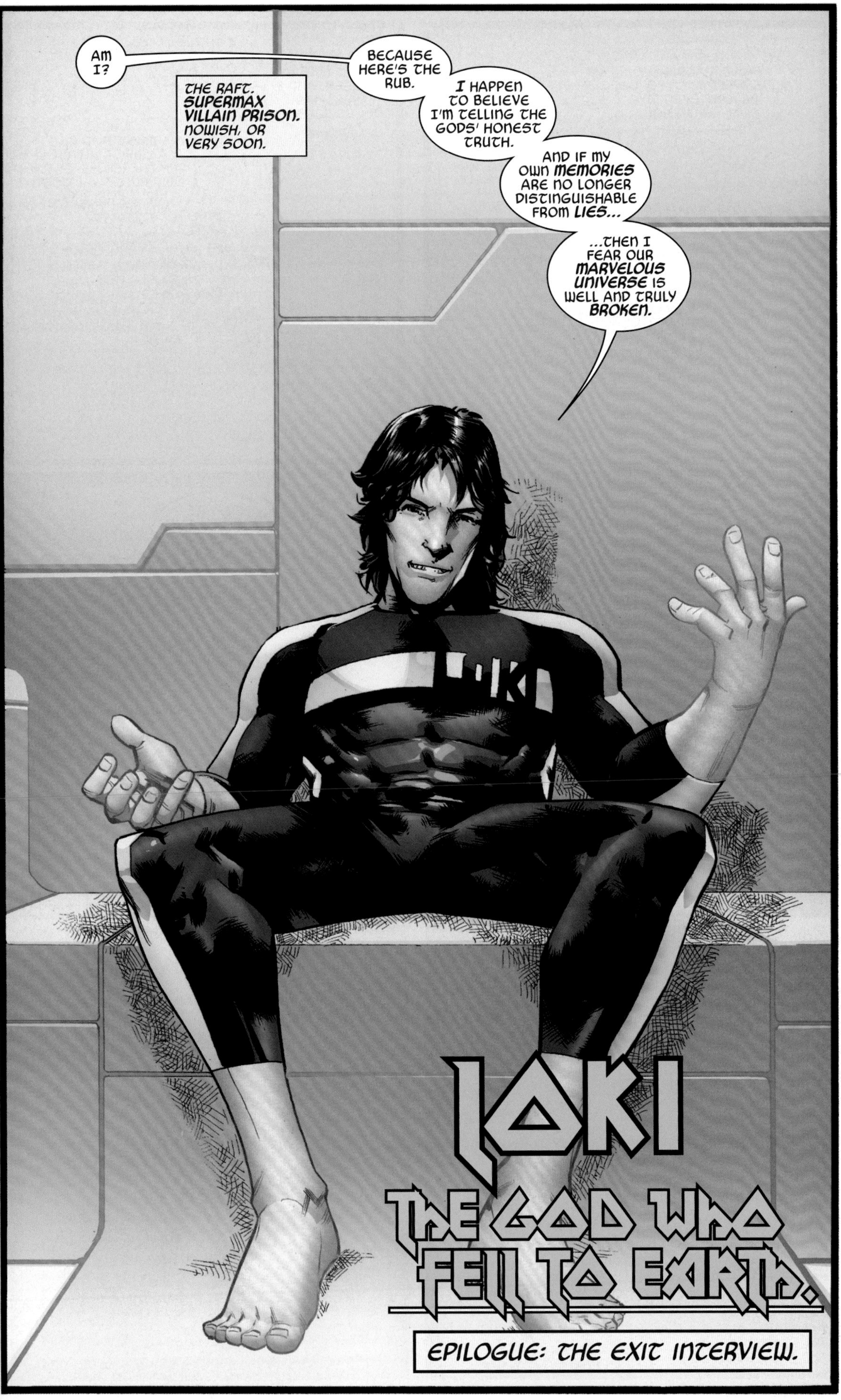
Am I?
THE RAFT. SUPERMAX VILLAIN PRISON. NOWISH, OR VERY SOON.
BECAUSE HERE'S THE RUB.
I HAPPEN TO BELIEVE I'M TELLING THE GODS' HONEST TRUTH.
AND IF MY OWN MEMORIES ARE NO LONGER DISTINGUISHABLE FROM LIES...
...THEN I FEAR OUR MARVELOUS UNIVERSE IS WELL AND TRULY BROKEN.
LOKI
LOKI
THE GOD WHO FELL TO EARTH.
EPILOGUE: THE EXIT INTERVIEW.

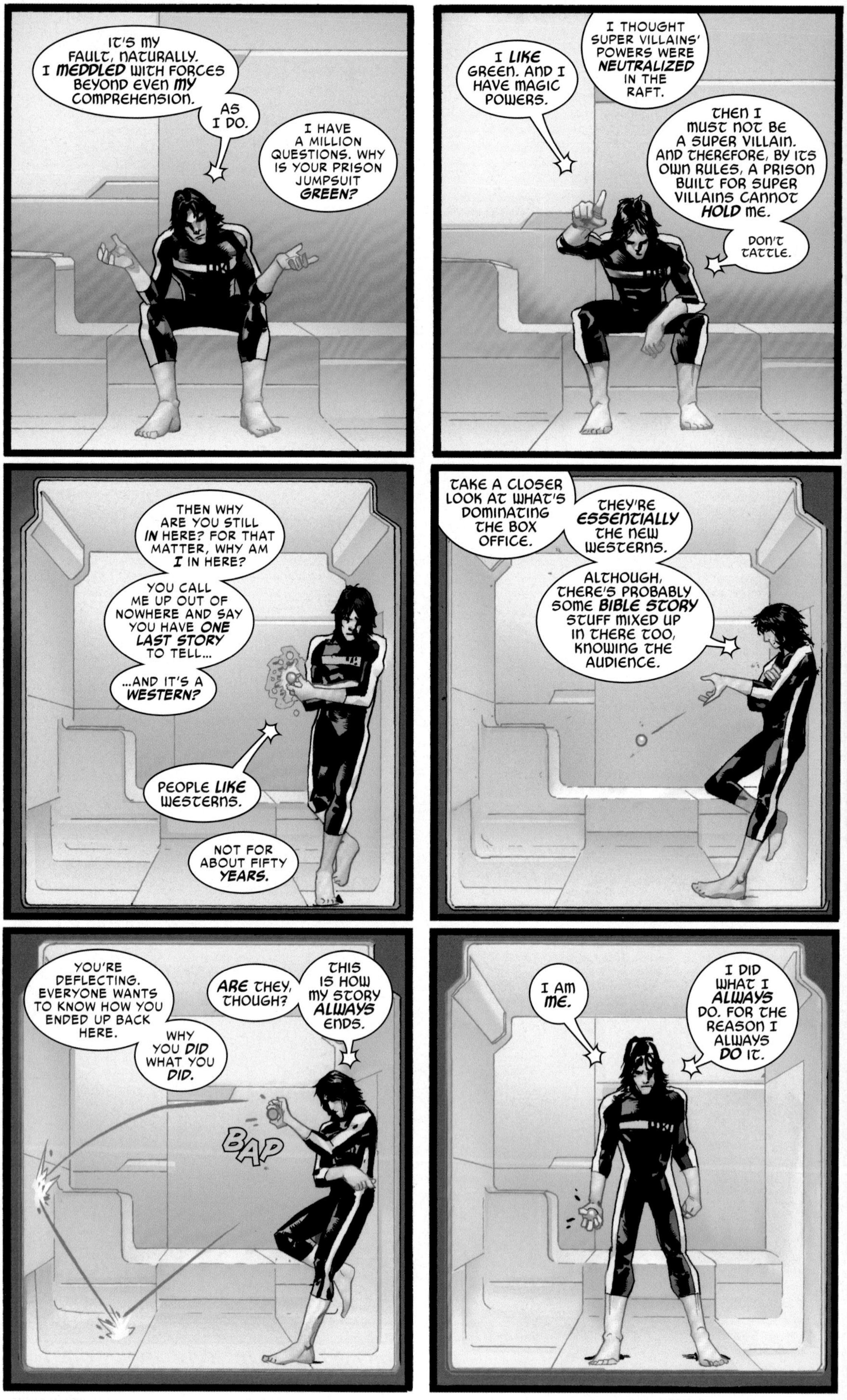

IT'S MY FAULT, NATURALLY. I MEDDLED WITH FORCES BEYOND EVEN MY COMPREHENSION.
AS I DO.
I HAVE A MILLION QUESTIONS. WHY IS YOUR PRISON JUMPSUIT GREEN?
I THOUGHT SUPER VILLAINS' POWERS WERE NEUTRALIZED IN THE RAFT.
I LIKE GREEN. AND I HAVE MAGIC POWERS.
THEN I MUST NOT BE A SUPER VILLAIN. AND THEREFORE, BY ITS OWN RULES, A PRISON BUILT FOR SUPER VILLAINS CANNOT HOLD ME.
DON'T TATTLE.
THEN WHY ARE YOU STILL IN HERE? FOR THAT MATTER, WHY AM I IN HERE?
YOU CALL ME UP OUT OF NOWHERE AND SAY YOU HAVE ONE LAST STORY TO TELL...
...AND IT'S A WESTERN?
PEOPLE LIKE WESTERNS.
NOT FOR ABOUT FIFTY YEARS.
TAKE A CLOSER LOOK AT WHAT'S DOMINATING THE BOX OFFICE.
THEY'RE ESSENTIALLY THE NEW WESTERNS.
ALTHOUGH, THERE'S PROBABLY SOME BIBLE STORY STUFF MIXED UP IN THERE TOO, KNOWING THE AUDIENCE.
YOU'RE DEFLECTING. EVERYONE WANTS TO KNOW HOW YOU ENDED UP BACK HERE.
WHY YOU DID WHAT YOU DID.
ARE THEY, THOUGH?
THIS IS HOW MY STORY ALWAYS ENDS.
BAP
I AM ME.
I DID WHAT I ALWAYS DO. FOR THE REASON I ALWAYS DO IT.

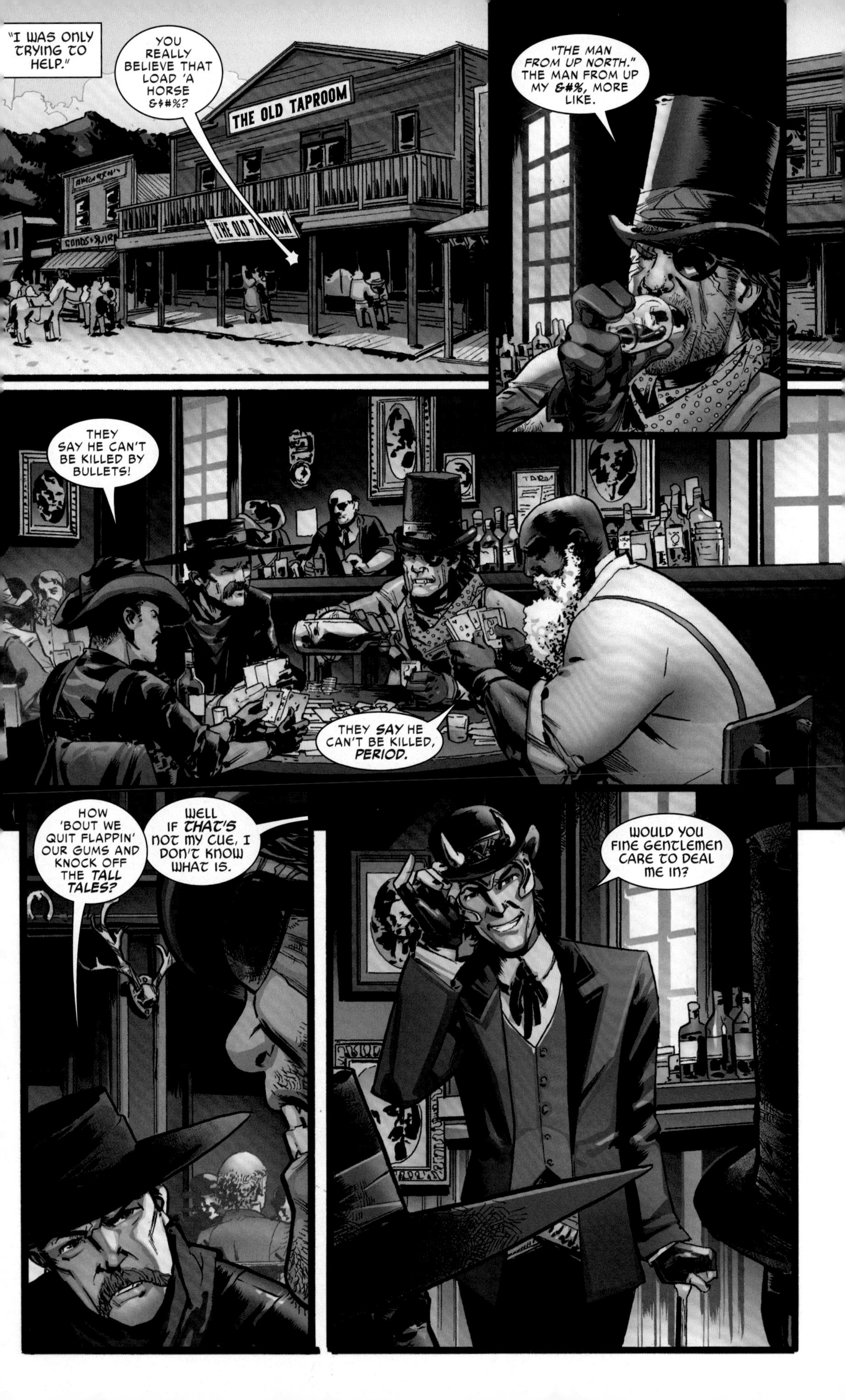
"I WAS ONLY TRYING TO HELP."
YOU REALLY BELIEVE THAT LOAD 'A HORSE &$#%?
THE OLD TAPROOM
THE OLD TAPROOM
"THE MAN FROM UP NORTH." THE MAN FROM UP MY &#%, MORE LIKE.
THEY SAY HE CAN'T BE KILLED BY BULLETS!
THEY SAY HE CAN'T BE KILLED, PERIOD.
HOW 'BOUT WE QUIT FLAPPIN' OUR GUMS AND KNOCK OFF THE TALL TALES?
WELL IF THAT'S NOT MY CUE, I DON'T KNOW WHAT IS.
WOULD YOU FINE GENTLEMEN CARE TO DEAL ME IN?

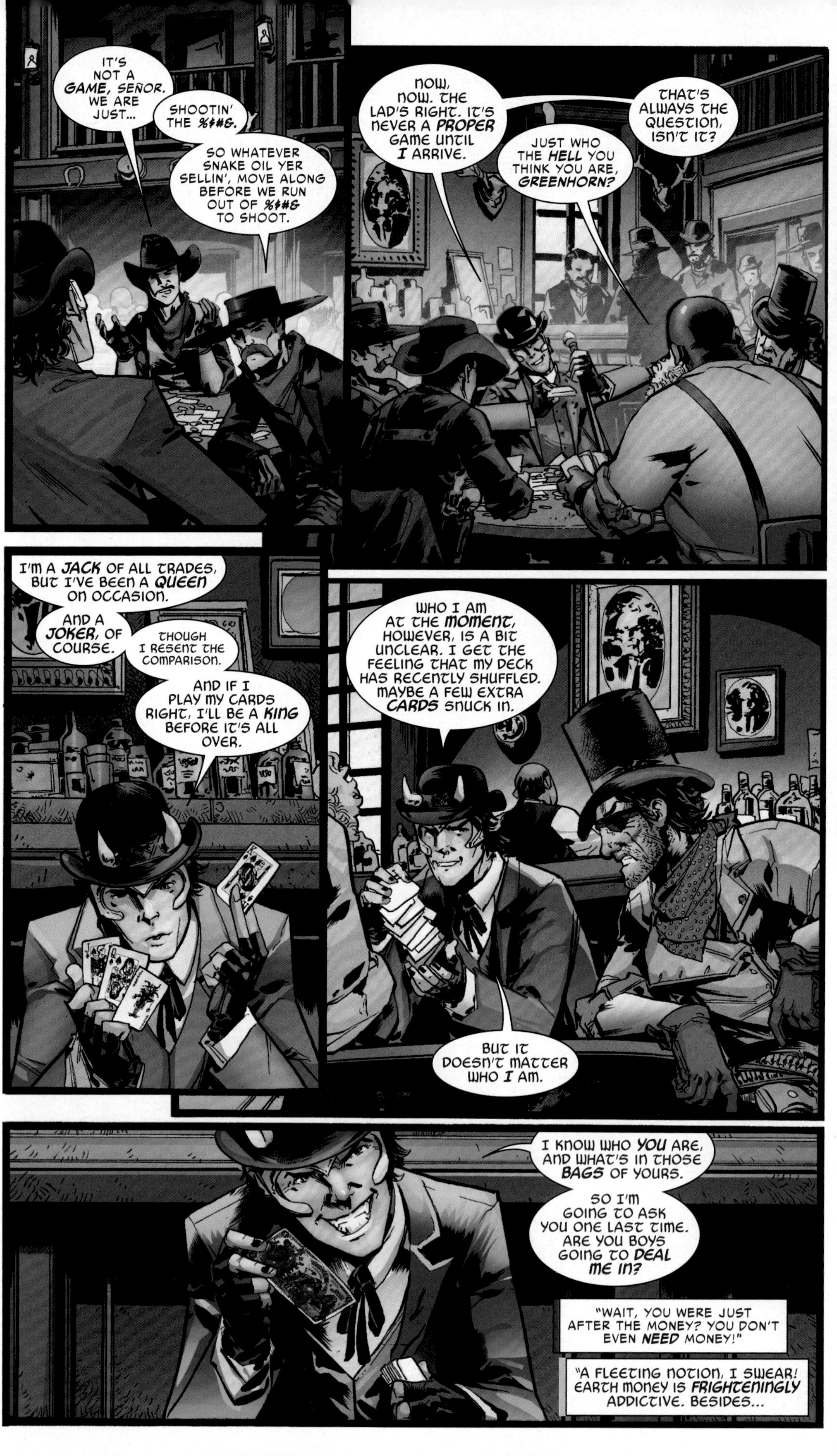
IT'S NOT A GAME, SEÑOR. WE ARE JUST...
SHOOTIN' THE %$#&.
SO WHATEVER SNAKE OIL YER SELLIN', MOVE ALONG BEFORE WE RUN OUT OF %$#& TO SHOOT.
NOW, NOW. THE LAD'S RIGHT. IT'S NEVER A PROPER GAME UNTIL I ARRIVE.
JUST WHO THE HELL YOU THINK YOU ARE, GREENHORN?
THAT'S ALWAYS THE QUESTION, ISN'T IT?
I'M A JACK OF ALL TRADES, BUT I'VE BEEN A QUEEN ON OCCASION.
AND A JOKER, OF COURSE.
THOUGH I RESENT THE COMPARISON.
AND IF I PLAY MY CARDS RIGHT, I'LL BE A KING BEFORE IT'S ALL OVER.
WHO I AM AT THE MOMENT, HOWEVER, IS A BIT UNCLEAR. I GET THE FEELING THAT MY DECK HAS RECENTLY SHUFFLED. MAYBE A FEW EXTRA CARDS SNUCK IN.
BUT IT DOESN'T MATTER WHO I AM.
I KNOW WHO YOU ARE, AND WHAT'S IN THOSE BAGS OF YOURS.
SO I'M GOING TO ASK YOU ONE LAST TIME. ARE YOU BOYS GOING TO DEAL ME IN?
"WAIT, YOU WERE JUST AFTER THE MONEY? YOU DON'T EVEN NEED MONEY!"
"A FLEETING NOTION, I SWEAR! EARTH MONEY IS FRIGHTENINGLY ADDICTIVE. BESIDES...

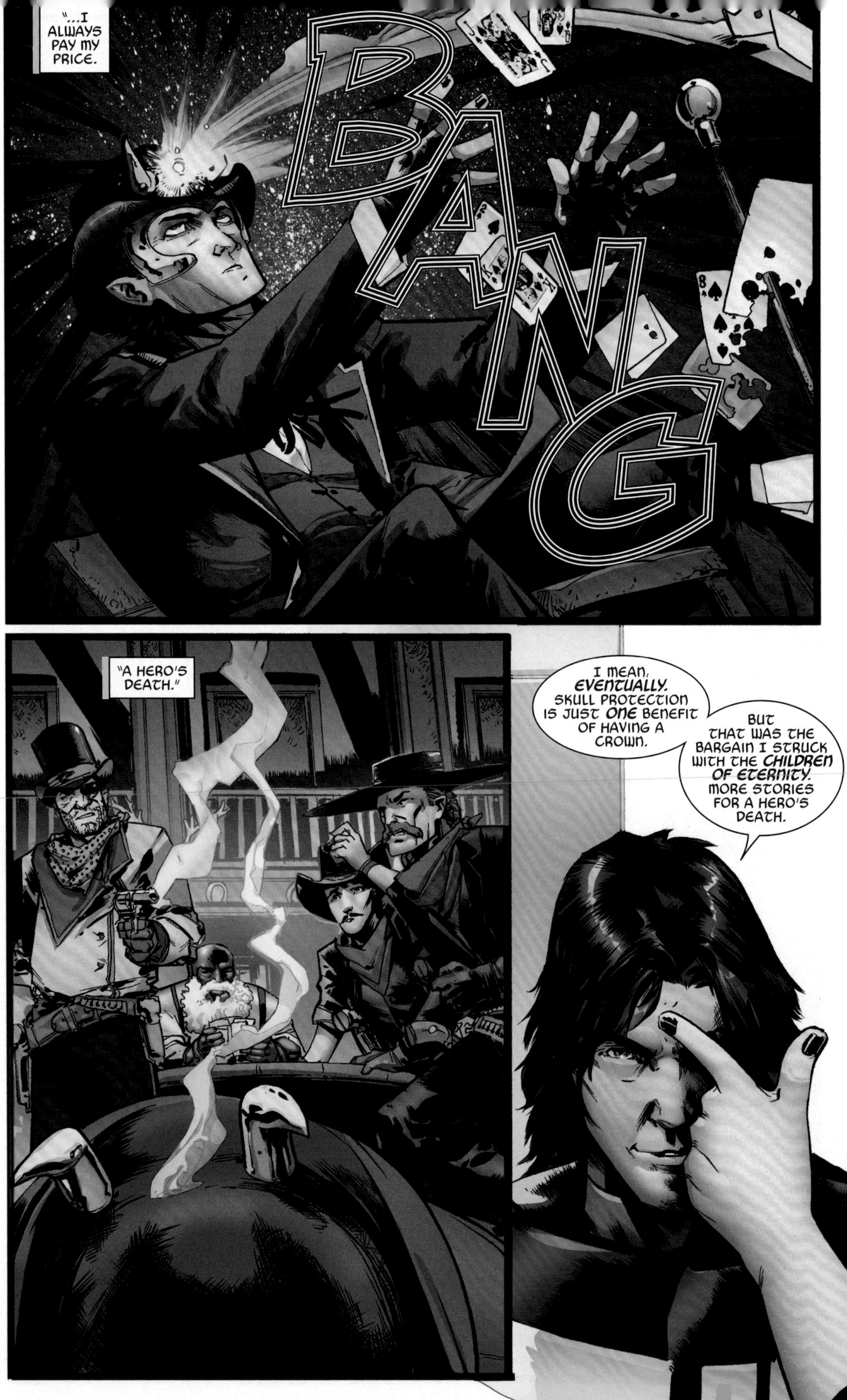
"...I ALWAYS PAY MY PRICE.
BLANG
"A HERO'S DEATH."
I MEAN, EVENTUALLY. SKULL PROTECTION IS JUST ONE BENEFIT OF HAVING A CROWN.
BUT THAT WAS THE BARGAIN I STRUCK WITH THE CHILDREN OF ETERNITY. MORE STORIES FOR A HERO'S DEATH.

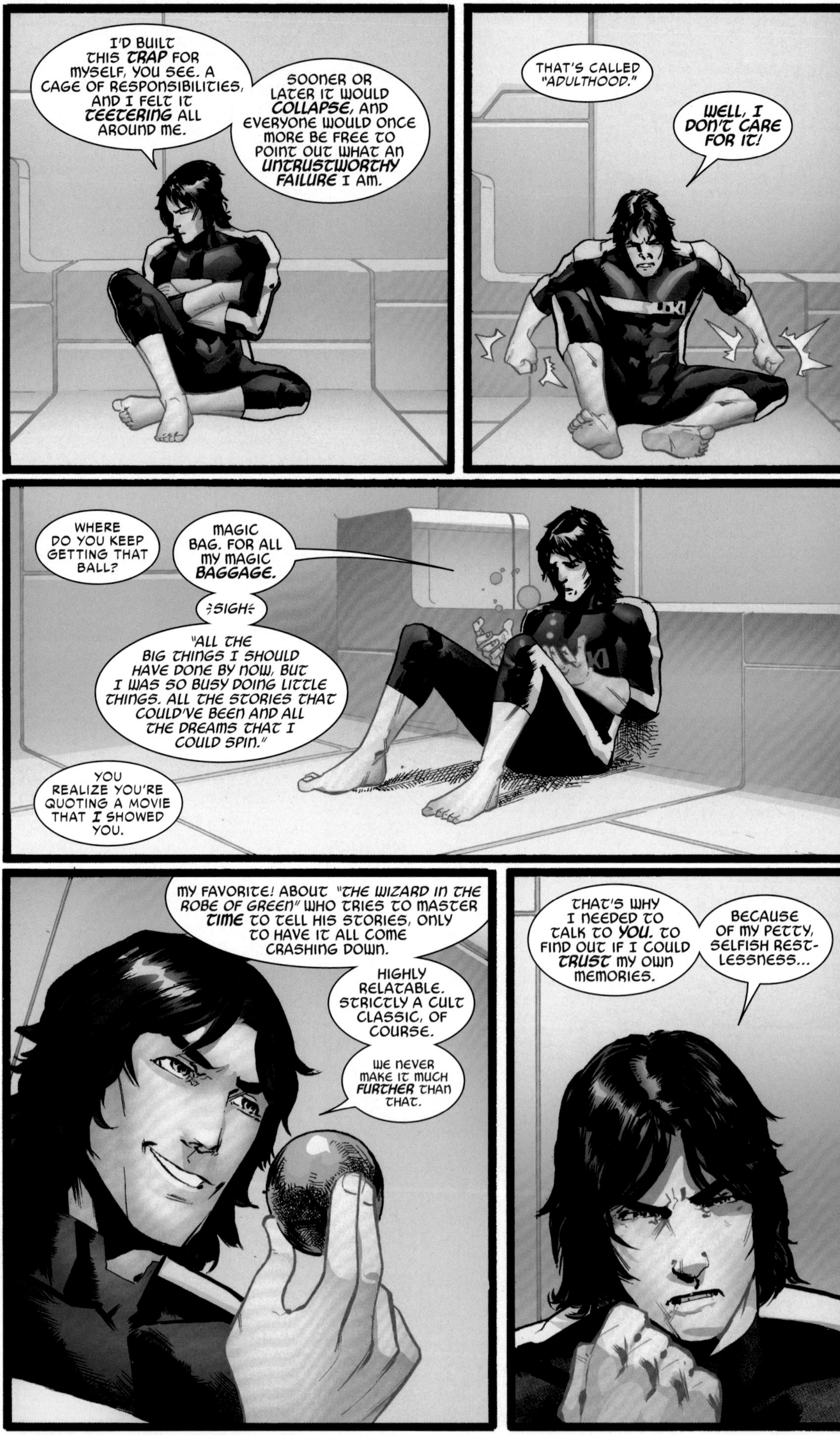
I'D BUILT THIS TRAP FOR MYSELF, YOU SEE. A CAGE OF RESPONSIBILITIES, AND I FELT IT TEETERING ALL AROUND ME.
SOONER OR LATER IT WOULD COLLAPSE, AND EVERYONE WOULD ONCE MORE BE FREE TO POINT OUT WHAT AN UNTRUSTWORTHY FAILURE I AM.
THAT'S CALLED "ADULTHOOD."
WELL, I DON'T CARE FOR IT!
WHERE DO YOU KEEP GETTING THAT BALL?
MAGIC BAG. FOR ALL MY MAGIC BAGGAGE.
SIGH
"ALL THE BIG THINGS I SHOULD HAVE DONE BY NOW, BUT I WAS SO BUSY DOING LITTLE THINGS. ALL THE STORIES THAT COULD'VE BEEN AND ALL THE DREAMS THAT I COULD SPIN."
YOU REALIZE YOU'RE QUOTING A MOVIE THAT I SHOWED YOU.
MY FAVORITE! ABOUT "THE WIZARD IN THE ROBE OF GREEN" WHO TRIES TO MASTER TIME TO TELL HIS STORIES, ONLY TO HAVE IT ALL COME CRASHING DOWN.
HIGHLY RELATABLE. STRICTLY A CULT CLASSIC, OF COURSE.
WE NEVER MAKE IT MUCH FURTHER THAN THAT.
THAT'S WHY I NEEDED TO TALK TO YOU. TO FIND OUT IF I COULD TRUST MY OWN MEMORIES.
BECAUSE OF MY PETTY, SELFISH REST-LESSNESS...

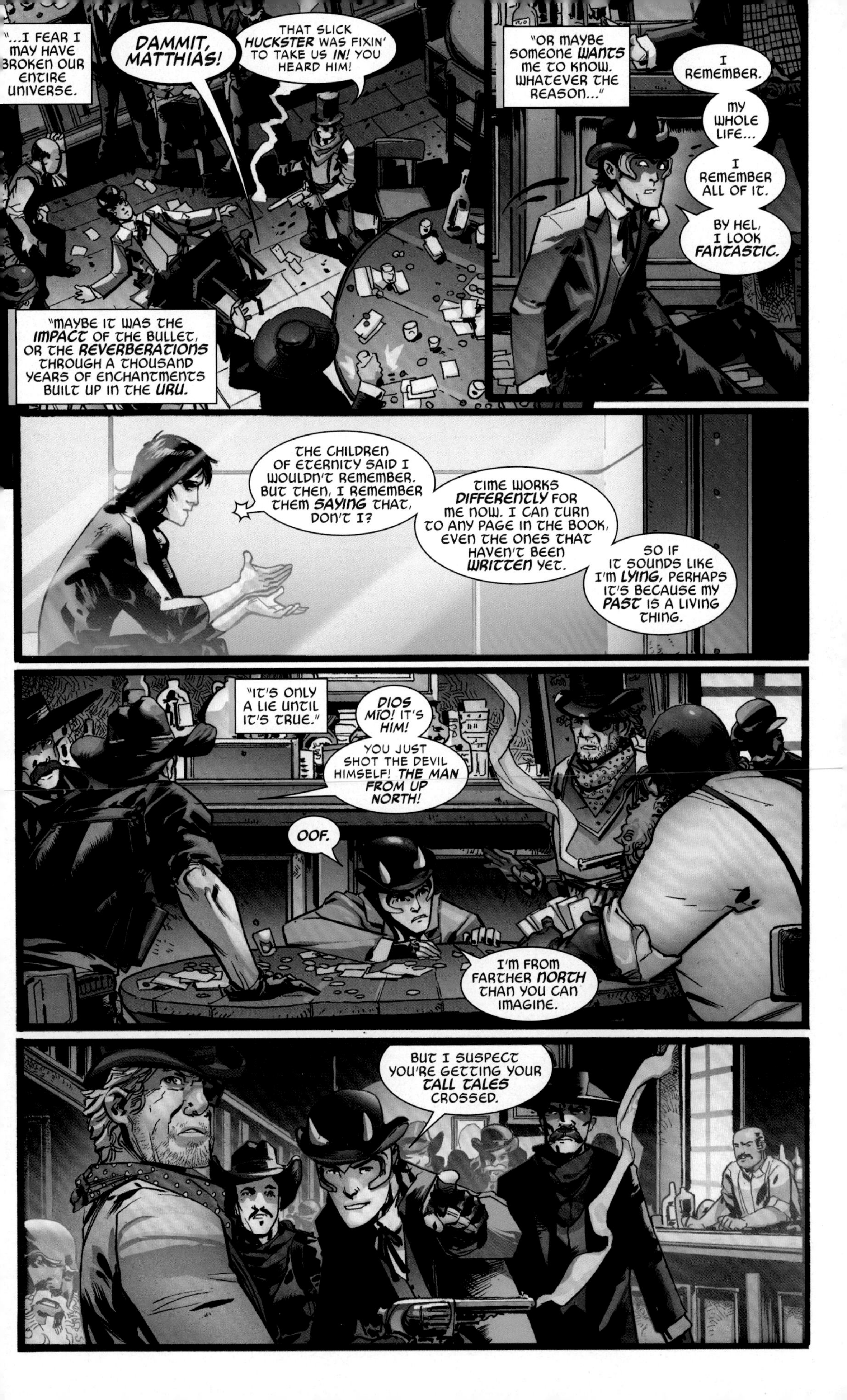
"...I FEAR I MAY HAVE BROKEN OUR ENTIRE UNIVERSE.
DAMMIT, MATTHIAS!
THAT SLICK HUCKSTER WAS FIXIN' TO TAKE US IN! YOU HEARD HIM!
"MAYBE IT WAS THE IMPACT OF THE BULLET, OR THE REVERBERATIONS THROUGH A THOUSAND YEARS OF ENCHANTMENTS BUILT UP IN THE URU.
"OR MAYBE SOMEONE WANTS ME TO KNOW. WHATEVER THE REASON..."
I REMEMBER.
MY WHOLE LIFE...
I REMEMBER ALL OF IT.
BY HEL, I LOOK FANTASTIC.
THE CHILDREN OF ETERNITY SAID I WOULDN'T REMEMBER. BUT THEN, I REMEMBER THEM SAYING THAT, DON'T I?
TIME WORKS DIFFERENTLY FOR ME NOW. I CAN TURN TO ANY PAGE IN THE BOOK, EVEN THE ONES THAT HAVEN'T BEEN WRITTEN YET.
SO IF IT SOUNDS LIKE I'M LYING, PERHAPS IT'S BECAUSE MY PAST IS A LIVING THING.
"IT'S ONLY A LIE UNTIL IT'S TRUE."
DIOS MIO! IT'S HIM!
YOU JUST SHOT THE DEVIL HIMSELF! THE MAN FROM UP NORTH!
OOF.
I'M FROM FARTHER NORTH THAN YOU CAN IMAGINE.
BUT I SUSPECT YOU'RE GETTING YOUR TALL TALES CROSSED.

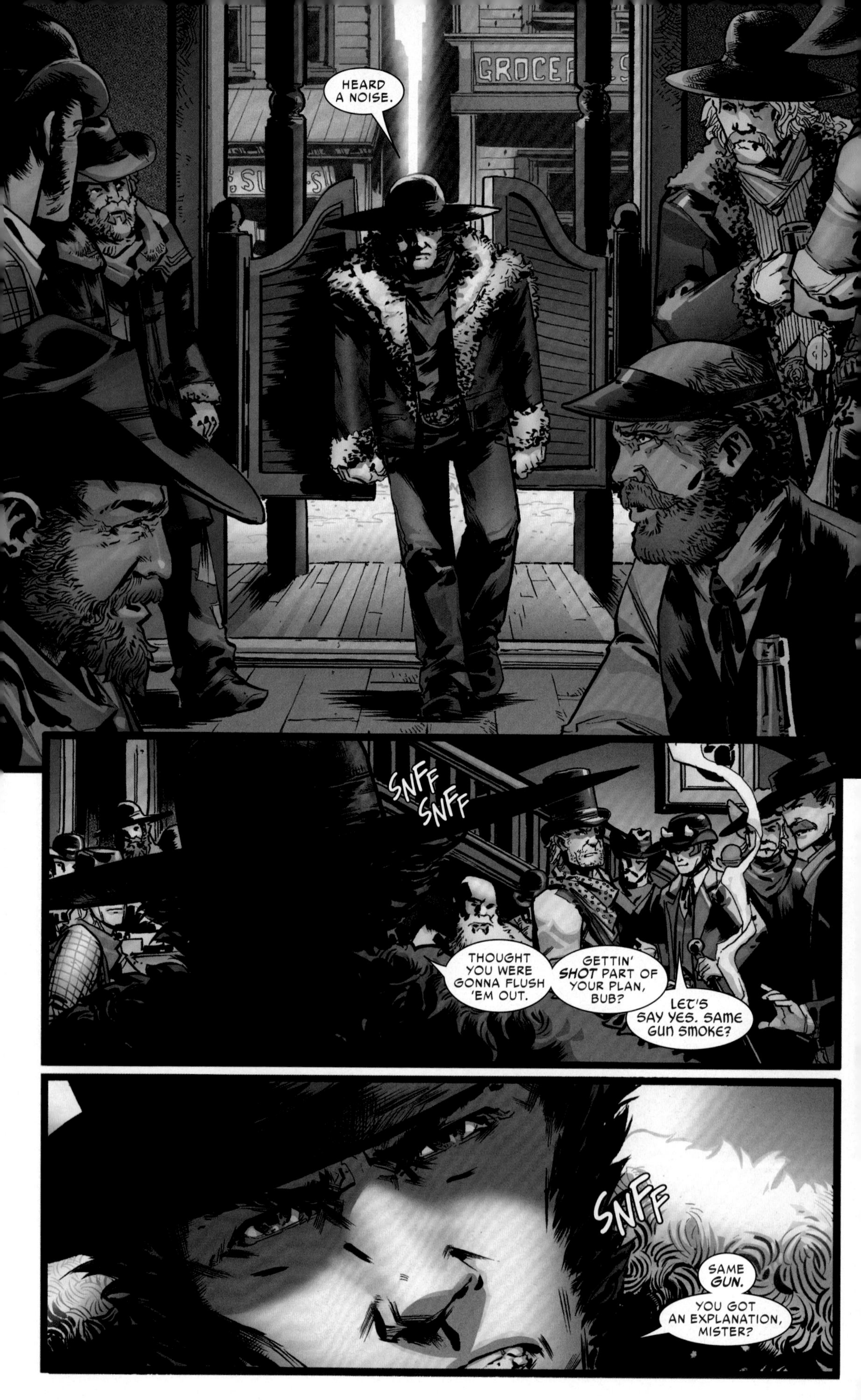
GROCER
HEARD A NOISE.
SNFF SNFF
THOUGHT YOU WERE GONNA FLUSH 'EM OUT.
GETTIN' SHOT PART OF YOUR PLAN, BUB?
LET'S SAY YES. SAME GUN SMOKE?
SNFF
SAME GUN.
YOU GOT AN EXPLANATION, MISTER?

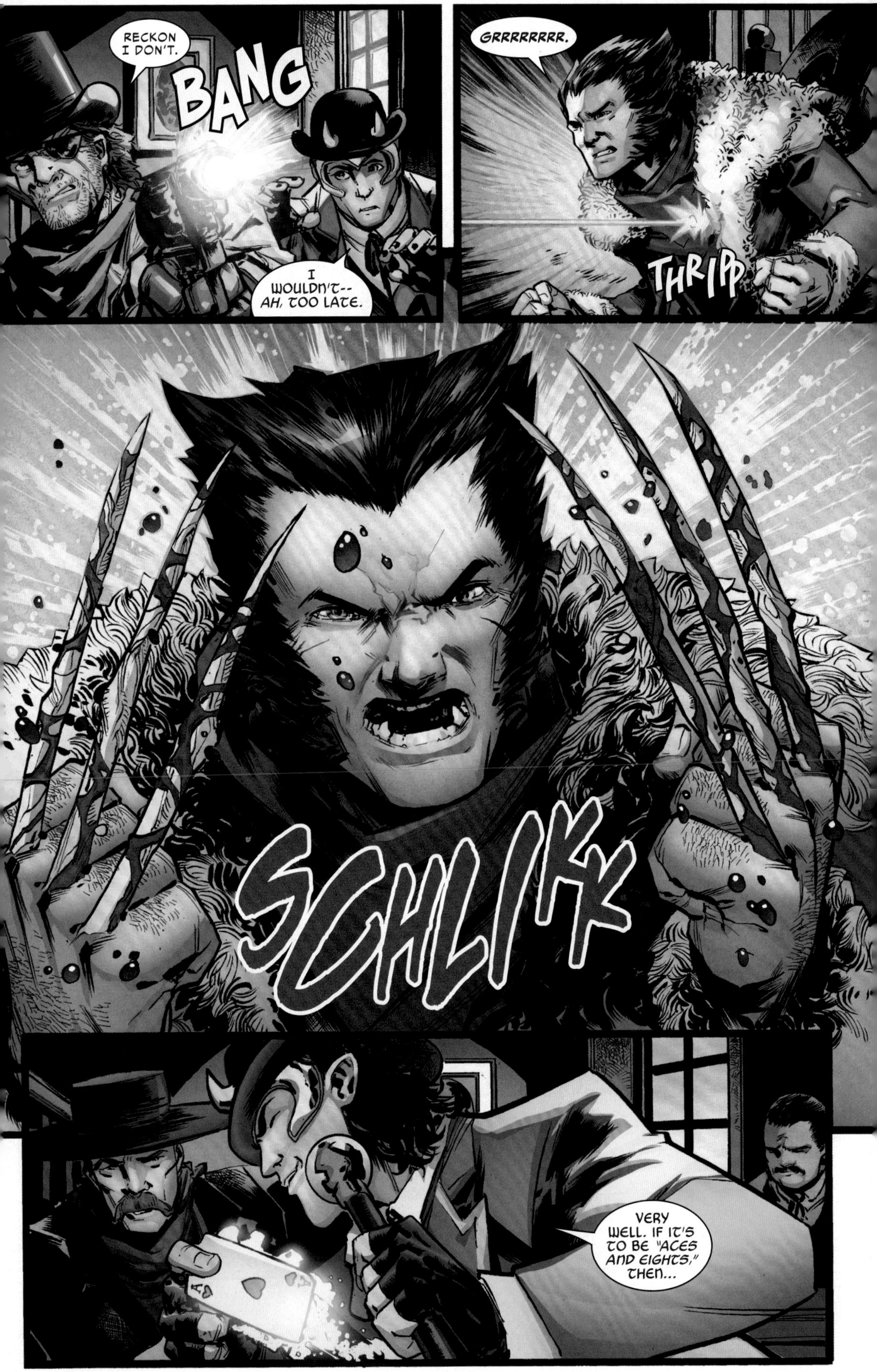
RECKON I DON'T.
BANG
I WOULDN'T--AH, TOO LATE.
GRRRRRRRR.
THRIPP
SCHLIKK
VERY WELL. IF IT'S TO BE "ACES AND EIGHTS," THEN...

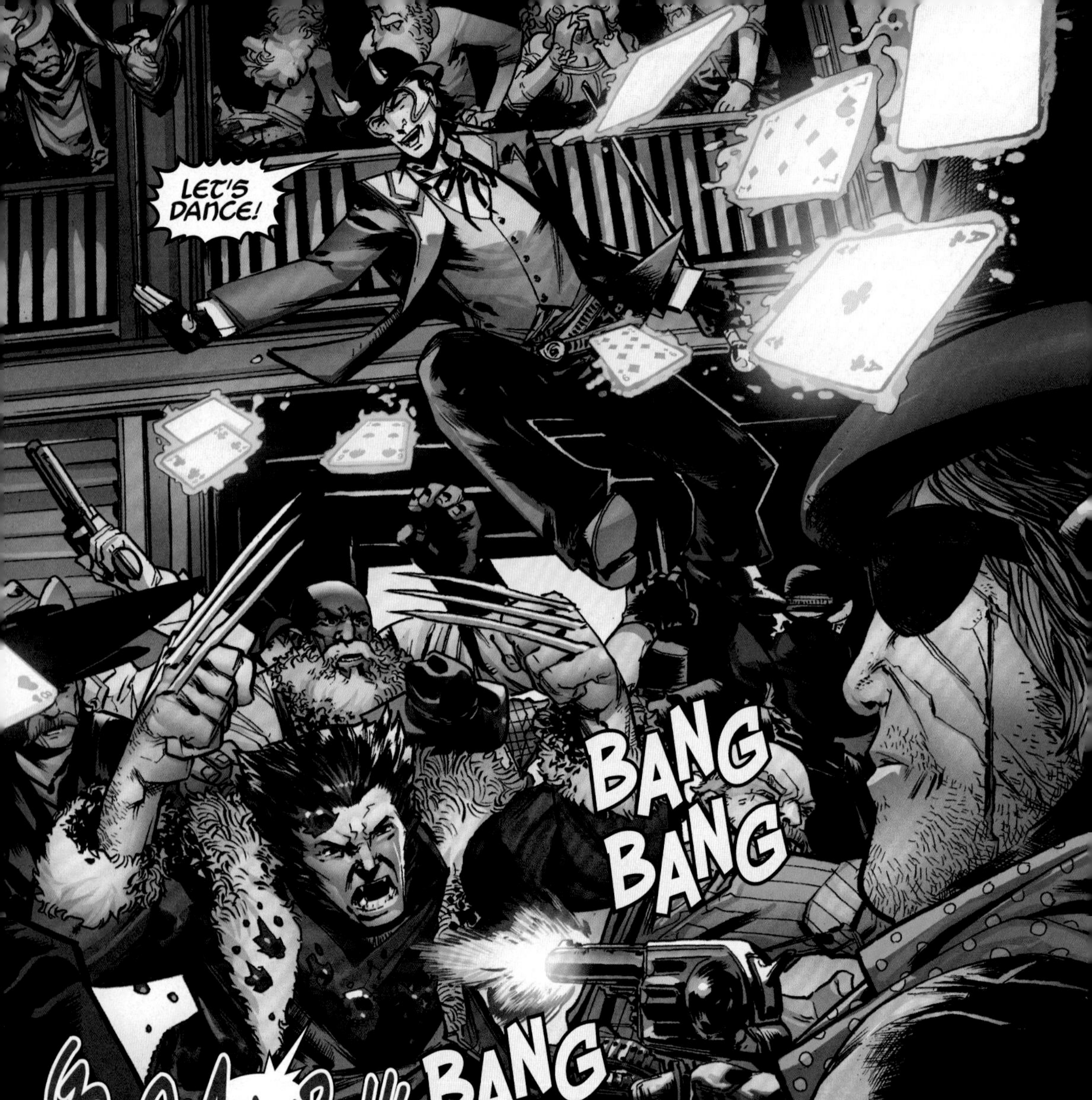
LET'S DANCE!
BANG BANG
GROOAAAWRGH!
BANG BANG
"WHY DO I GET THE FEELING THAT THIS STARTED OUT AS A DIFFERENT STORY ENTIRELY?"

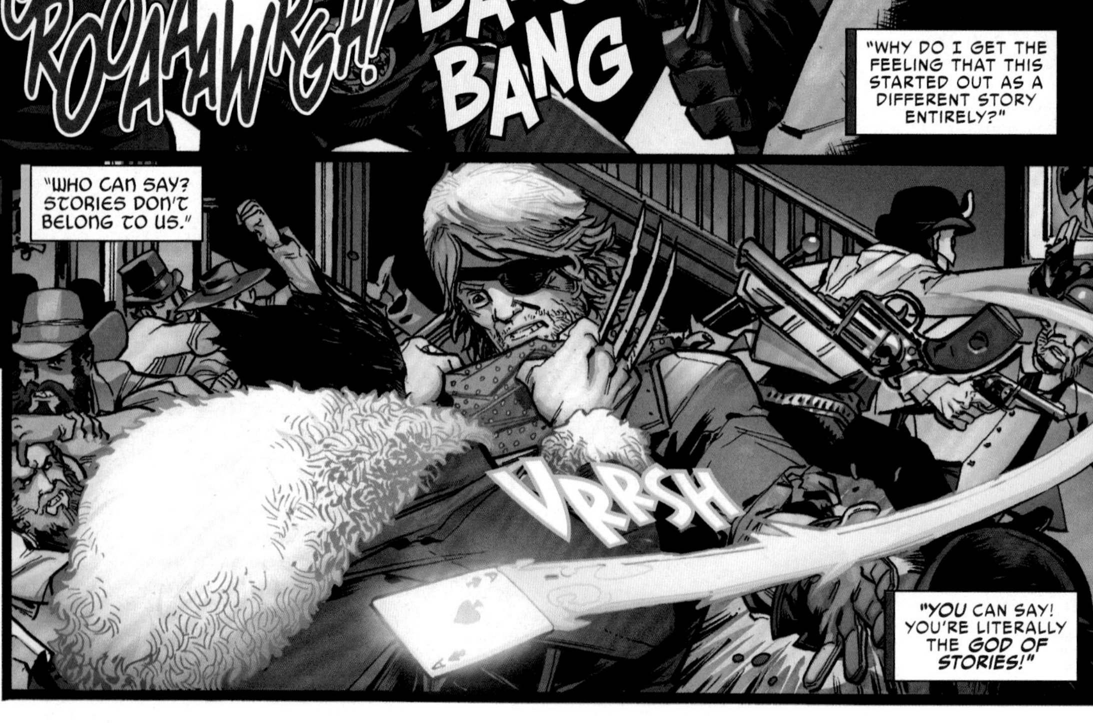
"WHO CAN SAY? STORIES DON'T BELONG TO US."
VRRSH
"*YOU* CAN SAY! YOU'RE LITERALLY THE *GOD OF STORIES!*"

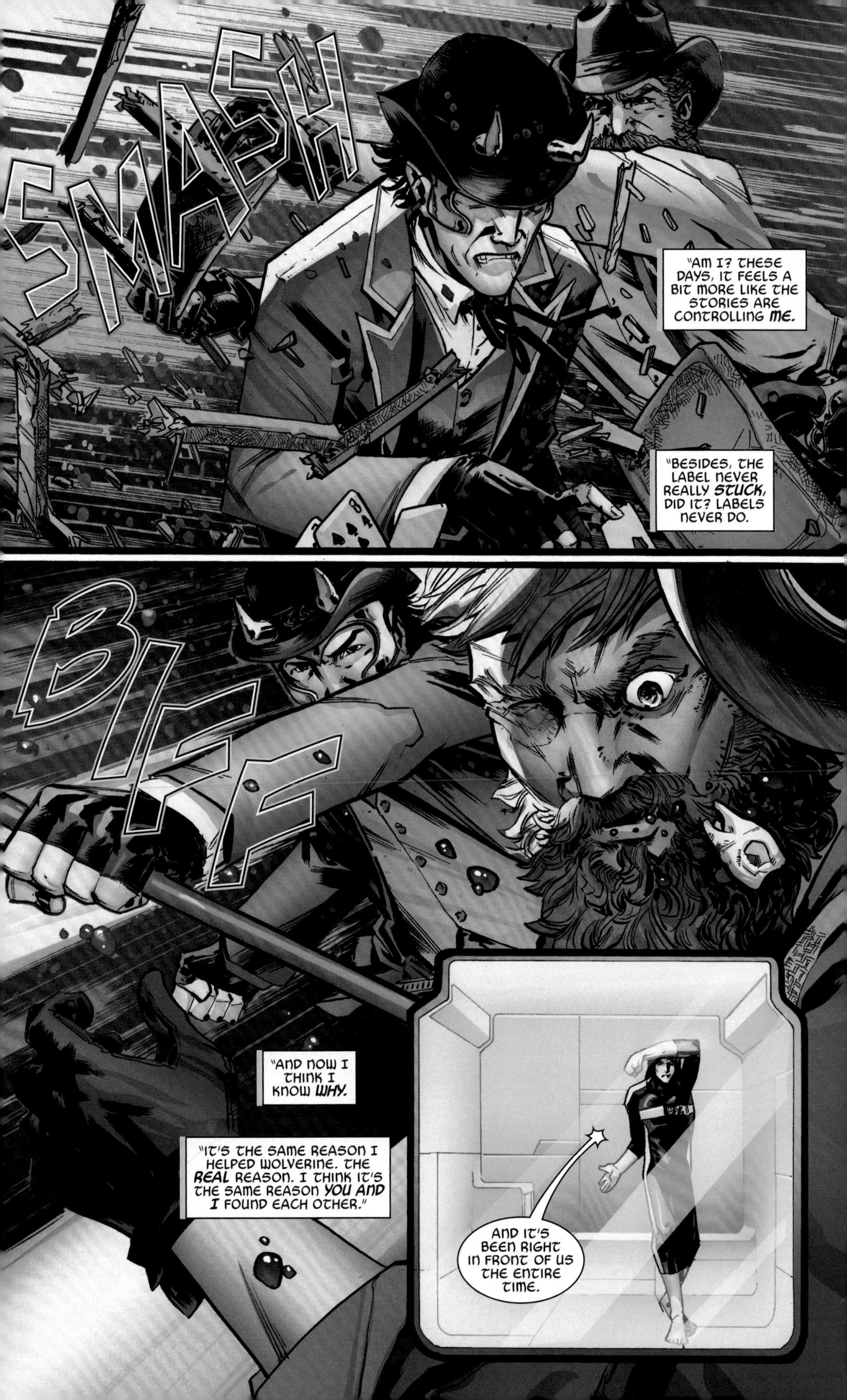
SMASH
"AM I? THESE DAYS, IT FEELS A BIT MORE LIKE THE STORIES ARE CONTROLLING ME.
"BESIDES, THE LABEL NEVER REALLY STUCK, DID IT? LABELS NEVER DO.
BIFF
"AND NOW I THINK I KNOW WHY.
"IT'S THE SAME REASON I HELPED WOLVERINE. THE REAL REASON. I THINK IT'S THE SAME REASON YOU AND I FOUND EACH OTHER."
AND IT'S BEEN RIGHT IN FRONT OF US THE ENTIRE TIME.

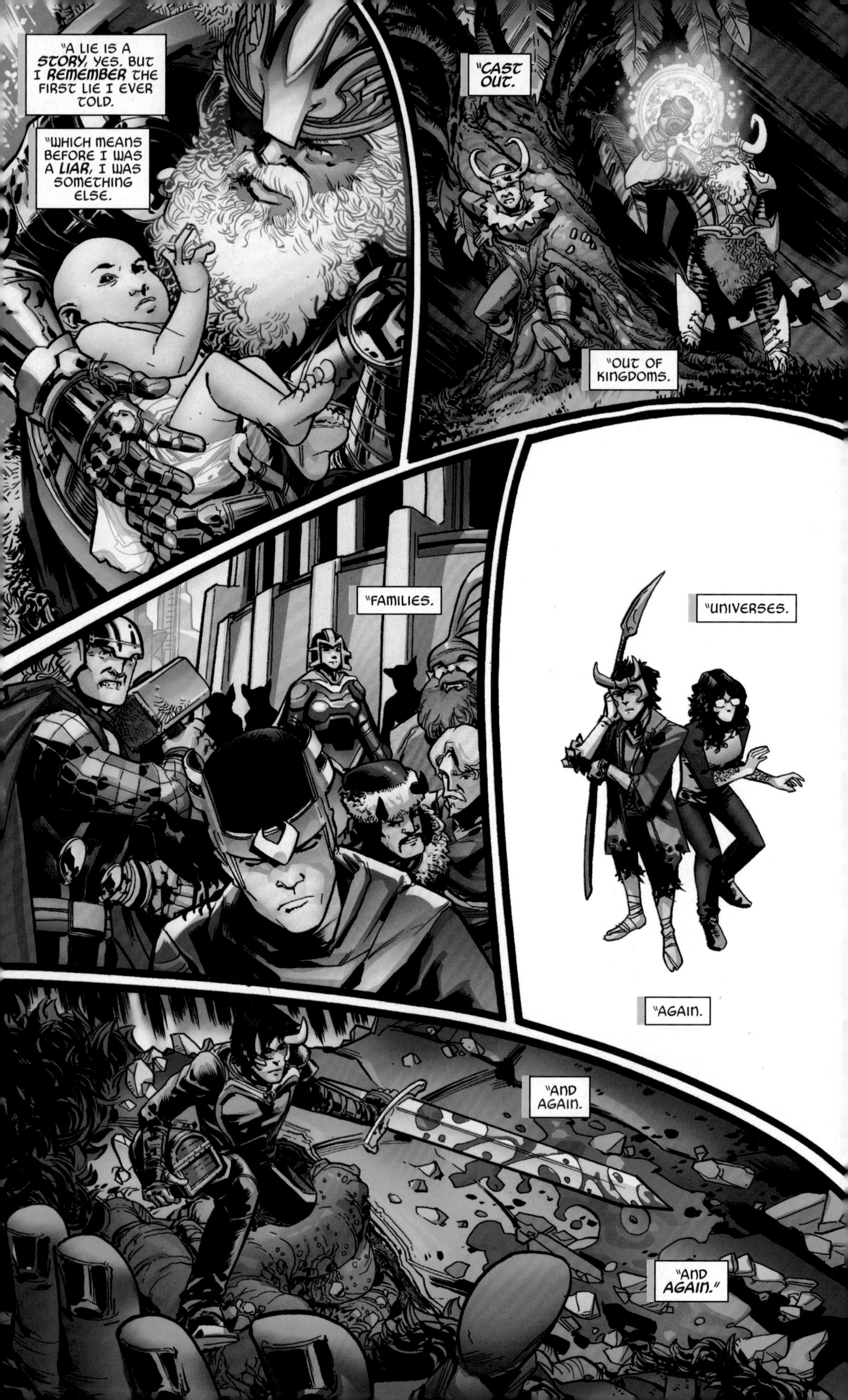
"A LIE IS A STORY, YES. BUT I REMEMBER THE FIRST LIE I EVER TOLD.
"WHICH MEANS BEFORE I WAS A LIAR, I WAS SOMETHING ELSE.
"CAST OUT.
"OUT OF KINGDOMS.
"FAMILIES.
"UNIVERSES.
"AGAIN.
"AND AGAIN.
"AND AGAIN."

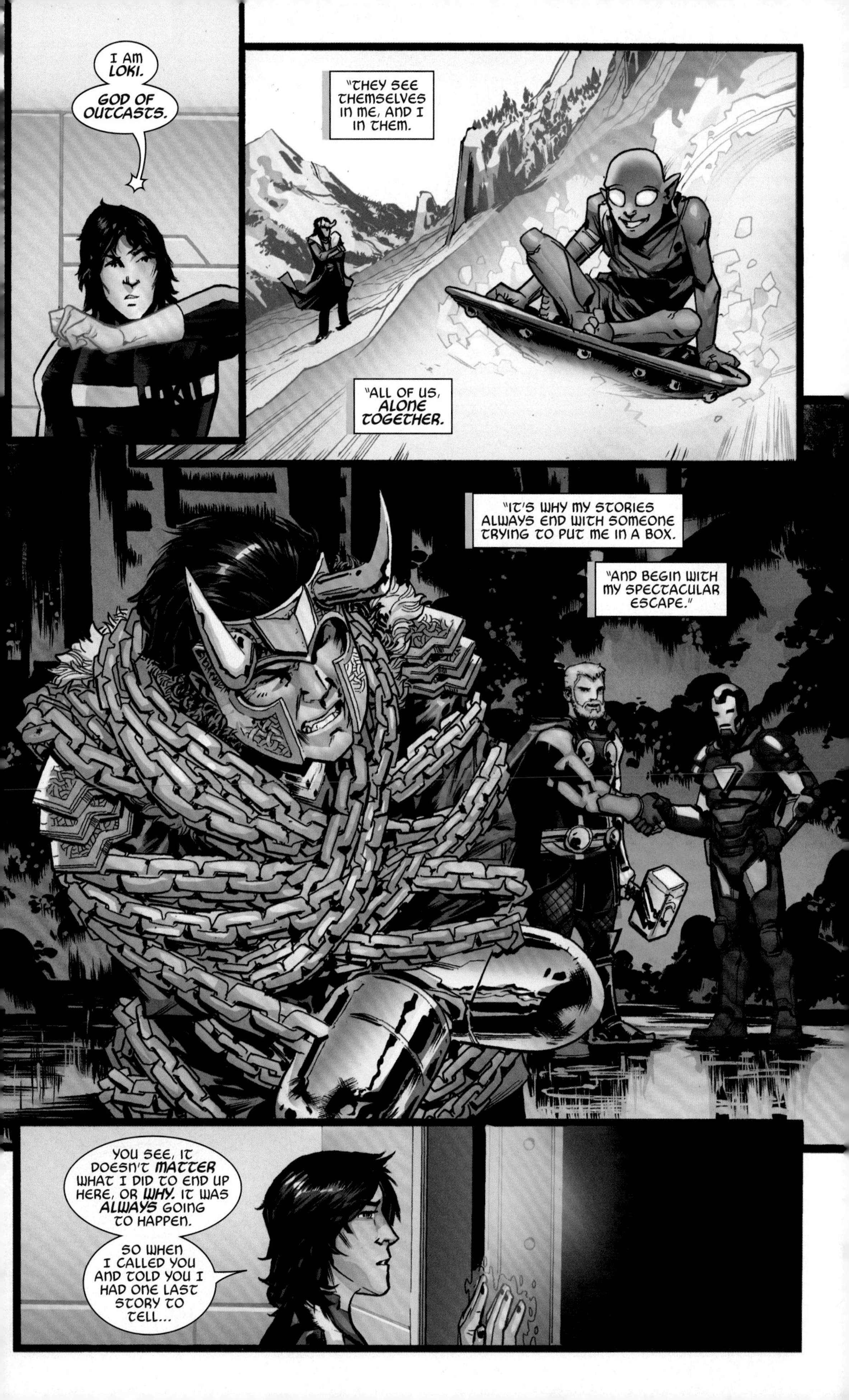
I AM LOKI.
GOD OF OUTCASTS.
"THEY SEE THEMSELVES IN ME, AND I IN THEM.
"ALL OF US, ALONE TOGETHER.
"IT'S WHY MY STORIES ALWAYS END WITH SOMEONE TRYING TO PUT ME IN A BOX.
"AND BEGIN WITH MY SPECTACULAR ESCAPE."
YOU SEE, IT DOESN'T MATTER WHAT I DID TO END UP HERE, OR WHY. IT WAS ALWAYS GOING TO HAPPEN.
SO WHEN I CALLED YOU AND TOLD YOU I HAD ONE LAST STORY TO TELL...

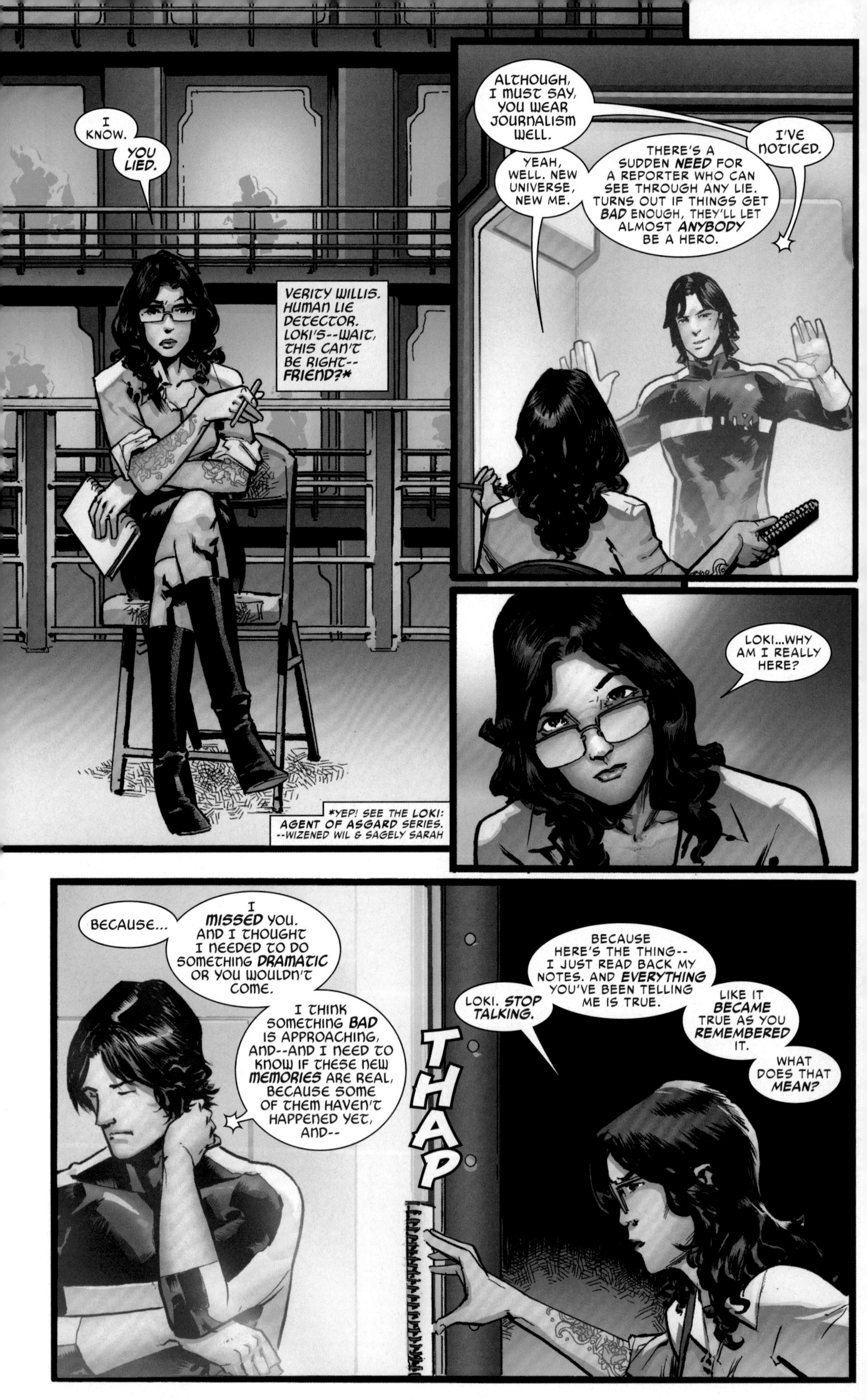
I KNOW. YOU LIED.
VERITY WILLIS. HUMAN LIE DETECTOR. LOKI'S--WAIT, THIS CAN'T BE RIGHT-- FRIEND?*
*YEP! SEE THE LOKI: AGENT OF ASGARD SERIES. --WIZENED WIL & SAGELY SARAH
ALTHOUGH, I MUST SAY, YOU WEAR JOURNALISM WELL.
I'VE NOTICED.
YEAH, WELL. NEW UNIVERSE, NEW ME.
THERE'S A SUDDEN NEED FOR A REPORTER WHO CAN SEE THROUGH ANY LIE. TURNS OUT IF THINGS GET BAD ENOUGH, THEY'LL LET ALMOST ANYBODY BE A HERO.
LOKI...WHY AM I REALLY HERE?
BECAUSE...
I MISSED YOU. AND I THOUGHT I NEEDED TO DO SOMETHING DRAMATIC OR YOU WOULDN'T COME.
I THINK SOMETHING BAD IS APPROACHING, AND--AND I NEED TO KNOW IF THESE NEW MEMORIES ARE REAL, BECAUSE SOME OF THEM HAVEN'T HAPPENED YET, AND--
THAP
LOKI. STOP TALKING.
BECAUSE HERE'S THE THING-- I JUST READ BACK MY NOTES. AND EVERYTHING YOU'VE BEEN TELLING ME IS TRUE.
LIKE IT BECAME TRUE AS YOU REMEMBERED IT.
WHAT DOES THAT MEAN?

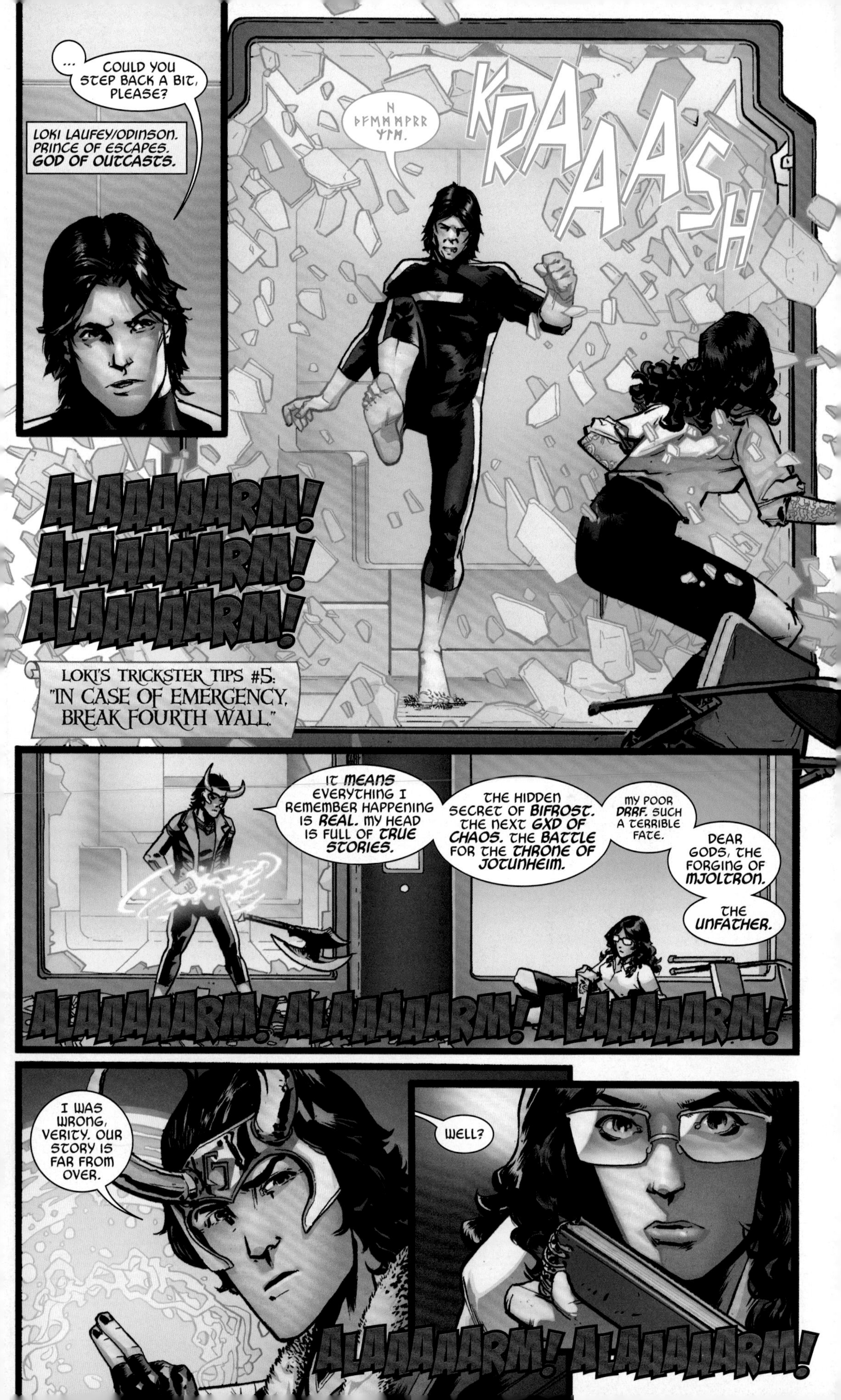

... COULD YOU STEP BACK A BIT, PLEASE?
LOKI LAUFEY/ODINSON. PRINCE OF ESCAPES. GOD OF OUTCASTS.
KRAAAASH
ALAAAAARM! ALAAAAARM! ALAAAAARM!
LOKI'S TRICKSTER TIPS #5: "IN CASE OF EMERGENCY, BREAK FOURTH WALL."
IT MEANS EVERYTHING I REMEMBER HAPPENING IS REAL. MY HEAD IS FULL OF TRUE STORIES.
THE HIDDEN SECRET OF BIFROST. THE NEXT GXD OF CHAOS. THE BATTLE FOR THE THRONE OF JOTUNHEIM.
MY POOR DRRF. SUCH A TERRIBLE FATE.
DEAR GODS, THE FORGING OF MJOLTRON.
THE UNFATHER.
ALAAAAARM! ALAAAAARM! ALAAAAARM!
I WAS WRONG, VERITY. OUR STORY IS FAR FROM OVER.
WELL?
ALAAAAARM! ALAAAAARM!

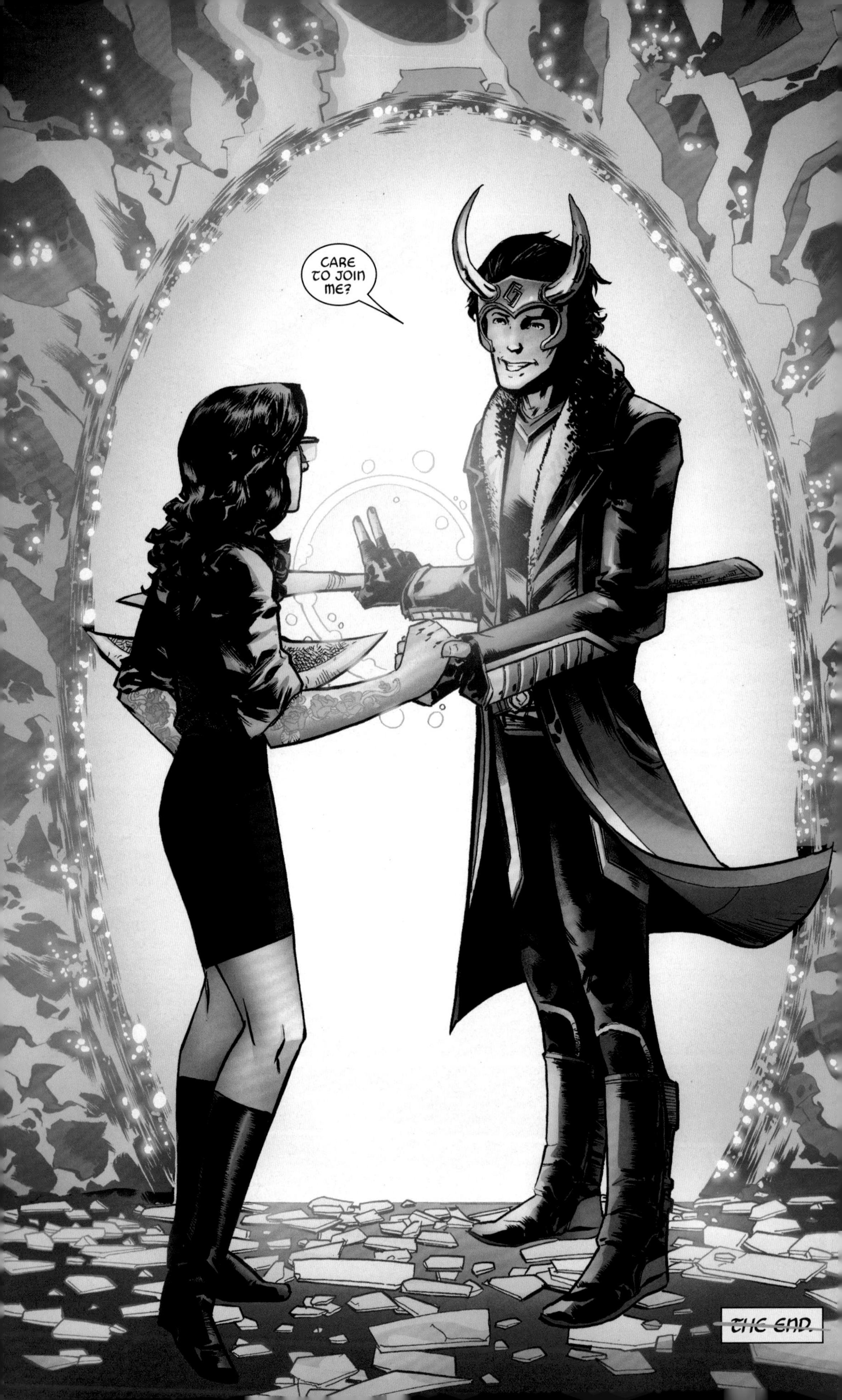
CARE TO JOIN ME?
THE END.

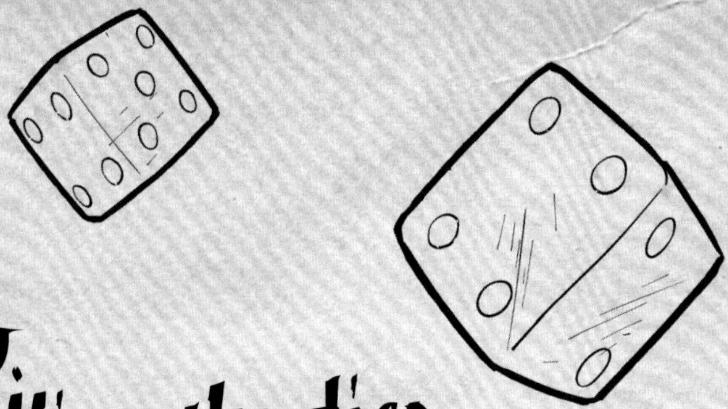

So. Rolling the dice.

That's the first image we have of Loki in our lovely little series, now ended on a perhaps incongruous note of a Wolverine-team-up-Western-flashback that may not be a flashback at all but indeed, something that is happening right now AND back then. One might surmise that we had a longer plan for this title, but if you've been reading along, you know that the plan doesn't always cooperate.

The movie we quote in this issue is *The Wizard of Speed and Time* (1988). My actual favorite movie and Loki's canonical favorite movie. It's the story of a stop-motion animator (a manipulator of time, in his way) who attempts to make a movie in a system that is stacked against him, whilst wearing, I kid you not, a green wizard's cloak. The whole thing is on YouTube, and of course Verity would be aware of it and simply HAVE to show it to Loki.

Verity! You didn't have to write in — she was always planned to return. But thanks for writing in. We had to hold the reunion much sooner than I expected.

Near the end of the film, "the Wizard" burns all his footage, saying, "It isn't the money or the time, it's just that we all worked so hard and made something really good."

And we truly did make something really good. My eternal awe and gratitude to our art team: artist Oscar Bazaldua, colorist David Curiel, our hilarious and surgical letterer, Clayton Cowles, and this issue's artist Andy MacDonald, who made my lifelong dream of writing a supernatural Western come vividly true. As well as our cover artist, Ozgur Yildirim, who turned the Bifrost into the Brooklyn Bridge and gave fans an instantly iconic image of Loki striding down a rainbow. And our beloved editors Wil Moss and Sarah Brunstad, who trusted us to have a plan. Which we TOTALLY did.

Either way, the damage is done. Loki is the unstuck-in-time God of Outcasts — which I imagine covers most of the people reading this. To all of you and all the Low-Key fans who supported our book, I am also beyond grateful. Remember, this is not the end of Loki's stories. "Head canon" is an oxymoron, an "imagined reality." And if the entire reality is imagined, who's to say what happened or what didn't?

We all are. And I'm still eager to find out what happens next. As one tween cosplayer told me at a convention: "I love the Children of Eternity. But I don't trust them."

Nor do I. Until then, one final trickster's tip…leave them wanting more.

Drrf lives,

Daniel Kibblesmith

2019. I think.

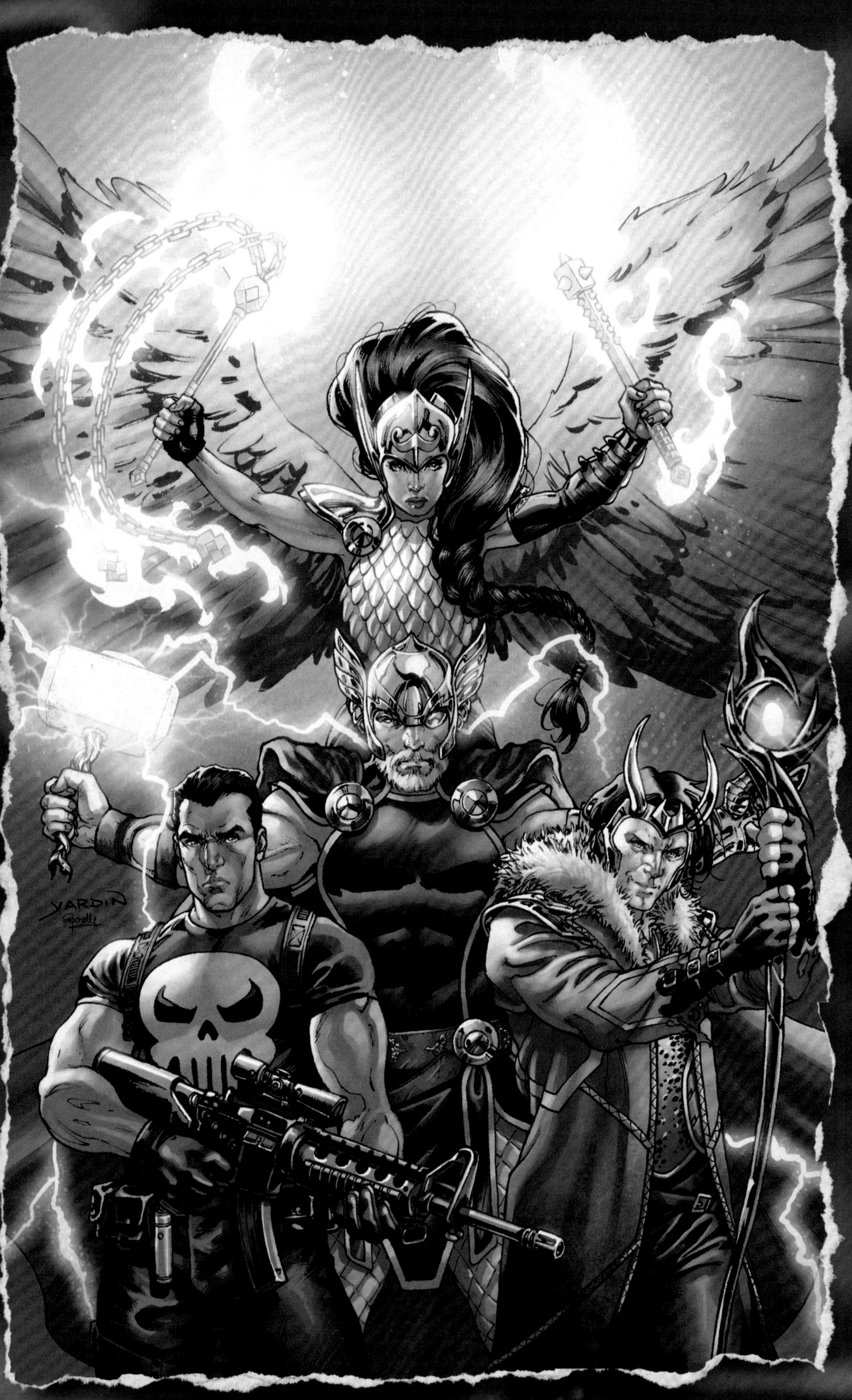
YARDIN

WAR OF THE REALMS OMEGA #1 VARIANT BY DAVID YARDIN & RACHELLE ROSENBERG

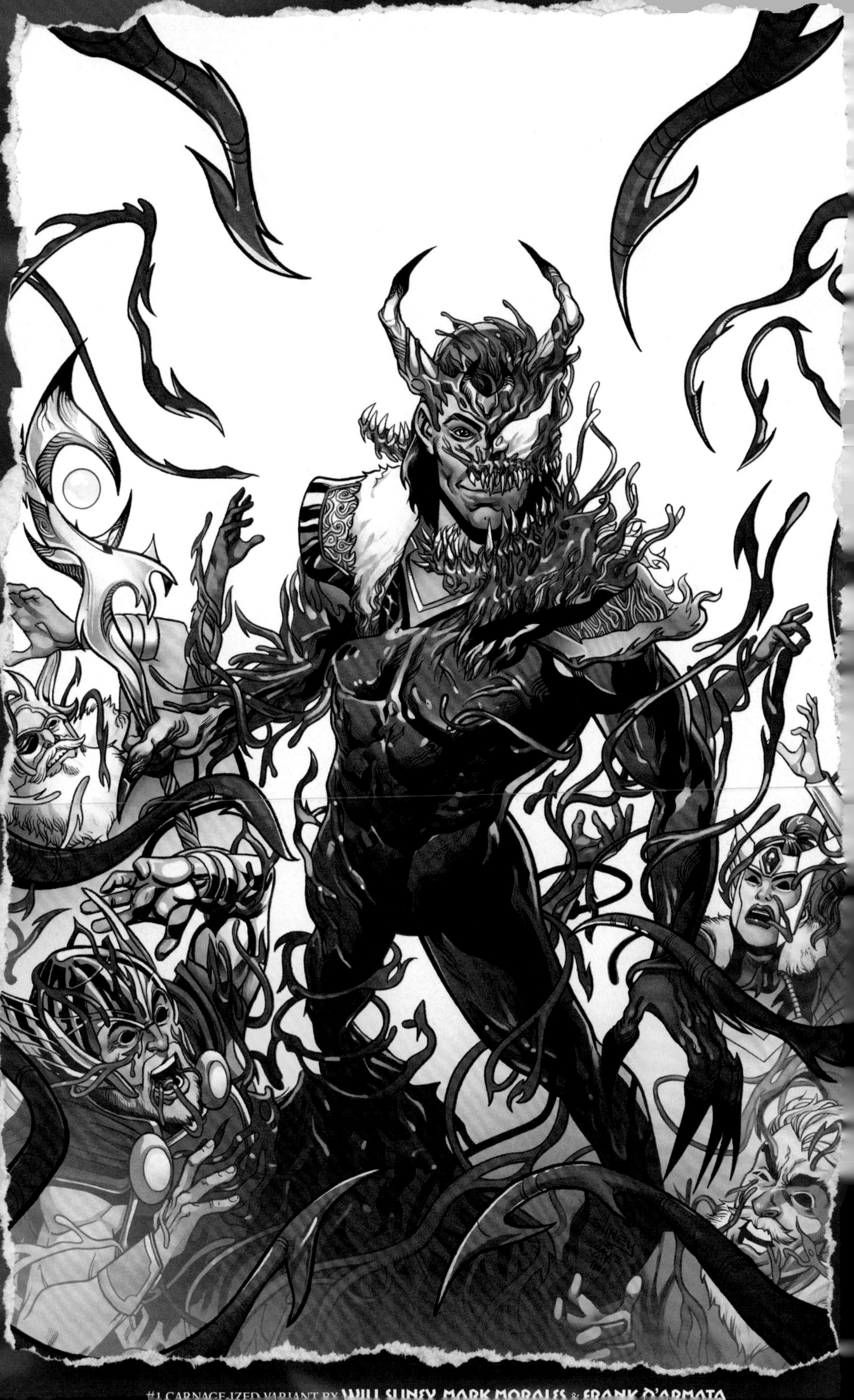

#1 CARNAGE-IZED VARIANT BY WILL SLINEY, MARK MORALES & FRANK D'ARMATA

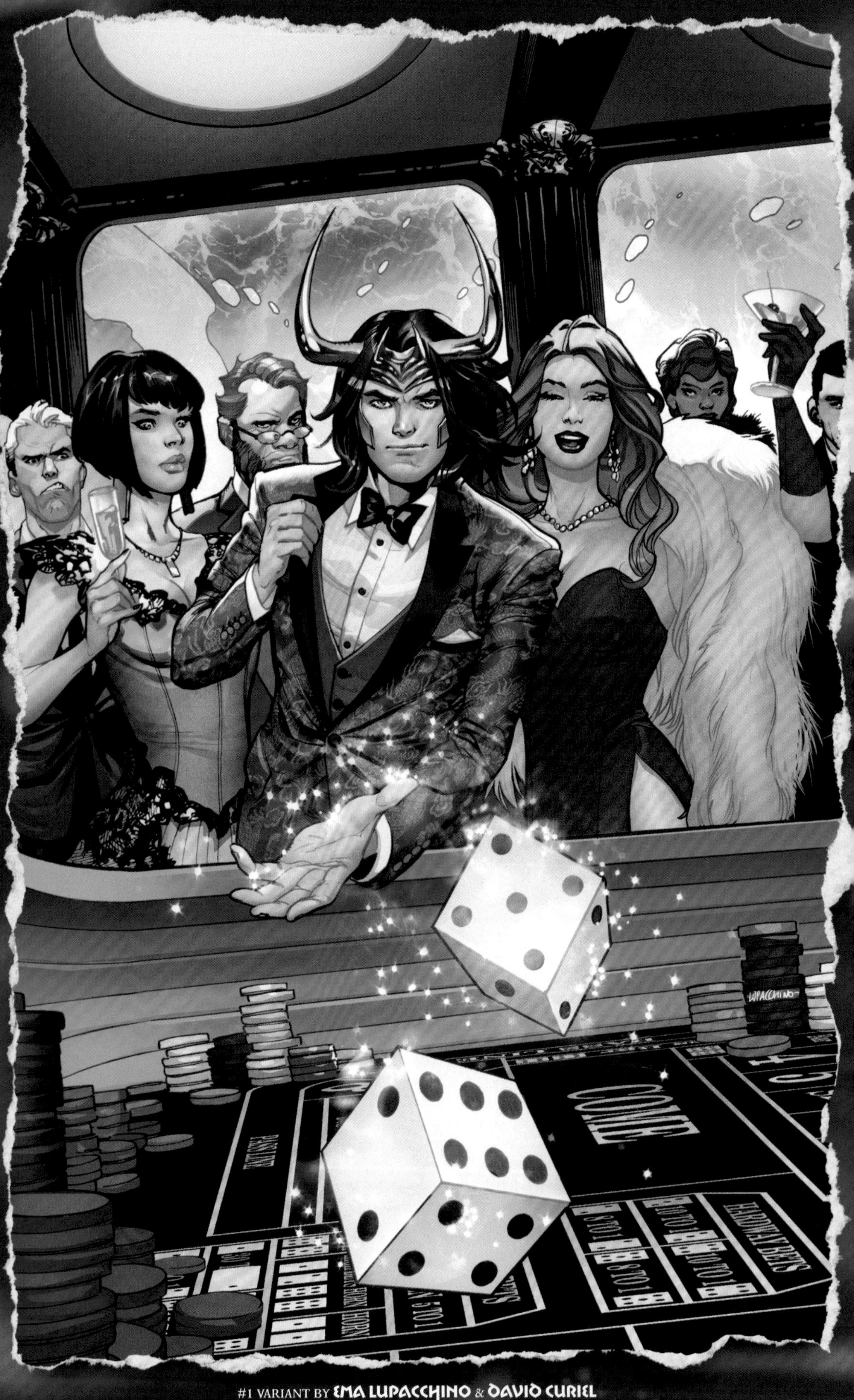

#1 VARIANT BY EMA LUPACCHINO & DAVID CURIEL

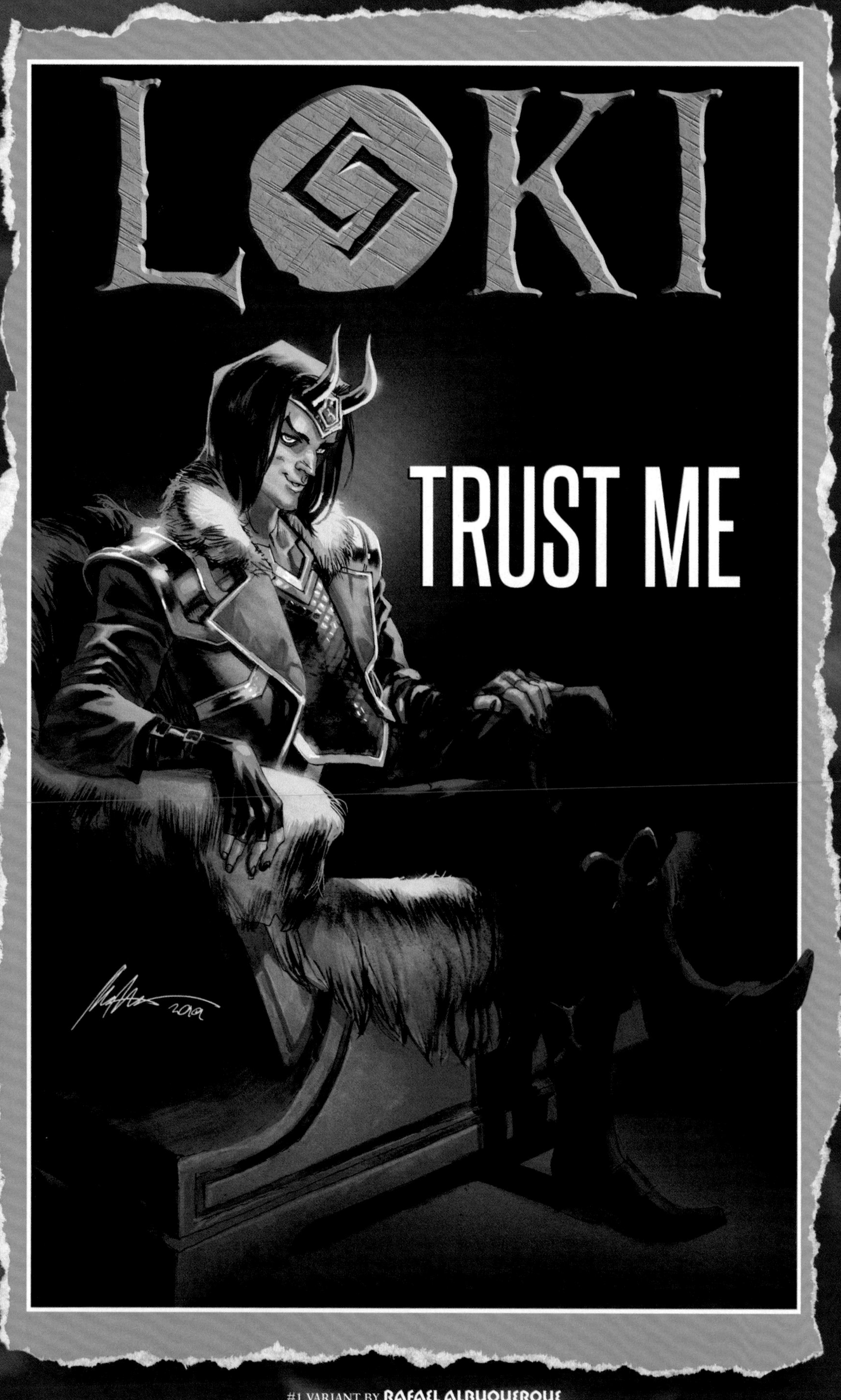
LOKI
TRUST ME

#1 VARIANT BY RAFAEL ALBUQUERQUE

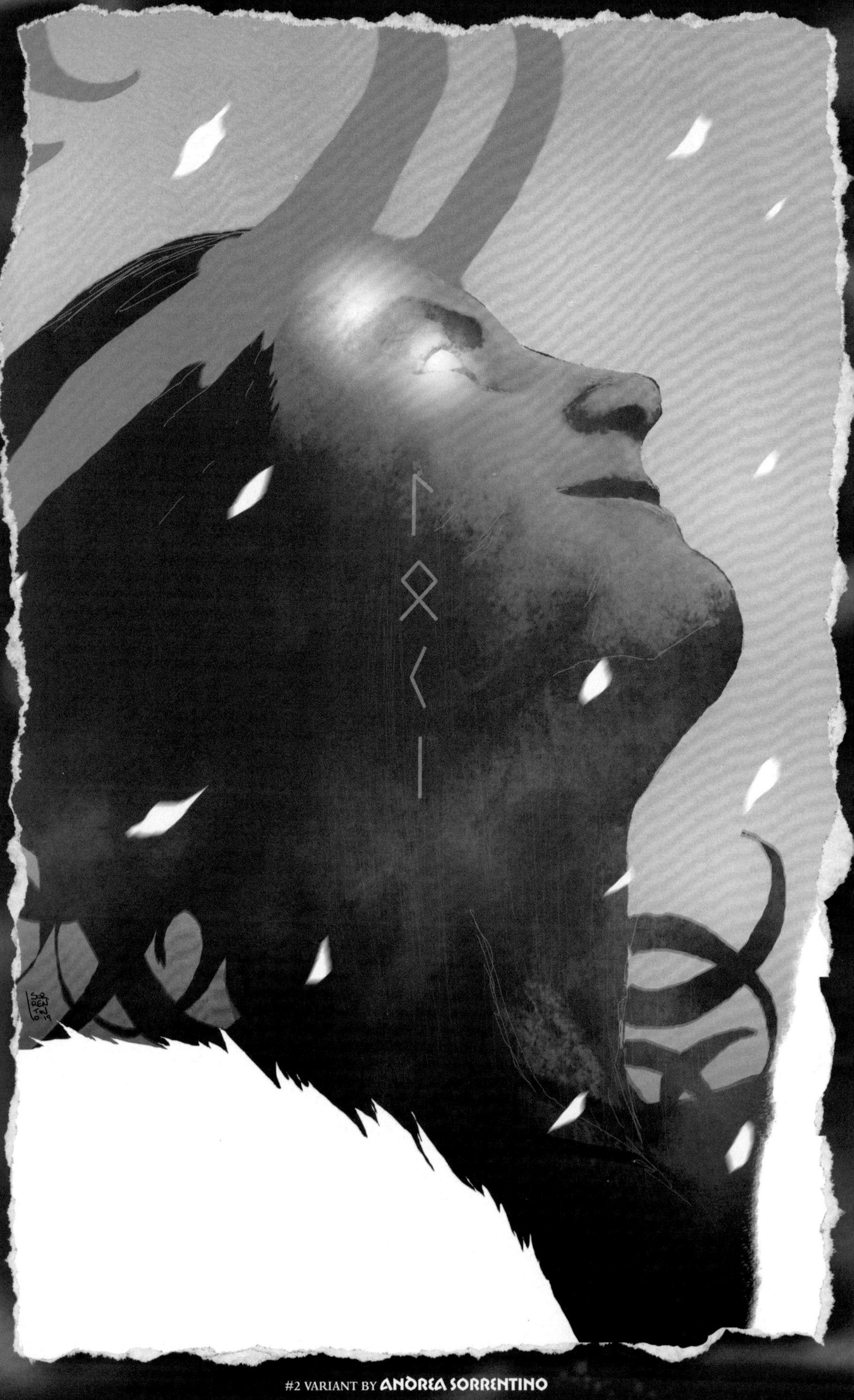

#2 VARIANT BY ANDREA SORRENTINO

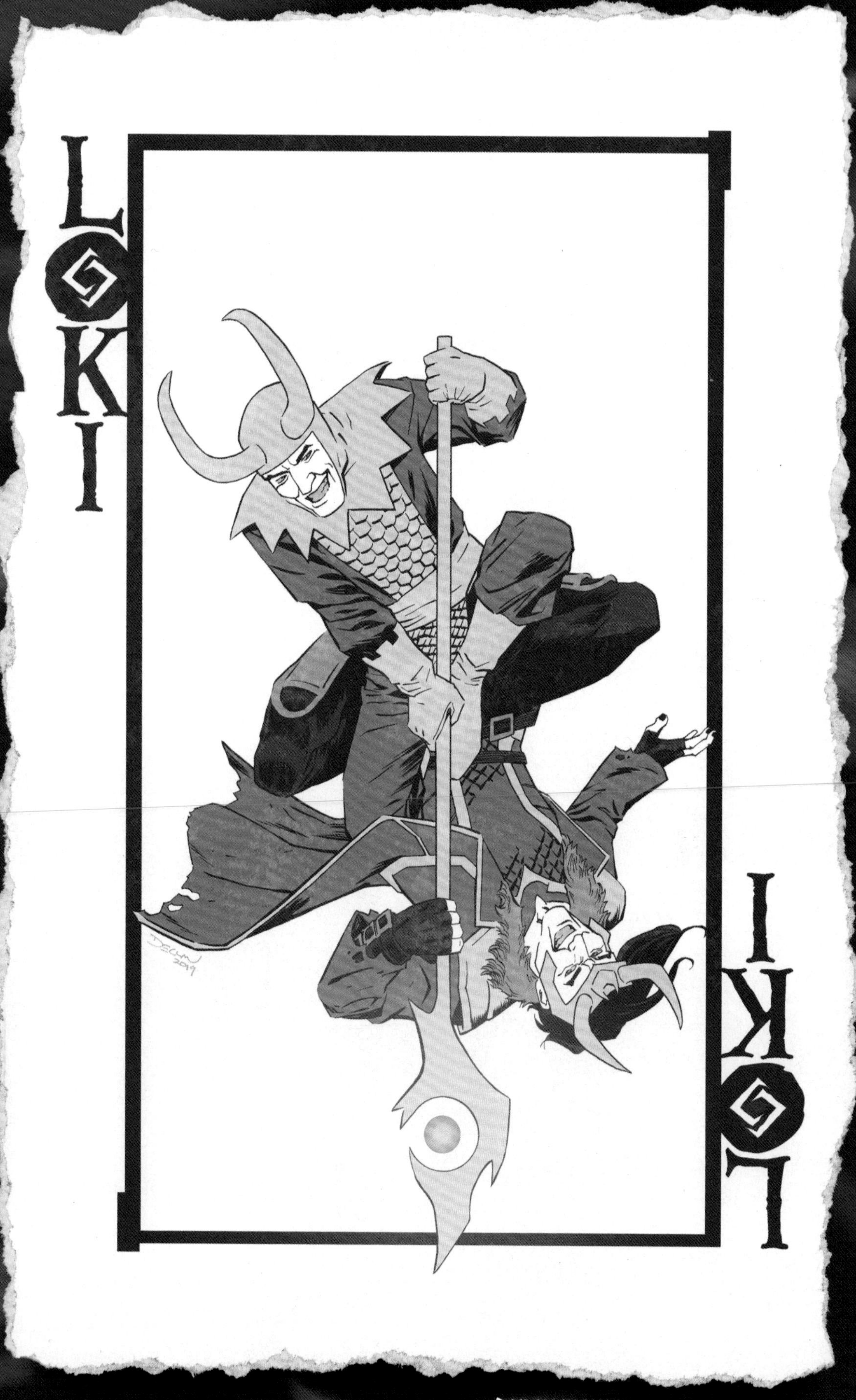
LOKI

#2 BRING ON THE BAD GUYS VARIANT BY DECLAN SHALVEY

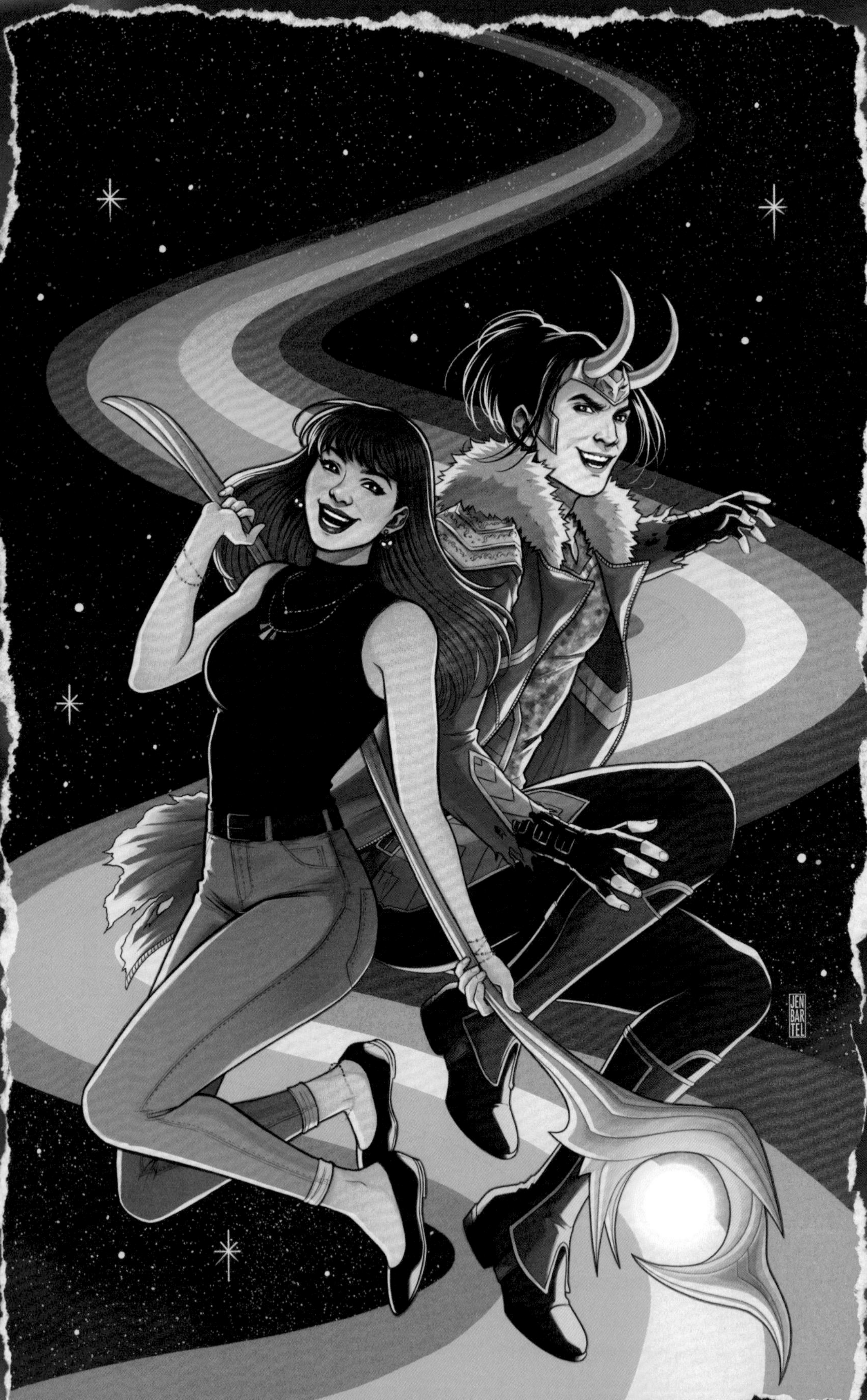
JEN
BAR
TEL

#4 MARY JANE VARIANT BY JEN BARTEL

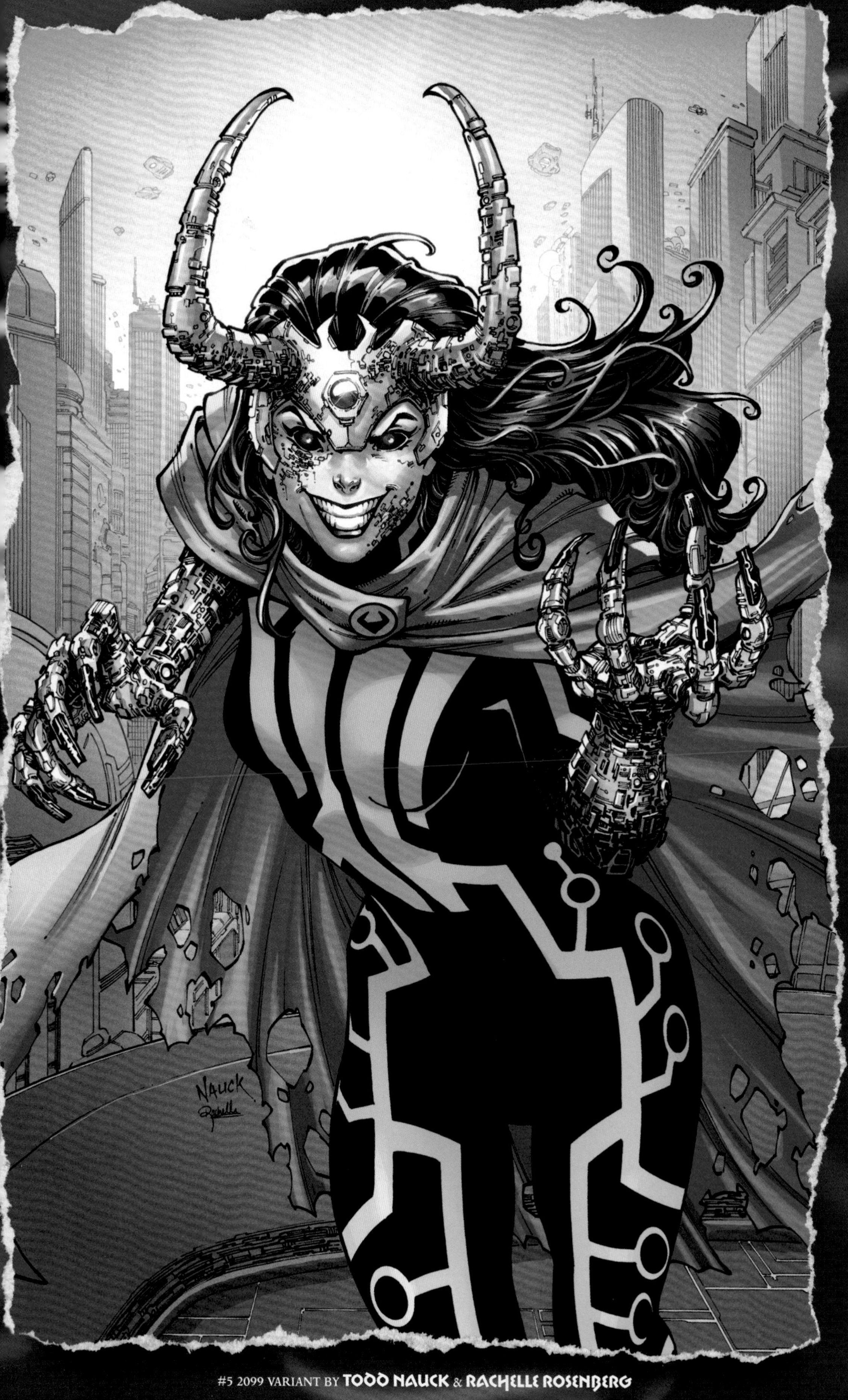
NAUCK

#5 2099 VARIANT BY **TODD NAUCK** & **RACHELLE ROSENBERG**

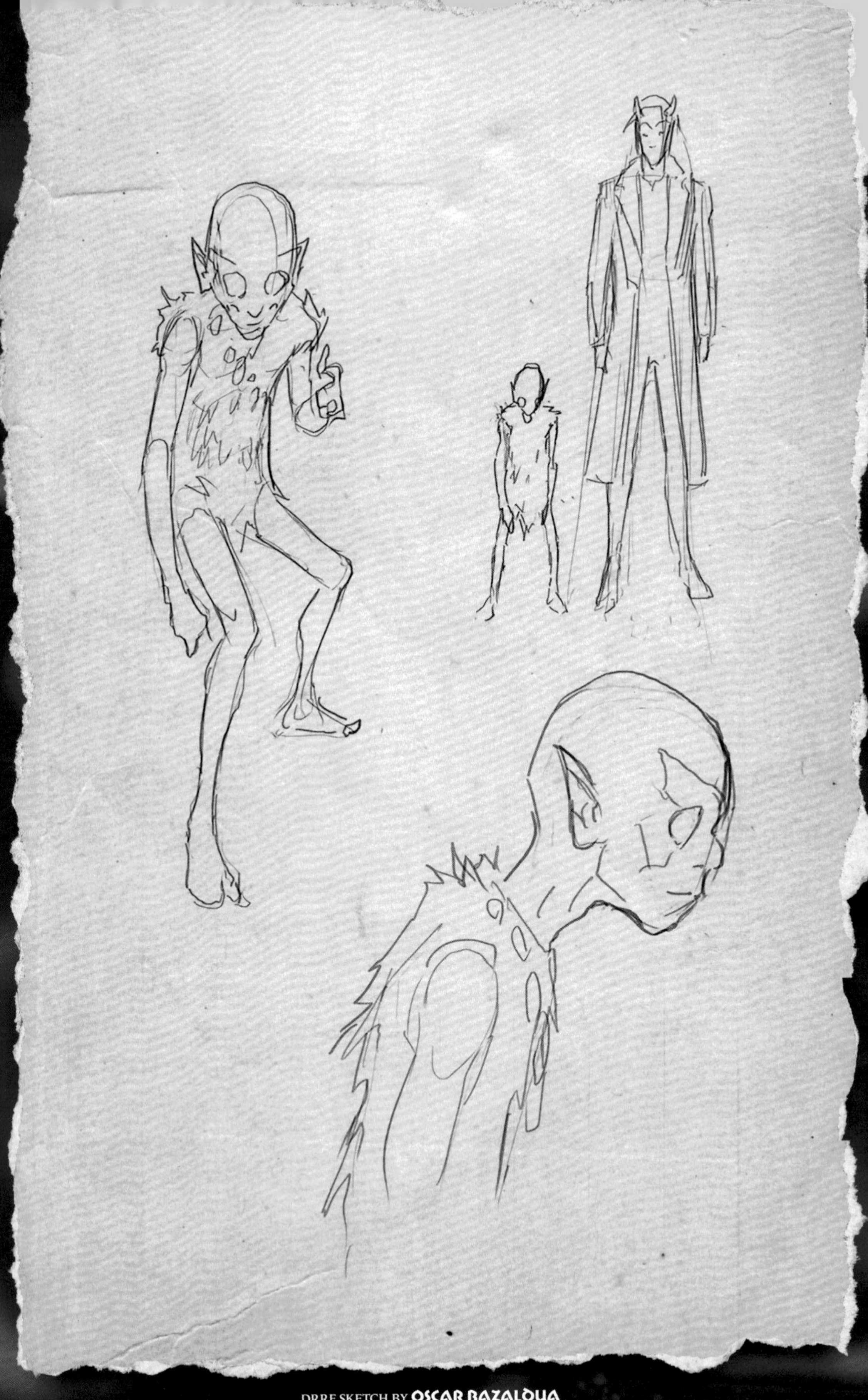

DRRF SKETCH BY OSCAR BAZALDUA